Jake Bernstein

STRATEGIC FUTURES TRADING

CONTEMPORARY TRADING SYSTEMS TO MAXIMIZE PROFITS

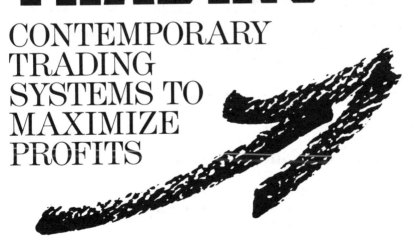

Dearborn
Financial Publishing, Inc.

While a great deal of care has been taken to provide accurate and current information, the ideas, suggestions, general principles and conclusions presented in this book are subject to local, state and federal laws and regulations, court cases and any revisions of same. The reader is thus urged to consult legal counsel regarding any points of law—this publication should not be used as a substitute for competent legal advice.

Publisher: Kathleen A. Welton
Associate Editor: Karen A. Christensen
Senior Project Editor: Jack L. Kiburz
Cover Design: Salvatore Concialdi

© 1992 by Jacob Bernstein
Published by Dearborn Financial Publishing, Inc.

Printed in the United States of America

92 93 94 10 9 8 7 6 5 4 3 2 1

Library of Congress Cataloging-in-Publication Data

Bernstein, Jacob, 1946-
    Strategic futures trading: contemporary trading systems to maximize profits / Jake Bernstein.
        p. cm.
    Includes index.
    ISBN 0-79310-290-1
    1. Futures. 2. Futures market.   I. Title
HG60024.A3B5 1992   92-6637
332.64′5—dc20   CIP

Dedication

This book is dedicated to every futures trader who strives for success in the markets. I identify with your struggles; I understand the pain of your losses, the frustration of your failures and the euphoria of your profits. I share in the knowledge that trading has revealed to you. I have lived and died with the markets for more than 21 years, learning their treacherous twists and turns, regularities and irregularities. I offer the tools in this book as my small contribution to victory in the quest for success in futures trading.

Because futures price trends are not static, the tools in this book will not continue to serve their purpose forever. Yet the concepts on which these tools are based are fundamental to all free markets. No matter how radically their external expression may change, their underlying structure will remain fixed as long as traders are ruled by emotion and markets are ruled by the laws of supply and demand. The astute trader will also be a "future-oriented" futures trader, using the tools and insights revealed in this book as a starting point for dynamic research that adapts to changing market conditions but never ignores the essential simplicity and importance of its roots.

This book is dedicated, therefore, to its readers. Only you can make the tools in this book work for you. And only you can adapt them to your individual applications. Please remember that there is a risk of loss in futures trading.

Acknowledgments

A special note of thanks to the following individuals and organizations for their assistance in making this book possible:

- Larry Williams for his permission to use and discuss some of his timing indicators, particularly OOPS, and for his valuable input through the years
- Dr. George Lane for developing stochastics and for his willingness to share knowledge and experience
- Bill Cruz for permission to use his TradeStation and SystemWriterPlus software and for his assistance in writing system parameters
- Joe Krutsinger for his excellent suggestions and advice regarding systems and indicators, and for his input on TradeStation and SystemWriterPlus programming
- Don Sarno for assistance in system and indicator testing, and for his recommendations regarding various timing indicators and their implementation
- Mark Silber, my partner in Bernstein Futures Inc., for his constructive criticism and support
- Marilyn Kinney for her constant efforts to keep distractions and interruptions from getting me off schedule
- CQG Inc. for permission to reprint charts from their System One™ quotation system
- Michael Steinberg, my literary agent, for his constant but well-intentioned badgering designed to help me meet my publication deadline
- And to my family, Rebecca, Elliott, Sara and Linda, for their forbearance during my many hours at the computer

Readers are welcome to write to me for assistance at the following address:

Jake Bernstein
MBH Commodity Advisors, Inc.
P.O. Box 353
Winnetka, IL 60093

Contents

Preface

I made my first trade in the futures market in the late 1960s. At that time I had little or no idea about the purpose of or internal workings of the market. Nor did I know the first thing about trading systems, timing indicators or systematic trading. My venture into the world of trading began several years earlier when a college friend convinced me to open a stock account to be used for speculating in low-priced gold mining shares. My stock market trades were based almost exclusively on fundamentals, wishful thinking, the recommendations of experts and the advice of my friend whose orientation was technical but not organized or systematic.

About two years later I was attracted to the futures market (then called the commodity market) by an advertisement for egg futures that made great claims for profit potential in trading eggs. Against my better judgment, I submitted to the high pressure sales tactics of the broker. I borrowed the $1,000 needed to open my commodity account. My broker traded eggs, eggs and more eggs. And he made money for me. His methodology was based on the seasonal tendency for egg prices to rise during the summer months. He called me frequently with weather reports and spoke with great gusto of heat waves, declining egg production and dying chickens. "The hotter it gets, the fewer the chickens, the fewer the eggs and the greater our profits," he would gleefully report to me. And all went well as long as we followed the seasonality of the egg market. But being only human, greed took over and I began to study the market.

My search for the ultimate trading tool led me to Gerald Gold's classic book *Modern Commodity Futures Trading*. Within its hallowed pages I saw for the first time a commodity price chart, trend lines, support and resistance, volume, open interest and point-and-figure charts. I was convinced that herein were all the answers I needed to turn the commodity markets into my personal money machine. Needless to say, my optimism was based on faulty assumptions, a lack of experience and the wishful thinking of a novice. I lost all my speculative capital within minutes trading pork belly futures. It was a sobering lesson, but one that was long overdue.

My initial success, based on ignorance followed by dismal but "educated" failure, led me to the serious study of futures trading. And my market studies have continued without interruption for more than 20 years. I have tested literally hundreds of systems that I have either developed or that originated with and have been promoted by other traders. *Only a handful of these systems have been consistently successful through the years, and only because they have undergone changes in response to varying market conditions. Profitable trading systems are not easy to find.* Many systems are advertised as profitable, however, upon closer examination they do not hold up in back-testing for an extended period of years. Frequently they have been *curve-fitted* to reflect the past. The process of fitting the system to test profitably in the past does not guarantee its profitable performance in the future.

The many years, thousands of dollars and hours I spent searching for the *right* trading systems and timing indicators have led me down numerous blind alleys; however, from each dead end I gleaned a small amount of new information. Eventually, success and failure merged and profitable results began to emerge. The lessons learned related not only to timing signals and system development but also to trading discipline and psychology. Early in my search I realized I was not alone; thousands of traders were also searching for the Holy Grail.

This book is about my searches for the grail. Some of my conclusions may surprise you. Others may not impress you. But, when all is said and done, I think this book will provide answers that will serve you well. If your trading has been a series of dead ends, my research will be valuable. If your search has produced marginal successes, my work may push you forward along the road to profits. And if you have been successful, my ideas may help you improve on what you are already doing.

You will read about advanced timing concepts and practical suggestions regarding risk management, trader psychology and performance maximization.

I don't have all the answers. The futures markets are doubly dynamic; they are constantly changing, both in terms of the supply and demand factors that affect price movement and in the political forces that exaggerate price movements. Although general principles can be applied consistently to futures trading, different technical and fundamental factors assume differing roles of prominence at different times. This is why trading systems vary in performance from year to year and from market to market.

A book is only as valuable as the ideas it stimulates and the successes it facilitates. I realize that everyone who reads this book will use it in a different way. Although I hope you will profit from the systems and indicators discussed, I know you can benefit from new directions in your own research. Here are a number of suggestions to help you get the most out of this book:

- Skim the book once, giving your main consideration to the technical concepts and test results.
- Make notes on particular ideas, indicators or methods consistent with your trading style or useful as adjuncts to techniques you are currently using.
- Return to the sections of the book you feel offer the most potential value in your trading.
- Apply the ideas and determine whether they have potential to improve your trading results.
- Develop variations on my ideas to see if they can further improve your results.

Above all, remember that I do not claim to have all the answers to successful trading. Although I have learned much in my more than 20 years of trading, my knowledge was not acquired in one or two lessons. Often my lessons were not learned even after the third or fourth time. I sincerely feel, however, that my experiences can help you no matter what your level of expertise in futures trading.

Tip

From time to time you will see sections marked TIP. These sections provide suggestions that are related to the topic at hand and may lead to other applications of the concepts, or to better understandings of them.

The Computer Trading Revolution

Futures trading is more competitive now than ever before. Personal computer systems have narrowed the information gap between professional traders and the trading public. The ongoing trend toward more effective trading systems is only now in its infancy. The computer revolution that began with the development of more efficient, faster and lower-priced hardware has now moved full speed into software development. Many advanced computer applications are taken for granted by schoolchildren today; and the days of artificial intelligence, neural networks and networking are upon us. Systems are "thinking" for themselves and "learning" from their own errors. Many traders, professional and nonprofessional alike, believe that these new software advances are the savior of the investment world. And their spending habits have reflected these hopes, as trading software sales have exploded in the late 1980s and early 1990s.

What does this all mean to the average trader? And what does it mean to the professional trader? I predict that, as traders become more focused on systems generated by computers, the markets will respond more frequently to their actions. The result will be numerous *false* signals as well as short-lived, self-fulfilling prophecies. The deterioration of trading systems will eventually open the door to opportunities generated by different types of signals and indicators. I would not be surprised to see many of today's most advanced computer trading systems replaced by more basic systems. Eventually revival of interest in the timing indicators of yesteryear may occur.

Why do I refer to the indicators in this book as *strategic*? Because they represent a combination of several different elements, each of which is strategic in its own right. The first aspect of these indicators is that they are time-tested. In other words, each indicator has been known in its basic form to futures and stock traders for many years and has been used successfully in traditional applications for many years.

Secondly, each indicator is based on or derived from valid theories of market behavior that are logical and based on a fundamental understanding of what drives prices. The extensive discussion of market personalities, for example, will add an important perspective to your trading repertoire, allowing you to be selective about the markets you trade and the systems you use in these markets. This aspect of market analysis has previously not been discussed in trading literature.

Finally, each method presented herein is essentially simple and easily applied by most traders. As a point of information I have not overly optimized the indicators in this book. There are inherent dangers in heavy optimization—dangers that traders often fail to realize until they attempt to use a system that back-tests brilliantly but leads to considerable problems in real-time application. What you choose to do with these systems is entirely up to you; however, I suggest you not optimize them since they may lose their strategic value and become a carbon copy of the past rather than a reasonable road map to the future.

I cannot guarantee that reading this book will help you achieve all the above understandings and goals. I do know, however, the power of attitude change. If my writings can help you develop a new and more direct attitude toward futures trading, your attitude will shape your actions and this will facilitate achievement of your goals. If my strategic methods can help you achieve profitable results when combined with your own disciplined trading, my job in writing this book will have been a success. But remember that markets change and systems must change as well. Traders must take their cues from the markets, for it is the ability to fit the right system to the right market that will be one of the primary keys to successful trading.

Part
1

Key Concepts and Structure

Chapter
1

An Overview of
Futures Trading

The search for profitable futures trading systems and timing indicators is as old as the market itself. Since the days of the primeval speculator in 16th century China, traders have sought ways and means to improve their success. Frequently, the search has been a fruitless one yielding uncertain solutions and specious techniques. Since the early 1960s a plethora of trading systems and methods has been unleashed on the public. In fact, the 1980s parented literally hundreds—if not thousands—of trading systems, methods and timing signals, as well as a veritable library of books, many purporting to reveal the ultimate "secrets" of profitable futures trading.

Many claims were undocumented or poorly researched since historical testing was, for many years, a laborious manual process. The ability to more readily verify the claims of systems developers and promoters increased markedly with the advent of advanced computer testing in the 1980s. Today virtually any system, method or timing indicator can be thoroughly back-tested by computer, often very quickly, once its algorithms and money management rules have been programmed. No longer must the trading public be victimized by the often fraudulent or erroneous claims that characterized preceding decades. If a system can be expressed in operational (i.e., programmable) terms, it can be tested by computer, and virtually any system can be perfected using the computer to test a variety of *if-then* scenarios using iterative processes.

Will New Technology Lead to Success?

The recent trend toward computer *neural networks* (the buzzword for computer software systems that learn from their own trial and error) has set into motion the wheels of what may prove to be the most significant advances ever in trading systems. Yet the advent of neural networks and so-called artificial intelligence leads to the inevitable question: Will highly effective trading systems become so popular that they will undo themselves, resulting in a backlash of simplistic systems and a return to the methods of yesteryear?

Given the rapid advances in neural net technology, it will not be long before we have the answer to this important question. Even before the answer is revealed, however, it is probable that neural networks, artificial intelligence and their advanced trading systems will do little to improve the average trader's lot. While these advances may stimulate the development of more efficient markets and better results for a select group of professionals, the average trader will still be a slave to emotion. And emotions gone astray will continue to limit the efficacy of systems as well as the success of traders who use them.

Time has proven only one solid fact about markets; they are ruled by fear, greed, insecurity and lack of discipline. Most investors and speculators are losers who contribute their funds to professional traders experienced in the ways of the markets. Consistently successful traders have one thing in common in addition to their success; they are not only experienced in the ways of the markets, but they are also intimately acquainted with the ways of their psyches. Time has demonstrated beyond any doubt that panic selling and bearish news characterize most market bottoms while panic buying and bullish news accompany most market tops.

The Weak Link

While systems, methods, techniques, computers, indicators and software may provide us with extremely helpful clues about how markets have behaved in the past and how they are apt to behave in the future, such advanced technology is the strong link in the chain, not the weak link. The chain will break at its weakest link, not at its strongest. Hence, we would do well to direct our energies toward strengthening the most vulnerable aspect of the trading equation, allowing the strongest aspects to rest on their laurels. The trader, ultimately the operator of his or her trading system, is the weakest link in the chain. Trading systems are void of emotion and judgment; they are either right or wrong. Systems do not feel insecurity, greed, fear or ambivalence. It is the trader who will either guide the system into the rocks or through the treacherous harbor to the open waters.

Misguided Masses

Most futures traders have long labored under the misguided impression that a completely automated trading program, one uncontaminated by the human element, will facilitate success. The mind imagines powerful computers whirring silently in a cold office, studying prices and patterns, generating buy and sell signals and placing orders directly to the exchange floors—the ultimate in mechanical trading. The computer solution should eliminate the human element from the equation, leaving only the perfection of bits, bytes, electrons, computer source codes, disk drives, modems and artificial intelligence!

Unfortunately, this Arcadian vision is flawed. As long as the *perfect computer* system trades markets with money that belongs to real human beings, the desire and possibly the need to override the system will continue to be a dysfunctional force. And the desire to undo the system will be greatest when the system is losing, increasing exponentially with each consecutive loss.

Assume that the computer system loses its starting capital. Will the trader fund the machine again? Or will the trader be inclined to alter the system—its parameters, its inputs and its outputs? If so, what has been gained? How is this system different from the original system, complete with the human weak link? Will the trader fund the "perfect system" with a vast amount of capital? Will the results be positive? Possibly so. In all probability the computerized trading system will be a neural network system that will have been *trained* to act in certain ways. There is no guarantee that its training will prevent it from significant draw-downs that may prompt the human operator to override the system, and its vast "intelligence" may not necessarily prevent the machine from losing its entire trading capital.

In theory the concept of completely mechanical trading is a good one. The desire to minimize or eliminate the human being from the equation is also a valid idea. It will be difficult, however, if not impossible, in actual practice to minimize the potentially harmful human effects from the trading equation. Experienced traders know that 10, perhaps 15 or more winning trades in sequence can be achieved, but it takes only one serious mistake to erase all the gains made on the winning series of trades.

Tip

Think about your trading. How many successive losses can you tolerate? Are you willing to quit a system after two successive losers? After three? After four? After five? If you're still *hanging in* after five successive losers, you possess more trading discipline than most traders. Consider that many outstanding trading systems have had as many as ten consecutive losers in their history, and you'll see how critically important persistence is in the formula for success.

What's the Answer?

What is the solution to this dilemma? Work with what exists, do the best with the tools that have been developed and hone trader behavior to the point that most serious trading errors will be minimized. Computer technology can help in this process; however, it is unlikely that computers will ever totally replace traders as the ultimate decision-makers. None of the purported advances in market analysis or computer technology has signifi-cantly improved the lot of the average trader in the 20 or more years during which I've been trading.

One thing that *has* vastly improved over the last 20 years is self-understanding. Intense psychological scrutiny has brought substantial progress in many areas of human behavior. The study of behaviorism, neurological processes and neurolinguistic programming has provided powerful tools for improving self-discipline, self-understanding, interpersonal relationships and business skills—tools that will improve trading results. Self-analysis and self-development in conjunction with new techniques provided by advanced computer-based trading research will ultimately prove to be the winning combination. An answer will not be found in any one area, but rather in the synergistic results of system testing and the development of trader skills, which, of course, include all aspects of trader psychology.

An Overview of Key Concepts

Many books teach the basics of futures trading. Since you probably are not a newcomer to futures trading, you may be inclined to skip this chapter. I suggest, however, that you read it carefully. While the concepts are basic, they are not elementary; they are the product of many trades and considerable research. My approach is not traditional and, given its divergent direction, may prove valuable in providing you with a new perspective.

Defining the Key Concepts

My trials and tribulations as a trader have led me to new understandings of the markets—understandings quite different from those I learned when I first began trading in the late 1960s. I realized early in my trading, although perhaps not early enough, that the way we define and understand the basic concepts of futures trading affects the way we trade. How we view the markets, or for that matter how we view any situation, shapes the way we respond. If we see life as a series of struggles, we will relate to life as a participant in the struggle and this identification will shape our behaviors. If we see the market as a challenge, we will treat it as a mountain climber treats his or her obstacle. We will seek the safest route to the top, always being aware that we must choose our steps carefully and that we might plummet earthward at any time unless our safety rope is secure.

This is the way most traders view the markets. Such a view injects an element of emotionalism into the markets that complicates the issue and is counterproductive. I would like, therefore, to offer a different point of view in the hope that it may inspire you to change your perception of the markets.

Purpose of the Futures Market

Contemporary approaches to futures trading theory and education seek to convince us that the futures markets serve an economic purpose. By standard definition, the futures market provides a vehicle that allows producers and consumers to buy and sell their products in an organized exchange using the public outcry system. We are told that speculators are valuable to the futures market inasmuch as they provide a buffer between producers and commercial consumers. We are told that the futures markets are the ultimate expression of a capitalist system and that they are essential to the effective functioning of our economy.

The collapse of Communism in the 1990s underscores the validity of capitalist vehicles such as our free market system, monetary system and futures trading, no matter how riddled with corruption and inefficiency they may be. And this solidifies traditional ideas about capitalism and the free market system.

Students of economics are indoctrinated with a variety of theories regarding the functioning of our economic system. They are educated in the laws of supply and demand; they are taught systems of macroeconomics, econometrics and economic forecasting. However, their tools are often useless in the market jungle where these rules do not apply. Where are those theories now as the killing wave of bankruptcies burns through the U.S. banking system? What happened to those Wharton and Harvard MBAs who helped lead their brokerage firms and insurance companies to ruin on a wave of junk bond investments? If our knowledge of markets and economics is so advanced, why do world economies experience continued volatility as well as periods of extreme boom and bust?

The Inadequacy of Old Knowledge

A college education is no longer sufficient for success in the markets and in life. The knowledge acquired from professors and books is merely a starting point for necessary life skills. The same holds true for the futures and stock markets. I propose that, for the purpose of the speculator, the market be considered a *black box*. I propose that the concepts of supply and demand be abandoned, and that the markets be seen in a new light. For those who must cling to the old ideas, I propose clinging to them in a new way, interpreting market behavior in terms of market behavior and not in terms that no longer suffice and may, in fact, never have served their theoretical purpose.

A Black Box Theory of Market Behavior: *The Money Exchange*

My understanding of the futures market is different from that of many traders. I suggest divorcing oneself from traditional understandings, viewing the marketplace as an organized vehicle for the exchange of money from weak hands to strong hands, from losers to winners, from the public to professionals. I propose understanding the market in terms of inputs and outputs. I see the basic input and output as one and the same: money. There are numerous small inputs and only a handful of major outputs. In other words, thousands of unsuccessful speculators contribute relatively small sums of money to the market, never to see most of it again, and a few successful traders remove large sums of money from the market. Between these two groups we have a host of other cost factors that remove money from both groups. Among these are brokerage commissions, market quotations costs, advisory services, commodity fund management fees, chart services, computer hardware and software costs, etc. Hence, the sum of the outputs will not equal the sum of the inputs unless we consider these cost factors as outputs.

The situation is clear and simple. Prices go up and down, traders take their positions, a majority of traders lose, and a minority of traders win. Your time as a trader is best spent not on understanding the precise nature of these inputs or the intricacies of their functioning, but rather on the tools that allow you to progress from the losing group to the winning group by knowing how to manipulate the inputs. I propose that we accept as fundamental market facts the following assumptions, and that once accepted we use them to achieve consistent success in the markets by skillfully manipulating them:

- The purpose of the futures markets is to provide a seemingly organized medium by which money can flow from weak hands to strong hands.
- Most traders will lose their speculative capital not just once or twice but repeatedly.
- Understanding market fundamentals is not necessary for success and may prove a hindrance in the quest for profits.
- Most of a trader's money will be made on a small number of trades while the higher percentage of trades will be losers or break-even trades.
- Some of a trader's worst losses will be a function of the self as opposed to the failure of a trading system.
- Success in the futures market will not be achieved by trading with a static system or method. Because markets constantly change the successful trader must also change. No single trading system will be effective in all markets at all times, or even in the same market at all times. I will provide suggestions later for monitoring and adapting to such changes. Trading systems and their operators must be dynamic.
- Traditional ideas regarding market entry and exit tools may be more myth than reality. These ideas must be abandoned in favor of techniques that can be thoroughly tested and evaluated in all types of markets.
- The traditional method of placing stop losses may not be the most efficacious. Stop losses should be placed according to the dictates of a trading system as opposed to a fixed percentage stop loss or a fixed dollar amount stop loss (with only a few exceptions).
- To stop losing and start winning, it is necessary to completely change one's *modus operandi* both operationally in the markets as well as personally in one's thoughts and actions.
- In addition to radically changing one's behavior and attitudes as well as one's goals in the markets, it will be necessary to become more mercenary, focusing complete attention on the goal of futures trading, which is, first and foremost, to make money.

- The idea that futures trading is primarily a form of entertainment, adventure, excitement, a gamble or a challenge must be abandoned.
- The market must be viewed as a treasure chest—a trader's job is to remove valuables from the chest skillfully, carefully and consistently. To do so the trader must know when the chest is most likely to open, how long it might remain open and when it is likely to slam shut.
- Each market has through the years acquired a "personality" of its own, which is most likely a reflection of the major traders involved in that market. An understanding of these unique and often revealing traits can assist you in your goals.
- The most successful trading methods are likely to be the most simple. Spend more time applying your methods as opposed to *optimizing* or complicating them.

Tip

It has been amply demonstrated that perception is a key, if not *the* key stimulus to many behaviors. There are many things you can do to alter your self-perception as well as your perception of the outer world. I suggest a thorough reading of Tony Robbins's *Unlimited Power* as an excellent source of information and training in this area. By altering your perception as well as your behavior, you will avoid the pitfalls of old and counterproductive habits, adapting new and profitable behaviors and perceptions.

Chapter
2

Systems Trading, Discipline and Profits

Cut your losses and let your profits ride.
The big money is made in the big pull.
Don't add to a losing position.
Always use stop losses.
Don't meet margin calls.
When in doubt stay out.
The trend is your friend.

The clichés are worn and weary. By now you've heard the rules about trading discipline at least a thousand times and you're tired of hearing them. To most traders these rules are nothing more than words—simple to understand but near impossible to implement. And there seems to be little anyone can do to drive the point home.

Traders are only human and, as a consequence, subject to the frailties of the human ego. We are unwilling to accept losses, unhappy when profits are small, afraid when prices are too low and too brave when prices are high. Regardless of how often traders take losses, they rarely learn from them. In one form or another, this subject has been the focal point of numerous books, tapes, seminars, courses and psychoanalysts' couches. Sad but true, few traders ever learn how to discipline themselves no matter how many losses they take.

Even more amazing is the fact that many traders are still convinced that their ticket to success is to find a better trading system. Actually, most traders will lose with any trading system no matter how well it tests, or how promising it appears to be. A disciplined trader can be highly successful with a mediocre trading system, and a bad trader can be a failure with an otherwise outstanding trading system. Clearly, there is only a limited positive correlation between trading system potential as revealed by historical testing and its actual performance in the hands of a trader. There is absolutely no doubt in my mind that *the trader makes the system and not vice versa*. This understanding should come as no surprise to any trader who has had a few years experience in the markets (and it already may be clear to those who have been trading for only several months).

Tip

During my years as a trader, I've drawn extensively on my experience as a clinical psychologist, my profession by education. My observations of trader behavior, including my own, have led me to the conclusion that to focus on improved trading systems before "healing" the self is to take the first step toward ruin.

Now that the problem has been stated, the issue is how to remedy it. To suggest that I can provide the answers in several pages of text would be the height of sophistry. I can, however, address the subject with considerable authority given my years of trading experience and my intensive observations of how others trade. Traders throughout the world have told me of the benefits they have derived from my 1980 book *The Investor's Quotient* and from my 1988 book *Beyond the Investor's Quotient*. Both books provided solutions to the behavioral and psychological problems shared by many traders. My work with trading systems both as developer and trader has given me a unique perspective on the discipline problems that face all traders. Although my suggestions can be very helpful, they are not to be taken merely at face value. They will need to be implemented, studied and refined to fit your trading style and your personality.

A Few Good Ways To Lose Money Trading the Futures Markets

E.L. Thorndike, the father of American learning psychology, noted that there are literally thousands of *wrong* behaviors and only relatively few *right* behaviors. His point was made in reference to the use of punishment as an aid to learning. While punishment has been used by parents, teachers and educators for many years, it is highly effective under specific circumstances but virtually ineffective in teaching new behaviors. If I punish you every time you do a particular thing I do not like, you will stop doing it; however, you may still do many other things that I do not like. I can punish you for each undesirable behavior, but my battle may be a lifelong one akin to picking dandelions from a lawn without removing the roots. While some new behaviors may be taught with punishment, the use of rewards for appropriate behaviors gets faster, better and longer-lasting results.

Consider the ramifications for education, effective child-rearing, personal development and positive interpersonal relationships. And consider the ramifications for the trader and investor. There are literally hundreds of investor behaviors and their variations that can lead to losses. However, there are few behaviors and their variations that can facilitate trading success. Unfortunately, most traders are prisoners of their faulty early-childhood education and are, therefore, also prisoners of their ineffective trading behaviors.

Although there are many ways to lose money in the markets, there are only a few ways to make it. And there are even fewer ways to keep it. While traders collectively spend millions of dollars every year attending seminars and buying books, tapes and trading systems, they focus little energy on learning behaviors that will facilitate success. Why? Because the rules of trading systems, methods and indicators are very specific, often objective, and frequently require nothing more than rote memorization. In other words, they're easy to learn and easy to apply.

Behaviors that contribute to success, on the other hand, are often intangible, somewhat subjective, situation relevant and individual dependent. No hard and fast rules apply to every trader. Frequently, traders are not in touch with the problems that require remediation. Not knowing what to change, they will surely be at a loss for techniques to help them make changes.

Perhaps my backdoor approach will be sufficiently unorthodox to get you started. Ignoring Thorndike and other outstanding behavioral psychologists, I'll tell you what you may be doing wrong. In so doing, I hope to break the monotony of *do this* and *do that* rules—rules that, although often heard, somehow fail to find their way to the cerebral cortex. Here, then, are some good ways to lose money in the futures (and stock) markets.

Plunge Headlong into the Market
Without a Plan of Action

This is an excellent way to lose money and lose it quickly. Why make a plan anyway? Would you drive from New York to Los Angeles without a map? You could. And you might be lucky enough to reach your goal without too many errors. You might even enjoy it! But each error would cost you, and some dearly. When your aimless travels end, you'll find that others have reached the goal faster and with less cost, both emotionally and financially. You want to take the ride for pleasure? That's fine, but don't expect to do it economically or quickly without a plan.

If you trade without a plan, your chances of success are slim to none. You may be one of the lucky few who hits it big the first time, but the odds of doing so are minimal. Without a plan, you will find yourself buffeted by the winds of chance, the opinions of others, the persuasion of newsletters and advisors, the pandering of brokers and the bias of the media. Your responses will be whimsical. But the greatest danger is that you will not learn anything from your behavior. If you are unaware of what you did wrong, the consequences of your actions will not be readily apparent to you. And you may run out of money before you learn your lessons.

But what exactly do I mean by a *plan*? Is it a trading system? A schedule? A set of rules? I define a trading plan as:

*A system or set of indicators that will permit relatively
objective evaluations of market entry and exit as well
as risk management.*

This could mean that you are following a computerized
trading system, signals from a chart book, newsletter, astrology,
random number generator, the *I Ching* or your broker. Regardless
of the source, the input must be treated as relatively unalterable
and followed as closely and as often as possible.

I do not advocate rigid adherence to any system. I do not favor
blindly following a totally mechanical system that might establish an unreasonable goal, which would surely result in failure
and a negative self-concept. I suggest instead employing a relatively mechanical trade entry system and a more flexible exit
system (to be discussed later on). In other words, I advise against
rigidity, against inflexibility and against blindly following any
plan. However, to stray from a plan intelligently, you must have
a plan at the outset.

There are various levels of adherence to a plan. Every trader
must find his or her own level of comfort in deviating from that
plan. Some traders will feel uncomfortable with only a minor
deviation from the course, while others will be able to tolerate
wide variances from their plans. The final determinant must be
your results in the marketplace. You alone can determine the
right formula by trial and error.

Read Many Publications, Watch the Television Business News and Follow the Consensus of Opinion

This is a surefire way to get confused and lose money at the
same time. I call this approach *Edsel trading*, named after the in-
famous Edsel that was designed by a committee attempting to
incorporate all of the changes and features recommended by
experts and consumers alike. While the Edsel may have been well
ahead of its time, it failed miserably as a product.

When you attempt to trade on the basis of the consensus of
opinion, you'll end up with an Edsel trading system, a system
that seems like it should work but doesn't. In fact, my research
with contrary opinion indicators strongly suggests that you are

better off trading against majority opinion rather than with it. Futures trading is a loner's game. You must find a combination of indicators and tools that works for you, and you must shut out as much outside influence as possible.

Add To Losing Positions To Average Your Cost

Here's a great method for losing your speculative capital. In fact, it works so well that many traders have virtually guaranteed themselves losses by following this time-tested strategy. The methodology is simple: whenever a position goes against you, hold on to it and add to it repeatedly to lower your average cost. When the market eventually moves your way, you will come out ahead. The reasoning is very logical in a game where no margin is required and time is not important. But in futures, and particularly in futures options, time passed is money lost. Contracts expire, margin calls continue, and the trend most often continues in its existing direction. While you may be right in the long run, you will most likely be broke in the short run.

Take Your Profits Quickly and Ride Your Losses

This is another popular strategy among losers. To see why this approach is so popular, let's examine its psychology. Most traders are anxious. They are so worried about the ego-deflating experience of being wrong and losing money that when they have a profit they are afraid it will not last. They are inclined to jump out of their profits quickly to get the gratification of knowing that they have banked the money and that the market cannot take it back. However, when there is a loss, things are quite different. Traders simply cannot admit to a loss. There is the perennial hope that things will eventually get better, that the market will turn around. And each small turnaround rewards the trader for hanging on. Unfortunately, it is often a classic case of one step forward and two steps back as the position continues to erode.

Several years ago I was hired to speak at the Alabama Farm Bureau. After my speech several attendees introduced me to an elderly gentleman whom they claimed was the best trader in the area. He was most eager to show me his trading system.

"It's really very simple," he said as he produced a small leather pouch from his pocket, removing a metal ball connected to a bead chain.

"I take this here pendulum and I hold it steady over a chart of the market I want to trade. Then I let the pendulum loose and I watch it closely. Most often it'll start to swing on its own. If it swings left to right, then I buy. If it swings top to bottom, then I sell. That's it!"

He was obviously very proud of his system and I certainly did not want to burst his bubble. So I nodded approval, hoping to hide my skepticism.

"Are there any other rules to your system, sir?" I asked with a serious and analytical tone.

"Well, yep, there's jus' one more part of this here program, but it don't amount to much," he drawled.

"What's that?" I asked skeptically.

"Well, it's a simple little thing. If'n at the end of the day my new position shows me a profit then I keep it. But if it's a loser then I kick it out. And any day after that if'n my position turns into a loser at the end of the day then I kick it out," he stated with an air of childlike innocence.

I realized immediately that in this last simple statement rested the essence of his success as a trader; he kept the winners and liquidated the losers quickly! He did the opposite of what most traders do. In essence his system of trade selection was a random system. The key to his profitable trading was that he *eliminated losing trades early in the game and rode winning trades until his system turned negative, or until they proved their lack of worth by becoming losers.* In so doing, he kept his losses small and his profits large by comparison. It was a simple system indeed, so simple that it worked well.

Start with Limited Capital and Attempt To Parlay It into a Fortune

This is the trader's utopian dream. The Horatio Alger story is still the image that inspires traders to take their shot at making it big in futures trading. Most traders begin with limited capital seeking to hit the one big trade that will propel them to success. However, the odds of doing so are slim. The simple fact is: the less you start with, the lower your odds of success. It's a matter of logic. If you're hoping to get on board that one big move, it may take ten consecutive losers before the winner comes. By then your capital could easily be depleted, and you'll miss the move you were hoping for.

My advice: be realistic. Begin with a good capital base. Be prepared for numerous small losses. Expect to be wrong five, even ten, trades in a row before you hit a big trade. When you do hit a big one, don't be too quick to get out. Remember that the less you begin with, the less likely will be your chances of success.

Find a Trading System, Advisory Letter or Money Manager That Has Performed Well and Latch On

Now here is another sure-fire way to lose your shirt. The time to go with a winner is when it has had a string of losses. Unfortunately, this is not the way most traders make their decisions. The temptation to go with a system or money manager is greatest when their performance has been outstanding, when they have attracted the most attention by their performance. I suggest that you find a good performer, wait until it has experienced a good-sized decline and go with it. However, please note that your incentive to get on board will not be very high when the decline in performance is in process.

Quit Your Job, Withdraw Money from the Bank, Get a Computer, Subscribe to a Quote Service and Begin Trading

I have seen more traders lose money this way than any other way. Futures trading is a profession. It takes time to learn the techniques, and it takes experience to implement those techniques successfully. There is no substitute for actual trading experience. It never ceases to amaze me how many doctors, lawyers and engineers quit their otherwise stable and lucrative professions to take up trading. Even more amazing is the sad but true fact that these professionals think they can make money by taking a few courses or seminars, or by reading a few books. When their efforts meet with losses, they are surprised that they have failed. What they have failed to understand is that futures trading is not like being a doctor, lawyer or engineer. The rules are not as well-defined, nor do they produce positive results as regularly as do the rules of their professions.

My advice is simple. Don't quit your job. Don't buy expensive quote equipment or computers. Don't fool yourself into thinking that the right system, the right computer or the right broker will make you successful. Trial and error, experience, self-discipline and consistency will, in the short run and in the long run, make you more money than will expensive equipment.

Use Spreads To Avoid Losses

This may seem like a sophisticated strategy. In actuality, it's just another way of avoiding a loss until it gets big enough to cause serious pain. While there's nothing wrong with trading spreads as spreads, there's everything wrong with spreading a position to avoid a loss. The only thing this will do for you is to lock in the loss. Often both sides of the spread will work against you, and you will end up increasing your loss. The time to take your loss is when the time to take your loss has come—it's not time to spread the position to avoid a loss. When used appropriately, spreads are good vehicles that may be used very profitably. They are vehicles used by professional traders by virtue of their consistency and adherence to seasonal patterns. However, when used to avoid a loss, they can be deadly.

Pyramid Your Position as It Becomes Profitable

Pyramids are burial vaults. Unfortunately, many traders mistakenly believe that as a market moves in their favor, they must add successively larger numbers of contracts to capitalize on the move. What happens, of course, is that the pyramid is built upside down. These individuals will buy one unit at the start of a move, add two or three more at a higher price, and add five or six more at an even higher price. The pyramid becomes top-heavy, and the slightest change in trend will send it crashing to the ground along with the trader's profits.

If you're going to build a pyramid, build it with a sound base. Establish your largest position at the beginning of a move and add successively smaller numbers of units as the market moves in your favor. You will still have a good-sized position when the move comes to an end, and your average cost will be much better than if you had built the top-heavy pyramid. In spite of all we know about futures trading and all that has been written about the ill-advised procedure of the top-heavy pyramid, there are still traders who think this strategy will work for them. In practice, success with this type of pyramiding is rare indeed.

Attempt To Pick Bottoms and Tops as often as Possible

After all, the better your entry and the better your exit, the more money you stand to make. The reasoning sounds good, and if there were a good way to pick tops and bottoms with a high degree of accuracy, the reasoning would be correct. But tops and bottoms are elusive, and they are dangerous. There is often a great deal of volatility associated with tops and bottoms. This makes them hard to find and hard to stay with once they have been found.

Larry Williams, perhaps the most prolific systems developer and one of the most aggressive traders I know, once shared his thoughts about top and bottom picking with me. He remembered the words of an old and experienced futures trader who told him, "Trying to pick a bottom or a top is like trying to catch a falling knife; it's very dangerous. Don't try to catch a falling knife. Wait until the knife hits the ground and digs its way into it. And then don't pick it up until it stops quivering." In the long run you will be much better off attempting to enter after tops and bottoms have been established, and better off trying to take a part of each trend than in attempting to pick a bottom or a top.

Buy Futures Options To Limit Your Risk

This is a wonderful way to throw your money into the deep dark hole. At first blush this strategy seems just as logical as do many others. Joe Granville used to say, "If it's obvious, then it's obviously wrong." This is especially true in futures options. In practice a vast majority of put and calls expire worthless. To buy a call when you expect an uptrend or to buy a put when you expect a downtrend is often a waste of time, money and commissions. Options lose time value quickly. Your timing with options must be even better than it is with futures; it's a case of double jeopardy. You buy an option because you think you're buying time. You think that your timing need not be as precise as it is with futures because you can only lose your premium plus commissions when you buy options, but this is the illusory aspect of the situation. Consider options strategies as opposed to an outright long or short in options.

Professional futures traders who make money with options are most often sellers of options since they know that most options expire worthless. They sell a deteriorating asset and the odds are clearly in their favor. Thus, if you're going to trade futures options, do it in a professional way by using options strategies and by being an options seller rather than an options buyer. Unless you're willing to approach options in a professional way, don't even bother getting involved in this market. The odds are against the options buyer.

Tip

Some of the worst abuses in the futures market have been perpetrated in futures options. Not only are the odds clearly stacked against the options buyer, but the commissions charged by some unscrupulous brokers are often much higher than what traders should pay. Remember this when you trade options.

How about Some Positive Suggestions?

Now that I have your attention, I will give you a few positive suggestions regarding trading discipline. Again, I will attempt to avoid standard recommendations. This is not to suggest that the time-tested methods do not work. Perhaps if explained and presented in a different way, they will make more sense.

Begin with a Simple Trading System

My years of research have revealed one important thing: the simplest trading systems often work best. Yes, I know all about the claims and the hypothetical performance records. I know all about the optimized systems and the black box systems and the virtues of artificial intelligence. But I keep coming back to the same conclusion as a result of my research: simple systems work best. They are easier to understand, implement and test. Once you have experienced profits using a simple method, you can experiment with complex systems and decide for yourself.

Be Independent, Isolate Yourself, Remain Pure

The trader's mind is a delicate machine. It is easily affected by the many inputs that daily impinge on the decision-making process. The futures market thrives on opinions, mass psychology, emotion, news and rumors. The less you hear, the better off you'll be. Your opinions are just as good as those of the next trader, and your systems, once tested, are as good as most. Most systems are correct between 50 and 65 percent of the time; however, even this 15 percent margin above chance occurrence is obviously not a large margin of safety. By allowing the input of others to affect you, this margin may be neutralized and you will lose your advantage. The ability to clearly see the markets is a great asset. The more you allow other opinions to influence you, the more you'll be like the rest of the trading world. You will not be in good company.

Don't Read the Market News   If you subscribe to one of the two daily U.S. financial papers, do so for technical data only. The news reports and opinions of the reporting staff are poison unless, of course, you can train yourself to do the opposite of what the majority recommends.

Don't Get More Than Two Advisory Services   Actually, you're better off with one or none. If you get one service, follow it as closely as you can. Don't pick and choose from among its recommendations. Follow all recommendations or follow none. Most traders pick and choose wrong.

Use a Discount Broker   Unless you do business with a broker who is also your advisor, use a discount broker who will not bother you with opinions or pressure you with trading ideas. If you decide on a broker who will also advise you, make sure it is one with considerable experience who is not in business for the simple purpose of generating commissions. Although difficult to find, such brokers are definitely out there.

Don't Discuss Your Trades with Anyone   Discussing your trades, signals, methods or indicators with other traders only infects them with your ideas and you with theirs. Confusion will be the end result.

Don't Read Popular Trading Magazines   Most are full of ideas that don't work. If you have arrived at your goal of self-discipline, read all you want. Otherwise, avoid trading magazines full of untested ideas, conjecture, heavy promotion, biased opinions, professional backbiting and advertisements that pander.

Don't Discuss the Markets with Friends   Your opinions are not important to friends and their opinions are not important to you. In stating your opinions, you will reinforce them to yourself, and you will be inclined to hold on to them in spite of what your system may say. A good trader will not express too many opinions, but will focus on actions, positions and signals instead.

Begin with Sufficient Capital, Trade Small Positions and Diversify Your Trading   Attempt to spread your risk over several different markets. Avoid the lure of large positions. The need to trade large positions essentially stems from ego and feelings of inadequacy. Many people need to compensate for negative self-concepts by asserting their power in the markets. They attempt to prove their *machismo* by being aggressive, trading large positions, taking chances and asserting their independence. You will be much better off beginning as a small fish in a big pond who seeks small reliable market moves as opposed to large, unreliable moves. Size creates problems. The larger your position the more difficult it will be to enter and exit trades with confidentiality and at good price fills. It's not the size of your position that's important, but how you trade your position that will make you a winner or a loser. Once you have learned how to trade, you can tackle the problems that come with large positions.

Change Your Perception of the Market   That's easier said than done! All organisms are captives of their perceptions. If you see the market as an adversary, you will approach it as a soldier approaches combat. If, however, you perceive the market as a vehicle that you must learn to operate, you will learn how to operate it to your advantage. I am not suggesting that the futures or stock markets are so predictable that you will be able to play them like a fiddle. I am, however, suggesting that your attitude about the market will shape the way you trade. It is far easier to go with the flow of the market than it is to fight the trend.

Do Your Homework   If you have settled on a particular trading system or method, you must be strictly dedicated to keeping your work up-to-date. When you've taken a few losses, you'll be tempted to abandon your system or forget about your market work. Then, when your work is out-of-date, the market will begin a large move. You'll quickly get your work up-to-date only to realize that you've missed the start of the move and it's too late to get on board.

Be Prepared for Numerous Consecutive Losses   One of the most frustrating, anxiety-provoking things a trader can experience is a string of numerous consecutive losses. These are the most difficult times for futures traders. They cause errors, inconsistency, lack of discipline and the search for new systems. If you are prepared for the worst before it happens, you will be able to cope with it when it actually does happen. And, believe me, it will!

Tip

Develop a list of your own trading rules and keep it convenient whenever you trade. While you may feel that you know your rules well, you'll be surprised at how often you slip into losing behaviors almost reflexively. Your list will serve as an excellent reminder. It will keep you on the right track, and it will help you remain honest with yourself. Keeping a list of your rules and reading it frequently will help you avoid the pitfalls of self-deception and misperception.

Part
2

Testing Signals and Understanding Test Results

Chapter

3

Systems Testing

The days of untested systems are gone forever. In fact, the pendulum is now swinging in the other direction. While unscrupulous operators "in the days of old" sold systems and methods for which they claimed fantastic results, today's unethical operators use statistics as a tool of deception. The public will always be easily duped by these individuals who, paradoxically, will benefit from the trend toward the statistical validation of systems. Manipulating statistics is not difficult. Just as Archimedes once said, "Give me a place to stand on and I can move the earth," the modern systems promoter would likely say, "Give me enough statistics and I can prove anything."

This sermonette on system validation makes the point that merely testing a system and generating highly favorable hypothetical results does not guarantee success with that system. Nor should such statistics be used as a security blanket or crutch by traders. Statistics can easily be manipulated—systems can be (and are) curve-fitted, and results, unless realistic, will not reflect actual performance when the system is implemented.

While many systems are developed to show optimum performance, it is imperative that systems be tested to show the worst-case performance.

Why Test Trading Systems?

Traders test systems for various reasons. Some test a system merely to say they've done so, only to disregard the outcome or to accept mediocre results, rationalizing the negative aspects of their "system." Other traders test systems in order to sell them to the public—their goal is to optimize systems in order to show maximum performance. Then there's the serious futures trader who tests systems to achieve several goals, including but not limited to the following:

- To determine whether a theory or hypothetical construct is valid in historical testing
- To summarize the overall hypothetical performance of a system and to analyze its various aspects in order to isolate its strong and weak points
- To determine how different timing indicators interact with one another to produce an effective trading system
- To explore the interaction of risk and reward variables (i.e., stop loss, trailing stop loss, position size, etc.) that would have returned the best overall performance with the smallest drawdown

Test Your Trading System

While it may seem that the last item listed above refers to optimization, you will see from the discussion of optimization later in this chapter that it is not optimization according to my definition of the term. The purpose of testing systems is simply to find what will work best for you based on what appears to have worked best in the past. In so doing, we must remember that what worked in the past in hypothetical testing may not necessarily work in the future.

A thorough test of your trading system should include at least the following information:

Number of Years Analyzed

Although it is desirable to test as much data as possible, many trading systems and indicators do not withstand the test of time. The farther back you test, the less effective most systems will be. Many system developers test only ten years of historical data since that best shows their systems. You must make your own decision regarding the length of your test.

Number of Trades Analyzed

More important than the number of years analyzed is the number of trades. You need not analyze many years of data if you have a large sample size of trades. I recommend at least 100 trades, provided your system will generate this number of trades in back-testing. If you are truly interested in determining the effectiveness of your system, the more trades you test, the better. Remember that there will always be a tendency to test fewer trades when you realize that the system is not holding up under back-testing. Some traders argue that the factors underlying futures market trends 25 years ago were distinctly different from those during the past ten years. They feel that testing 25 years of data distorts the picture. If they are correct, how would we know when the current market forces change and that we must therefore change our trading systems? We are much better off finding systems that work in all types of markets.

Maximum Drawdown

This is one of the most important aspects of a trading system. A very large drawdown is a negative factor since it eliminates most traders from the game well before the system would have turned in its positive performance. Since most traders are not well capitalized, they cannot withstand a large drawdown. However, drawdown is a function of account size. Obviously, a $15,000 drawdown in a $100,000 account is not unusual; however, the same drawdown in a $35,000 account is serious. You may decide to risk large drawdown in order to achieve outstanding performance, but this is your decision.

Consider also the source of the drawdown by examining the largest losing trade. If the majority of the drawdown occurred on only one trade, you will be better off than if the drawdown was spread out over numerous successive losses.

Maximum Consecutive Losses

This performance variable is more psychological than anything else. An otherwise excellent trading system may have lost money on many trades in succession. Few traders can maintain their discipline through four or more successive losing trades. Even after the third loss, many traders are ready to either abandon their system or to find ways of changing it. However, at times it is necessary to weather the storm of ten or more successive losses. If you know ahead of time what the worst case scenario has been, you will be prepared. That's why it's important for your system test to give you this information.

Largest Single Losing Trade

This important piece of information indicates how much of the maximum drawdown is the result of a single losing trade. And this allows you to adjust the initial stop loss in retesting the system so as to see how large the average losing trade has been. If the average losing trade, for example, was $1,055 and the largest single loser was $8,466, you can readily see that a good portion of the average losing trade was a function of the largest loser. This shows that if you had a better way of managing the large loser (in hindsight, of course), your overall system performance would have been considerably better.

I strongly recommend close examination of the actual trade that resulted in the single largest loss if this loss is clearly much higher than the average losing trade. Another question to ask is: Why was the largest single losing trade so much larger than the stop loss selected? A single largest losing trade that is several times larger than your selected stop loss points to a potential problem, perhaps with the system test. You must investigate further in such cases.

Largest Single Winning Trade

Perhaps more important than the largest single losing trade is the largest single winning trade. If, for example, your hypothetical profits total $96,780, and $33,810 of this is attributed to only one trade, you have a distorted average trade figure. It's often a good idea to remove this one trade from the overall results and recompute them in order to show the performance without this extraordinary winner. You may find that the system you have tested is mediocre, perhaps even a loser, when the single largest trade has been eliminated from the performance summary. If you can wait ten years for the one big trade, then use the system—but do so against my advice. What you're looking for in any system with regard to average winning and losing trades is consistency—far more important than one or two extremely large winning trades that give a distorted performance picture.

The performance summaries shown later list the largest single winning long and short trades. Frequently these two trades alone account for a considerable portion of the net system profits. While some traders feel that this somehow diminishes the value of the system, I disagree. As long as at least one-half of the overall system performance is due to trades other than the largest single winning long and short trade combined, the system is valid. As far as numbers are concerned, I would not use any system that, after deducting reasonable slippage and commission as well as the largest single long and short winners, does not show at least $100 average profit per trade.

More importantly, because a large portion of profits in many systems derive from a very small number of trades, it is imperative that you follow each and every trade as closely to the rules as possible. Trading systems are not money machines; they don't grind out one profit after another. Trading systems make their money on the bottom line. There are many losers and few winners. The losers are kept in check by using money management stop losses that must, in most cases, be reasonably large. And the winners, only a few of which are very large, make the game worth the candle. The trader who can't stick with a position, or let it ride, is the trader who will be sorely disappointed with the results because the big winners will be cut short.

Later in this book I will make a case for systematic market entry and less rigid market exit. Bear in mind, however, that when this procedure is followed you must stick with the original system as closely as possible for market entry. Such adaptations are recommended for the skilled trader only!

Percentage Winning Trades

This statistic is not nearly as important as one might think. In actuality few systems have more than 65 percent winning trades; and the more trades in your sample, the smaller this figure will be. Systems that are correct as little as 30 percent of the time can still be good systems; and systems that are accurate as much as 80 percent of the time can be bad systems. It's easy to see that even a high degree of accuracy with a large average losing trade and small average winning trade does not make a good system.

Average Trade

This statistic will tell you what the average hypothetical trade has been. You must make certain that when you test your system you deduct slippage and commission from your average trade. Commissions add up, even discount commissions. And slippage is an important factor when determining system performance. As a rule of thumb I recommend deducting between $75 and $100 per trade for slippage and commission. Once this has been done, you will often significantly reduce the average trade figure. As I pointed out earlier, you must also pay close attention to the largest winning trade and the largest losing trade when evaluating the average trade. The average trade figure is important since it considers all profits, all losses, slippage and commission.

Optimization and Retesting

There has been considerable controversy about trading system optimization. What exactly is wrong with optimizing systems? Can you go too far? Is there a happy medium?

What Is Optimization?

The real issues in system optimization are complex, and they've been exacerbated by the tendency of systems developers to optimize their programs above and beyond any reasonable degree. To optimize a system is to discover the parameters that provide the best results in hypothetical back-testing. In other words, optimization is a form of discovering what would have produced the best results using numerous *if-then* scenarios.

Before low-cost computer hardware and software, optimization was a long and laborious procedure. To discover the best *fit*, the systems developer would need to repeatedly backtrack and test several variables. If the system parameters were numerous, the process was virtually impossible. Obviously, computers have made this a quick and efficient task.

Such ease of testing and optimizing is both good and bad. On the one hand it allows traders to develop, test and refine (i.e., optimize) systems much more rapidly. On the other hand it has opened the door to what is called *curve-sitting*. The simple fact is that the powerful system-testing programs now available allow traders as well as systems vendors to repeatedly test a host of timing variables, stop losses and other risk management schemes in order to determine which combinations would have produced the best results. In effect this procedure fits the best parameters on past history to produce the best hypothetical results. However, the conclusions reached by such methods are often deceptive and specious.

The trader who tests and retests to find the best fit will eventually reach his or her goal, but the goal itself may be nothing more than a reflection of the curve-fitted results. Tests tell us what has worked in the past, but may not reveal anything worthwhile about the future. Since the past is not a carbon copy of the future, it is doubtful that the optimized parameters will work in the future. The more parameters in the decision-making model, the less likely they are to work in the future.

Overly optimized results lead to false conclusions. The result will likely mean losses. For those who develop and sell futures trading systems as a business, optimization is an amazing tool that allows the creation of outstanding hypothetical performance results that in turn allow systems developers to make incredible claims. And claims sell systems.

Time will tell if I am wrong about overly optimized systems. Vast personal experience, however, strongly validates my conclusions. I recall recent developments regarding several popular trading systems sold by a software developer. The advertised claims were fantastic. Systems were sold for T-bond futures, S&P and currency futures. The outstanding performance claims provided a strong media campaign.

Naturally, all of the proper disclaimers were made to comply with the then current regulatory requirements. There were no disclaimers regarding optimized results, however, nor was it disclosed that *not all buyers of the systems would be using the same system parameters.* Because the systems were continually optimized for best results, the hypothetical track records were truly impressive. However, the results did not necessarily jibe with results experienced by those who had old versions of the software—versions that did not reflect the new optimized parameters. This is high-tech deception. Recognizing that there might be legal liability, the systems developers eventually disclosed this fact in small print. Few buyers understood the meaning of the disclosure and even fewer cared, given the impressive hypothetical performance record. Naturally, buyers of the software felt that they could match the hypothetical performance.

In many cases these traders did well initially. A customer in my brokerage firm purchased one of these programs and began trading it strictly according to the rules. The results were impressive. I began to watch intently every time a trade was made. It was uncanny how well the system entered and exited trades. It was as if the system had internalized a sixth sense about the market. Then, after several months and excellent results, the system began to unravel. Numerous large losses occurred and performance deteriorated more rapidly than it had climbed. The dangers of an overly optimized system became apparent once again.

A Rational Approach to System Development

I do not totally oppose optimizing trading systems. I do favor a rational approach to this procedure. My rule of thumb is simple: your trading system should have no more than four to six variables. You should search for the best combination of entry and exit variables as well as a reasonable combination of stop loss and trailing stop loss amounts. But this is where the optimization should end. The more variables you build into the system, the less likely will be the future performance of the parameters.

Another aspect of system development relates to market personality—a topic that has received little attention by most traders and market analysts. Rather than heavily optimizing a system, I recommend tailoring your system to the personality characteristics of the individual markets, provided that such characteristics exist and that they are sufficiently stable. The analysis that follows in Chapter 4 includes my evaluation of market personality types, and contains some suggestions on which types of systems might be used in the different markets.

Chapter
4

Personality Characteristics of the Futures Markets

Market personality has not received sufficient attention over the years. Since every futures market is affected by numerous and diverse fundamentals—fundamentals that are at times radically different from one another, it seems logical that markets would behave differently when evaluated technically. That markets appear to have individual personalities has long been known to traders. While my choice of the term personality to describe the markets may seem inappropriate, I am convinced, based on my experiences, that there couldn't be a better choice.

During my years of practice as a psychologist with the State of Illinois, I worked extensively in intelligence and personality testing. My experience with personality evaluation of psychiatric patients has been a valuable asset in understanding futures traders and has provided considerable insight into the personalities of markets.

In the clinical evaluation of human personality, the psychologist can choose from numerous assessment tools that gain a glimpse into a certain aspect or aspects of human personality. The psychology of tests and measurement provides practitioners with a variety of tools ranging from the purely technical to the intuitive. While most lay people are familiar with the Rorschach or *ink blot* test, they are unfamiliar with such tools as the MMPI (Minnesota Multiphasic Personality Inventory) or the TAT (Thematic Apperception Test).

The MMPI requires simple yes or no responses to several hundred specific items such as *My father was a good man*. The responses are evaluated by computer and compared to a series of base responses of various diagnostic categories. A given individual's response pattern might most closely resemble those of anxiety neurotics or phobics, and a diagnosis is made on this basis. Although the MMPI has been one of the most widely studied and administered technical inventories, there is still considerable controversy (as in virtually every area of psychology) regarding its accuracy and efficacy.

Tools such as the Rorschach and TAT are more open-ended. They require a free associated verbal response to a set of standardized ink blots or, in the case of the TAT, concrete pictorial situations (i.e., two people in close proximity). The individual in⁺erprets what he or she feels is taking place, and the nature of these responses, called projections, provides evidence regarding the subject's internal mental processes.

In studying market behavior, the trader who evaluates systems is doing essentially the same thing. The technician evaluates market personality by imposing a set of standards (i.e., timing indictors or a trading system) on the market and by determining how well the indicators evaluated the personality of the market. A system that worked well on the basis of hypothetical back-testing is assumed, right or wrong, to be a system that will continue to work (i.e., produce profits) in the future. In other words, the system test will relate the personality of the market.

The Intuitive Approach to Market Evaluation

Another way of evaluating market behavior is more intuitive, although with intensive study and examination the intuitive process could no doubt be quantified. An intuitive approach to evaluating the futures markets might consider many variables. Here are some of the questions in my intuitive market evaluation:

Who Are the Major Players?

The wheat market, for example, is dominated by large producers and grain companies. All grain complex markets are affected by weather, which has always played a dominant role in determining price trends. Knowing this about the personality of wheat futures, a trader would be more inclined to use seasonally based indicators. If the key players in wheat futures are larger (i.e., highly capitalized) traders, the market may be in a reasonably good state of balance most of the time (i.e., supply and demand in balance) and prices might, therefore, be at a fair value most of the time. Hence, wheat futures might not be a good vehicle for most speculators other than at times when weather is a factor. The same might hold true for the other grains.

Soybean oil and soybean meal, on the other hand, are markets that work well on a spread or ratio basis. More demand for soybean oil causes end users to pay higher prices for soybean oil, which in turn causes more beans to be crushed and creates an oversupply of soybean meal. The spreads and ratios between soybeans, soybean oil and soybean meal are important in understanding these markets, and a technical trading system might also consider these factors as part of the overall system. And, of course, there is the important consideration of competitive oilseeds such as cottonseed oil, palm oil, canola oil, etc. Problems with these crops will affect the price of soybean oil. And this will be reflected by the buying and selling actions of large commercial traders, both producers and end users. A thorough understanding of these facts can be helpful in understanding the personality of the soybean oil market and in developing a trading system that will be effective in this market.

The platinum market, for example, has had two big players—the Soviet Union and Japan. The Soviets are the world's largest producer and supplier, and the Japanese have been one of the world's largest buyers. This makes platinum a volatile market that has exhibited numerous large price swings. Once platinum prices begin a major trend, they tend to continue in that trend. Knowing this, the trader could use a volatility breakout system on platinum futures since it would be imperative to avoid the many small whipsaws in such a market.

What Are the Political Factors?

Do political factors help shape the personality of a market? Yes! The machinations of the G7 and the EEC have had a significant impact on currency futures. Since they are closely correlated with the interest-rate trend in their respective countries and by virtue of the interrelationships between interest rates in different countries, currency futures have had a history of strong trends. Why? Because central banks (i.e., government banks) tend to change their interest rate policies slowly. Once set into motion, a trend in interest rates tends to continue for a fairly long time, and this in turn results in fairly lengthy currency trends. This is an important revelation about market personality since it clearly directs the trader to use trend-following systems in the currencies. And we know from experience that such systems work well in the interest rate and currency markets.

As another example, palladium futures, although not actively traded, could one day become explosive since over 95 percent of all world supplies are the result of Soviet production. A supply cutoff could send the price of palladium into the stratosphere should the Soviets ever decide to exercise their power. This is most revealing concerning the personality of palladium as a sleeping giant. Volume is thin, but one day prices may explode. What to do? The astute trader would avoid palladium most of the time while closely monitoring trading volume. A sudden rise in trading volume and open interest would be *prima facie* evidence that something big is in the works. In this case knowing the personality of the palladium market could prove to be extremely profitable to the speculator.

Does the Market Tend To Follow Through, or Does It Fizzle?

Some markets tend to continue moves for a long time once they break out in one direction or another. Coffee, Japanese yen and lumber are among the best in this respect. Other markets such as wheat, corn and oats tend to have large moves over relatively brief periods of time. Knowing this, the futures trader would adjust the type of system and signals used in the different markets to suit their propensity for trends or lack thereof.

How Are Tops and Bottoms Typically Established?

Some markets tend to form climactic tops and bottoms. Among these are gold, silver, cotton, soybeans and pork bellies. Some markets tend to establish rounding or base-building bottoms. Among these are sugar, live hogs, corn, wheat, oats and Canadian dollar. Knowing these traits enables a trader to be patient in awaiting bottoms. Quick exit of long positions or prompt entry of short positions near tops in markets such as gold, silver, cotton, soybeans and pork bellies is also advisable given the nature of these markets to establish climactic tops.

Is the Trading Public More Active in Certain Markets Than in Others?

And if so, of what value might this information be? Some markets are dominated by the trading public while others have more of a professional following. Lumber futures, for example, are not particularly popular with the trading public; however, the market is one of the most seasonally predictable and strongest trending markets. If we observe that the public has suddenly acquired an active buying interest in lumber futures following a sustained uptrend in price, it is safe to assume the price move is nearing its end.

Is the Market Dominated by Day Traders or Position Traders?

The S&P futures market, for example, is dominated by day-time frame traders. Why? The contract margin is so high it dissuades many traders both on and off the floor from carrying a large or at times even a small position overnight. Hence, S&P futures are dominated by considerable intraday activity and volatility. Knowing this aspect of S&P futures personality can easily point the futures trader in the direction of short-term and day trading using intraday timing systems to catch the short-term swings.

This introduction has only scratched the surface of market personality evaluation. I've compiled my thoughts regarding the personality of each major futures market in greater detail on the following pages. Knowing these traits may help you considerably in researching trading systems and methods that are effective. Bear in mind that the personality of a market may change; however, this process usually takes a considerable amount of time and there is often sufficient warning that things are changing. Those who actively traded shell egg futures in the late 1960s and early 1970s, for example, will recall that this was the pre-eminent seasonal market for a number of years, but when egg production facilities were upgraded and temperature controlled, the market began to fade and trading volume eventually dwindled to nil. And, of course, there were onion futures in the 1950s and potato futures in the 1970s, each with their unique personality. Just as human personality can change, so can market personalities, but the process usually takes time.

A Thumbnail Sketch of Markets by Their Personalities

What follows is a personality evaluation of each market as I have come to know it during my years as a trader. Remember that these evaluations are subjective, but not entirely so, since they are based on observation, first-hand experience and technical studies. You may not agree with my analyses since your experiences with each market may have been different. I offer you these analyses, however, in the hope that they may lead you to profitable avenues of systems research.

Live Cattle

This is a highly seasonal market that can sustain trends for a considerable length of time. Of all the futures markets, live cattle (and feeder cattle) exhibit the most regular and predictable price cycles, which are a function of the production process, gestations, and the time required to raise animals to market readiness. These cycles, measured low to low, are approximately 9 to 11 months, 20 to 24 months and 10 years. These trends, both up and down, are not without substantial and fairly lengthy corrections that often prohibit riding the trend too long.

Trading systems here should, therefore, be more swing-oriented, attempting to play the numerous uptrends, down-trends and cycles within the longer term or secular trend. Because the cattle market is dominated by hedgers and commercial users, the downside corrections in a bull market tend to last longer than expected, while the upside corrections in bear markets can be quite strong. In general, cattle producers are slow to admit to errors and inclined, therefore, to hold on to livestock without hedging them until prices have fallen considerably. Then, at a low ebb they are often pressured by their bankers to sell their animals, often at a loss, which gives the market its tendency toward a final and strong push down. The market produces *holes* of supply caused by such forced liquidation. The holes, both up and down, account for some brief but fairly strong moves both up and down. Timing indicators should focus on cyclical lengths as valuable guidelines.

Live Hogs

Since the fundamentals of hog production differ from those of cattle production, the hog market is quite different from the cattle market. The life cycle of hogs is considerably shorter than that of cattle, which makes the hog market more immediately responsive to fundamentals. While the hedging element still accounts for sharp and sudden changes in trend, the market is an excellent trading vehicle provided the trader approaches prices from a shorter-term perspective. Technical trading systems that are short-term oriented have good potential. By short term I mean an approximate 5-day to 15-day perspective.

As a point of information, hog futures are among the most seasonally reliable of the futures markets. The tendency for hog prices to bottom in late October and to move higher until late November is among the ten highest probability seasonal tendencies in the entire futures market complex. This tendency has occurred over 80 percent of the time since the start of trading in hog futures. And there are several other seasonal tendencies that are highly reliable as well.

A combination of short-term timing indicators as well as seasonal indicators is very effective in hog futures given this market's well-established personality. And the size of the hog contract in terms of dollars per tick is attractive to new futures traders who won't need to risk as much as they might in other futures markets.

Pork Bellies

The personality of pork bellies is akin to that of a jet-setter. The best way to describe this market is: *live fast, die young*. In the 1970s it was the preeminent market for speculators. Although trading volume has declined significantly as traders turned their attention to more volatile markets such as currencies and stock index futures, pork bellies remain high on the list of higher risk, high reward markets. Bellies are suitable for day trading, short-term trading, cyclical trading, technical trading, seasonal trading and spread trading.

The unique personality of pork belly futures is shaped by the nature of its storage fundamentals. The only futures months traded are February, March, May, July and August. From August through February there are no delivery months. This is due to the production cycle of pork bellies. Because demand slows once the summer is over, producers reduce bacon production. Bellies are placed in storage for delivery against the February contract. Specifications of the belly contract, however, prohibit the delivery of August bellies against the February contract. In other words, pork bellies in storage during August cannot be delivered against the February contract. This makes for some interesting price moves. It is not unusual for August and February bellies to move in opposite directions. The August/February pork belly spread is one of the most volatile spreads is one can trade. There is also a high degree of seasonality in this spread.

In addition to the above characteristics, the belly market has been the whipping boy of health-conscious consumers and physicians for many years. Everything about eating bacon is unhealthy—it's high in fat and cholesterol, high in salt and loaded with nitrites that purportedly increase the risk of cancer. The eating of pork is not permitted by the Moslem and Jewish religions. These objections and events relating to them have exacerbated the volatile personality of bellies.

Finally, the pork belly market has for many years been dominated by a handful of aggressive pit readers who frequently drive prices to considerable extremes even on an intraday basis. Tops and bottoms in this market, therefore, do not form slowly. They are often violent and dynamic. It has not been unusual for pork belly prices to move up several hundred percent following an extreme and sustained bear market.

Given the nature of the pork belly market, I advise against using market orders unless absolutely necessary. Stop limit and stop limit orders with a few ticks discretion are recommended alternative as are *fill or kill* orders. Be particularly cautious with *market if touched* (MIT) orders since they are frequently filled a distance from the specified price in "fast market" conditions.

Most technical trading systems should prove effective in pork bellies as should seasonally based trading systems. In addition to the above there has been a strong cyclical component in pork bellies that affords for successful trading using the approximate 9-month to 11-month cycle as well as the approximate 3-year to 4-year cycle. More information about both cycles (and many others) can be found in my *Handbook of Economic Cycles.*

Corn

This market has been the mainstay of the grain and soybean complex commodities. Its futures history is a long and reliable one based both on seasonal and cyclical patterns. Due to the dependence of corn production on weather factors, the market has often violently responded to such conditions. The rallies have been relatively brief but very dynamic when there has been drought, disease, excessive rainfall or an early frost. These are, however, the exception rather than the rule.

The overall personality of corn futures is relatively mild-mannered. The market tends to make slow and steady moves in both directions interspersed with periods of violent up and down moves due to the previously described factors. Hence, the speculator has two choices—either trade corn futures when weather becomes an important consideration, or trade corn from an extremely long-term orientation using wide stop losses to avoid the substantial market corrections that characterize the long-term bull markets in corn.

If you use a short-term system that keys in only on weather-related markets, be prepared to take profits quickly. Most weather-related bull markets in corn run their course in six to ten weeks.

Oats

Experienced futures traders will recognize the expression *gentlemen don't trade oats.* I emphatically disagree. While there is no doubt that trading activity in oats is very limited, it is also true that the oats market tends to lead the other grain markets. In addition to this tendency, the oats market also exhibits strong seasonal tendencies as well as strong uptrends and downtrends. There has also been a tendency for oats to react violently to weather developments; however, the bull and bear markets tend to be longer lasting than they do in corn and some other grain complex markets. Given these characteristics of the oats market, I recommend a trend-following system and advise traders who have not studied or traded in the oats market to do so.

Wheat

While the wheat market is one of the oldest U.S. futures markets, it is not among the best trading vehicles. In fact, I have found very few systems that produce consistently good results in wheat other than those based on seasonal tendencies. When Burton Pugh wrote his classic series of booklets *The Science and Secrets of Wheat Trading,* he discussed wheat futures in considerable detail noting their tendency to fluctuate with the lunar cycle. During the early 1900s the market was extremely active, which contributed to liquidity and made wheat futures an excellent trading vehicle. Things have changed, however, and now wheat futures are not the premier grain market. While there are several periods of highly reliable seasonality during the year, wheat is generally a difficult market to trade from a technical standpoint.

Soybeans

Soybean futures have become the preeminent agricultural futures market. The market has both a strong speculative following as well as diverse commercial and hedger components. Trading activity is quite good and the market tends to establish fairly good trends lasting for longer periods of time. In both the American and South American growing regions, weather is a primary factor in soybean futures. Bull markets inspired by weather have been very volatile but tend to last for a relatively short time. Traders who are able to withstand considerable price corrections both up and down should participate in the market using a trend-following system.

Because soybeans are crushed for the production of soybean meal and soybean oil, there are spread relationships between the price of soybeans, soybean oil and soybean meal that can affect the markets considerably over the short run. Some knowledge of the soybean crush spread would, therefore, be helpful in evaluating the personality of soybean futures and determining which type of trading system and signals might work best.

Naturally, soybeans also have a strong seasonal component. For a complete picture of the market, the serious futures trader should be familiar with the soybean seasonals. Since seasonals are primarily a function of weather, most market up moves begin in late October to early November and are frequently over by the middle of July.

As with most of the grain complex markets, soybean futures are difficult to trade from a purely technical standpoint due to their often erratic nature. Soybeans may be traded on the basis of technical systems, however, many of the traditional approaches are not effective when considered on a longer-term basis.

Soybean Oil

While soybean oil futures are subject to many of the same influences that affect soybean prices, the market tends to be a better trading vehicle in terms of trends. It has been easier to find effective trading indicators in soybean oil than in soybeans or soybean meal. At $6 per tick this is a good market for short-term traders, and trends last longer than in some of the other grain complex markets. Frequently, simple or weighted MA techniques are effective in soybean oil. Because the bean oil market is very responsive to developments in other oilseed products around the world, it can be highly volatile at times. However, there is an important relationship between soybeans, soybean oil and soybean meal. The so-called *crush* spread can, at times, distort the individual behavior of soybean oil and soybean meal as supply-and-demand factors affect the spreads. Those who are willing to study the spread and combine it with their technical trading system in soybean oil and soybean meal could greatly improve their results.

Soybean Meal

Meal has been more of a professional market than a public market. Commercial activity is dominant and many trading systems will not fare well. However, a system that takes into consideration the activity of large traders can do well in meal. Hence, such methods as on-balance volume (discussed in Chapter 11) and the Market Profile® should prove very successful in forecasting and trading soybean meal. The market has had a strong ten-year cyclical tendency with major lows established during the first year of each decade.

Gold

Precious metals have been among the most widely followed markets. Given the international interest in gold, it is the premier metals market. But this does not automatically mean that gold is a good trading market or that technical trading systems will work well at all times. The core issues are volatility and trading volume. When trading volume and speculative interest are high, trading systems will do well; when there is little interest in gold, the market will slip into a narrow trading range, rendering most trend-following systems virtually useless.

Gold has other aspects to its personality as well. It has been regarded as a safe haven during times of crisis and often responds dramatically to political and financial crises both domestically and internationally. Such reactions, however, are often short-lived if they are not consistent with the existing trend. Hence, one good short-term method for trading gold is to buy on expectation of a crisis and sell on the news that a crisis has actually developed. There are a number of intraday timing tools that can be used effectively in such cases.

There has also been an important seasonal tendency in gold prices. For many years gold futures have made their low in the late summer and turned higher through year end. Many of the largest up moves in the history of gold futures have taken place from mid to late August through mid to late September. There has been an uncanny tendency for important news events to occur in August, and these events often, but not always, result in a price spike for gold. Two recent events have been the Gulf War and the aborted Soviet Coup.

Silver

For many years silver futures traded in a narrow range. But with the assistance of a bull market in gold, inflation and the Hunt brothers, the market moved sharply higher only to establish a major peak in 1980. Since the dynamic bull market of the late 1970s and early 1980s, silver has become a quiet market, spending more time in long stretches of ennui than in volatile bull moves.

Silver has come to be known as the *poor trader's gold* since it is often traded by those who are either fearful of gold or who prefer to trade silver due to the usually lower margin requirements. However, the personality of silver is shaped as much by the nature of its traders as it is by the nature of its dual usage. Silver is not primarily a precious metal nor an industrial metal—it is both. Hence, silver prices have the dual ability to rise in a demand market based on utilization as well as in an inflationary market in sympathy with gold. It should be observed, however, that silver can often be a leading indicator to tops in gold and platinum. When public speculative activity reaches a state of frenzy, a top in gold cannot be far off.

Silver futures are also a good market technically, provided, of course, that there is sufficient range to allow for speculative activity. Silver has been an excellent trending market, which is ideal for systems traders using trend-following systems. When silver futures become active, the market can also be an excellent vehicle for day traders. A day-trading method called Critical Time of Day (CTOD), described in my *Short-Term Traders Manual*, has been extremely effective in day trading silver futures when the trading range averages ten cents or more.

Given its speculative personality as well as its dual role, silver has proven an excellent trading vehicle. I advise all futures traders to trade silver when the market has reasonable volatility. When it does not allow for short-term or position trading, I recommend watching its activity closely so that you can get on board once trading conditions become optimum. A number of the trading systems described in Chapter 5, in particular the Consecutive Closes System, should work well in silver. Trend-following systems have also worked well.

Platinum

Just as silver is known as the poor trader's gold, platinum is known as the rich trader's gold. The platinum market is highly specialized, affected strongly by developments in the Soviet

Union and Africa, its two major producers, and by economic trends in Japan, its largest consumer. Platinum can make very large price moves over relatively short periods of time; however, it is not suitable for day trading since trading volume is often comparatively thin.

Given platinum role's in industries such as automobile manufacturing and petroleum production, the market has important industrial applications. While one might think that Japan is a large consumer due to its preeminent role in auto production, the fact is that Japanese investors have long favored platinum as an investment vehicle. Hence, Japanese involvement can drive prices sharply lower or higher based on two significant factors.

Trend-following systems work well in platinum provided one is willing to accept rather large risks in initial and trailing stop losses. The market needs plenty of leeway due to its volatility. I recommend platinum trading for experienced traders only. Order placement is very important in this market given its volatile and relatively thin trading.

The importance of the platinum versus gold ratio or spread in shaping the personality of this market should not be overlooked. Platinum prices spend most of their time at a hefty premium to gold. On occasion, however, platinum prices fall under gold prices. While there is no hard-and-fast rule about the ideal spread relationship, it is generally felt that a spread of more than $75 premium to gold is usually a precursor to platinum lows (i.e., gold $75 higher than platinum). At these levels platinum prices are relatively cheap and long-term accumulation of platinum is usually a wise investment. While platinum can often fall under gold for many months, the rise in platinum prices relative to gold from spread lows has frequently been extremely large. Speculatively inclined traders should consider following the spread when it falls below even. Track the spread using trend indicators to detect a turn, and when the turn comes, enter the spread by buying platinum and selling short gold. Since gold and platinum have a different point value, remember to buy two platinum futures contracts for every gold contract you sell. Since the markets are traded on different exchanges, you'll need to margin both sides as opposed to being given the advantages of spread margins.

In summary, platinum is a higher risk market recommended for journeymen traders only. Whether you trade platinum for the long term or short term, or whether you trade the platinum versus gold spread, I recommend careful use of price orders and stop orders. You'll also need to be careful about the size of your position since open interest and trading volume are often relatively small.

Palladium

Although one of the most thinly traded of all markets, this market should be closely watched by all speculators. The fundamentals of palladium are unique since well over 95 percent of the palladium is produced by only one country—the Soviet Union. From this important fundamental derives the unique personality of palladium futures, and in spite of it, the strategic value of palladium continues to increase. As a substitute for platinum in various industrial applications, palladium, which is considerably lower in price than platinum, will continue to grow in popularity and usage. In the event of a production cutoff by the Soviet Union, prices will soar virtually uncóntrollably and speculators on the long side of the market will reap tremendous profits as long as the government or the exchange allows trading to continue.

However, palladium spends most of its time as a thinly traded market dominated by professional traders. Given the low volume of activity, there are few trading systems that work well unless they are intermediate to longer term in their orientation. Naturally, price fills and position size will be problems unless the market becomes more active. While I do not recommend trading this market unless you are quite experienced, I do advise watching palladium closely for signs of an impending breakout to the upside. Due to thin volume and low open interest, any attempt by insiders to accumulate a large position will not go undetected and you may be able to enter the market before a large move.

Copper

Copper futures have a long history. Of all the metals copper is the most stable and also the most seasonal. The use of copper in housing, automobile production and many other industries, combined with the instability of mining operations in South

America and South Africa, have directly influenced copper price trends. Copper has, therefore, been a relatively good trading market both seasonally and from a long-term position perspective. It has had a generally stable but, at times, violent personaltiy.

Because some of the highest reliability seasonal trades are found in the copper futures market, I recommend applying a short-term trend-following system to copper during the window of up and down seasonals in order to fine tune timing. Copper prices have also correlated well with trends in the stock market. Figure 4.1 shows the relationship between copper futures and the Dow Jones Industrial Average from 1980 to 1991. While the correlation between these two markets is not 100 percent, it certainly suggests that systems that work in trading stock index futures should also work in copper futures.

The characteristics of copper futures do not qualify it as a day trader's market, however, there are often good short-term opportunities. While trading volume is rarely very high, it is often extremely stable with few extreme peaks or troughs. And open interest is often sufficiently high to permit relatively good price fills and sufficiently large positions.

Japanese Yen

Developers of trading systems know that the yen is the one market that has shown the best historical results using virtually any reasonable trading system. The market has a history of strong and lasting trends, up as well as down, and technical indicators are very effective. If a system won't work in the yen, the odds are it won't work in most other markets. The yen is a speculative market, that attracts traders from throughout the world including banks, individual trader hedgers, cross-rate traders and others. Due to the stable and often heavy trading volume as well as the high open interest, I recommend that all traders study, follow and trade yen futures. The market has enjoyed a stable, active and good trending personality.

Swiss Franc and DMark

These markets are not far behind the yen in terms of volume, trend, open interest and the applicability of technical trading systems. Of the two I prefer the Swiss franc. While the yen and the

Figure 4.1 The Correlation of Copper and the Dow Jones Industrial Average 1980 to 1991

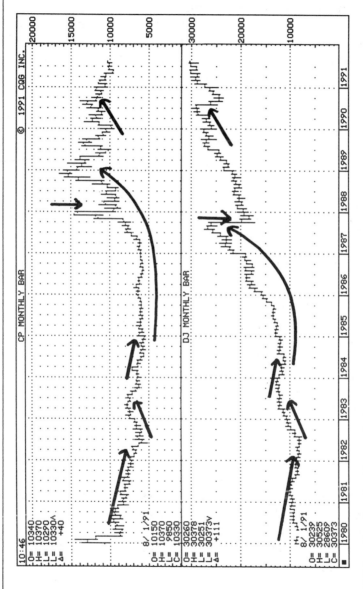

Swiss franc are excellent day-trading vehicles as well as position-trading vehicles, the Dmark is less desirable from the day-trading perspective. As in the case of the yen, I strongly recommend tracking and trading these markets using a variety of trend-following systems, most of which should produce good results as long as the markets remain relatively active and volatile. Both markets exhibit stable trend personalities due to their broad base of international participation.

British Pound

Unless you are interested in position trading, I do not recommend this market. While you may find some success in day trading the British pound, other currencies previously mentioned are preferable to this end. Technically speaking, the pound is a good market that acts well using trend-following indicators. Due to comparatively thin trading volume, some intraday moves prompted by news can be exaggerated.

Canadian Dollar

While the Canadian dollar has had some very strong up and down trends, they have not been without significant interruption. Trading volume is very light compared to the other currencies making this market unsuitable for day traders. Technically, however, the Canadian dollar is a good market for trend trading and should produce good results using trend-following systems. The overall personality of this market is stable, conservative and quiet—just like Canada itself.

Treasury Bond Futures

T-bond futures have become one the most active financial markets in a relatively short time. In spite of heavy volume and extremely high open interest, the market has not been one of the best performers technically on a position-trade basis. On a very short-term and day-trade basis, however, T-bond futures have performed extremely well. Given the heavy participation of banks and other financial institutions as well as numerous well-capitalized traders and the general public, T-bond futures have been highly liquid, permitting very large positions to be transacted with little or no slippage in price. The personality of T-bond futures is stable and ideally suited to systems trading for short-term as well as long-term perspectives.

As long as international and domestic economies continue in their erratic and often unstable trends, T-bond futures will continue to provide excellent short-term and day-trading opportunities. A variety of trading systems are, therefore, applicable. Note that whenever there has been a "flight to quality" due to international events or stock market declines, T-bond futures have moved up quickly and sharply.

Treasury Bill Futures

This market is often less volatile than the T-bond market; however, it tends to exhibit better trends and technical performance. While it is not necessarily a viable substitute for those who wish to trade interest rate futures for the short term, it is a good market for those who are intimidated by the large price swings so common in T-bond futures. In terms of personality, the T-bill market is a very subdued version of T-bond futures.

Eurodollar Futures

The market is heavily traded by financial institutions, and although not generally known, trading volume can often be extremely large with numerous large blocks exchanging hands. Although this is not a day trader's market unless, of course, you are trading on the exchange floor, Eurodollar futures have been prone to establish long-lasting and technically reliable trends. They are also responsive to "flight to quality" events, although not nearly as strongly as are T-bond and T-bill futures.

Coffee

Among the food commodities coffee ranks as the king of the speculators markets. In his book *The Blue Lion*, Robert Lynd claimed that the most obstreperous nations of Europe were addicted to coffee. Lynd's comment could also have applied to coffee futures, which may very well be the most obstreperous of all markets. Coffee may also be the most profitable.

Coffee is to the agricultural markets what yen is to the financials. Although trading volume can become thin at times, coffee futures have shown some of the most reliable up and down trends of the futures markets and have been among the most profitable markets. But coffee futures are not for the thin-skinned or inexperienced trader. Volatility is substantial, seasonal factors and weather play a large part in the game, and coffee production cartels play a major role in large price moves.

Given the speculative nature of coffee trading, I recommend it only for those who have both the experience and capital to trade effectively. I advise against day trading due to the typically poor price fills, particularly on market orders. Virtually all trading systems discussed in this book should work well in coffee futures.

Cocoa

The market tends to run in spurts of strong moves up and down with alternate periods of dormancy. While not nearly as good a market as coffee, cocoa can do well with a variety of technical trading systems provided there is sufficient price range to limit whipsaw signals.

Orange Juice

The major aspect of this market is seasonal. Typically, seasonal lows tend to develop during summer months, although most traders are unaware of this fact. By the time many traders realize that frost or freeze conditions are developing, the market has often made its up move from humble beginnings in the summer months. Unfortunately, trading volume is thin most of the year; I advise against day trading and against market orders unless unavoidable. Few traders are aware that the exchange may reject even stop loss orders during periods of extreme price volatility. This is why I recommend great caution in trading OJ futures. The growing role of South American producers is adding yet additional volatility to the already thin and volatile market. As with other thin markets, I recommend exiting long positions on strength when it is relatively easy to sell as opposed to attempting exit when prices are declining and it is difficult to sell. Limit up and limit down moves are quite common in OJ during late autumn and into mid-winter months.

Sugar

Sugar futures have been traded for many years and have spent much of their time languishing in a narrow price range.

There have, however, been several exceptionally explosive bull markets followed in every case by equally strong bear markets. Day trading is not recommended; however, position trading during big bull and bear markets is advised. Short-term swings can also be traded due to each price tick relatively high value.

The tendency for sugar prices to remain in a relatively narrow trading range from a low of about three cents per pound to a high of seven cents per pound for many years serves as a natural type of support and resistance. When prices break out of this range to the upside, they often move higher, sharply and forcefully, making the market very amenable to the Quantum Trading approach discussed in Chapter 9.

Cotton

Cotton has been a speculator's market for many years. Weather is the main determinant of price. With a one cent move being $500 in value, the cotton contract has been a favorite of higher risk traders for many years. It is a market in which many legendary traders such as Jesse Livermore and Arthur Cutten learned their skills, often the hard way. But today's cotton is not the same as yesterday's cotton. The market is still a highly speculative vehicle; however, it is not as technically reliable as it was during the 1920s and 1930s.

Cotton has had a close relationship to war. Cotton prices have moved sharply higher in proximity to every war both in the United States and abroad (Figure 4.2). The synopsis on page 60 summarizes this curious relationship.

There has been a strong tendency for important tops and bottoms in cotton prices to be signaled by island patterns. When the price for any given day or group of days is entirely out of the range of the previous day and the subsequent day, an island pattern occurs. A few ideal island top and bottom patterns are illustrated in Figure 4.3. An island top and an island bottom pattern in cotton prices is illustrated in Figure 4.4. While such patterns are not unique to cotton, they do have a higher frequency of occurrence in cotton than in most other markets.

Lumber

I find it strange that more traders are not interested in this highly seasonal market. Lumber futures have exhibited some of

Figure 4.2   A Synopsis of Cotton Prices and War

Cotton Prices and War

Cotton prices tend to move higher during war. While it's one thing to tell you that this is true, it's quite another to graphically illustrate it. Naturally, there are only a limited number of observations to support this finding. However, when examined, the historical data below will show how solid the correlation has been. The probing mind will ask: Why is there a relationship? There are at least three obvious reasons why cotton prices increase during wars:

1. Armies need to be clothed. This increases demand; hence, prices rise.
2. Clothing, severely damaged during combat, must be replaced thereby increasing demand and prices.
3. Cotton production is hampered by land being taken out of production and fewer farmers to tend crops.

Consider the following very interesting price and historical facts:

1. Previous to 1775, the start of the Revolutionary War in the United States, cotton prices were in the 16¢ to 18¢ per lb. range. Although no price quotes are available for the years during the war, the price in 1782 was in the 38¢ to 40¢ range, a substantial move to the upside.
2. At the start of the War of 1812, cotton prices were in the 8¢ to 10¢ range. When the war started, prices shot almost straight up to about 31¢ per lb. during the next few years, again a significant move to the upside.
3. Previous to the Civil War, prices were in the approximate 11¢ to 12¢ range. Then came the BIG move. Prices moved to over 50¢, a move to the upside of over 37¢ in a matter of several years, again confirming the very close relationship.
4. At the start of the Spanish-American War in the late 1890s, cotton was at its lowest level since previous to the Civil War in the 6¢ to 7¢ range. By 1910 the market had moved to about 15¢, more than doubling in price and again confirming the relationship between war and bull markets.
5. Prior to World War I cotton prices were in the range of 9¢ to 10¢. When the war broke out, prices began a strong bull market, and by 1919 they had moved to as high as 39¢, again a major increase correlated with war.
6. Prior to World War II, cotton prices were in the approximate 10¢ range. Again they began a very strong move that brought them to as high as 27¢ by 1945. Following the war cotton moved to near 40¢ by the late 1940s, again a very strong move correlated with war.
7. Before the Korean War in 1950, cotton prices were at approximately 32¢. They began an upmove correlated with the Korean War rallying to over 46¢ within several years. While this was one of the smaller moves, there's no doubt that it upheld the correlation.
8. We can safely say that the Viet Nam War began in 1964. At the time cotton prices were at about 24¢. By the time the war was over in 1973, cotton prices had reached to as high as 67¢, yet another major move.
9. When the Gulf War started, cotton futures were at about 76¢. They rallied to 94¢+, yet another conformation of the correlation between war and cotton prices.

Figure 4.3   Ideal Island Top and Bottom Formations

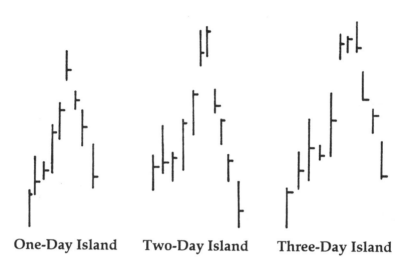

Island Tops

One-Day Island   Two-Day Island   Three-Day Island

Island Bottoms

One-Day Island   Two-Day Island   Three-Day Island

Figure 4.4 Island Top and Bottom Formations in Cotton Futures

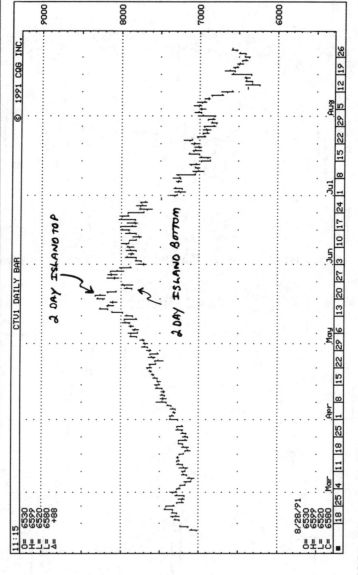

the most reliable seasonal trends of any market and rank near number one with copper in seasonal predictability. There has also been a close relationship between lumber prices and the trend in residential building. Hence, lumber fluctuates on the basis of two powerful fundamental forces that are reflected in strong, reliable and technically valid price trends that are amenable to systems trading.

While not a market for day traders, lumber futures are clearly the market of choice for seasonal trading when combined with technical timing indicators to fine tune the approach of seasonal turns. Trends are relatively long-lasting and are, therefore, amenable to trend-following systems (described in Chapter 7).

Petroleum Complex

One of the better markets for technical trading is crude oil. Trend-following systems as well as day-trading systems are often very effective and the market is international in scope. In addition, the highly seasonal nature of petroleum futures makes the markets ideal for the seasonal trader who can apply timing to the seasonals. The reliability seasonal price tendencies are truly impressive. As an example Figure 4.5 shows the tendency of cash fuel oil on a monthly basis since 1938. It illustrates the over-whelming tendency for prices to bottom in summer and move higher most through year end. The personality of these markets has, for the most part, been very stable with crude oil being the leader. It enjoys broad international participation and heavy volume—making it the market ideal for all types of trading.

S&P Futures

I've saved the best for last. However, the term *best* is clearly subjective. What's best for one trader may be worst for another trader. In this case, I define best as the most technical, most liquid and most volatile. In spite of these outstanding features S&P futures trading is not for everyone. There are alternatives such as the Major Market Indicator and the NYFE Index, but neither offers as much liquidity as does the S&P.

S&P futures are the preeminent day trader's market of the 1980s and 1990s to date. The market makes large price moves during virtually each trading day, liquidity is often exceptionally

Figure 4.5   Cash Seasonal Tendency of Fuel Oil 1938 to 1991

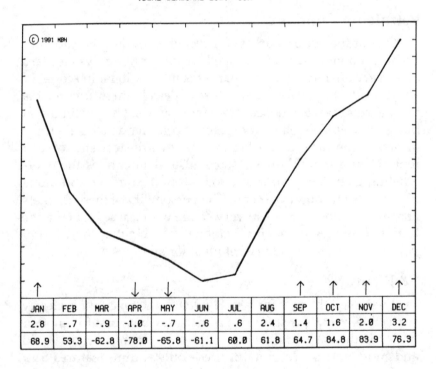

MONTHLY SEASONAL CASH TENDENCY: FUELOIL   Years 1938 - 1991

HIGH % SEASONAL UP MONTHS: JAN SEP OCT NOV DEC
HIGH % SEASONAL DOWN MONTHS: APR MAY
IDEAL SEASONAL HIGH: DEC
IDEAL SEASONAL LOW: JUN

© 1991 MBH

JAN	FEB	MAR	APR	MAY	JUN	JUL	AUG	SEP	OCT	NOV	DEC
2.8	-.7	-.9	-1.0	-.7	-.6	.6	2.4	1.4	1.6	2.0	3.2
68.9	53.3	-62.8	-78.0	-65.8	-61.1	60.0	61.8	64.7	84.8	83.9	76.3

good, tick value is high, and there is rarely a dearth of news to move the market. But the high margin requirement prevents many traders and floor traders from holding their positions overnight, and this contributes to the high volatility. Furthermore, many floor traders do not own their own memberships, but rent them from other members. This forces them to trade frequently in an effort to generate sufficient profits for their monthly rental fee. S&P futures, therefore, are the best of all markets for day trading.

Given its dominant role, I have given considerable attention to S&P futures. However, the systems I've shown in this book should work equally well in other volatile markets as well as new markets not yet being traded.

A Word about Futures Options

Perhaps the most creative marketing program in futures trading history was the exchange-backed campaign to popularize futures options. Now that these markets have existed since the mid-1980s, we can evaluate their role as a speculative vehicle and as a protective vehicle to the hedger. They do not serve either purpose very well. Frequently, options are priced unfairly and their liquidity is often insufficient to permit prompt entry and exit at the market unless price fills are of no concern to you. In both the 1987 and 1989 stock market crashes, stock index futures options were not viable trading vehicles since floor traders were not held liable for market orders, often refused price orders, and often refused to make a market at all.

Those able to employ options strategies using spreads and writing options (i.e., selling options short) have fared well. However, this has not been so for the general public. Rather, the professional side of the market has been dominated by a select few who have reaped considerable profits by employing options strategies that are either unknown to, or generally unavailable to, the average trader.

While I've provided the highlights of my market personality analysis, there are many other subtle aspects of individual market behavior, many of which can only be acquired by direct experience. The more knowledge you accumulate about the personality of markets, the more strategic will be your trading. Consider, for example, that cotton futures are prone to establish island top and bottom patterns while such patterns have been extremely rare in interest rate and in stock index futures. Also consider the personality of wheat futures as a market that tends to defy most trading systems. These important facts can be used to refine your current trading systems, to develop new market specific trading systems, or to avoid certain markets, directing your energies and funds to those areas with the greatest potential for success.

However, don't assume that market personalities are written in stone or that a market cannot change its personality. This can happen, but it is rare. When it does occur, it often takes many weeks or months to develop. The shell egg futures market, for example, was a very active market that had a strong seasonal bias. It was both a good position and day-trading market in the 1960s and 1970s. But the market changed its personality and during a period of several years ceased to be a viable market not only for speculators and position traders but for hedgers as well.

Potato futures, both Maine and Russet, were also seasonal markets. Prices were relatively low for many years and with fairly good regularity prices moved sharply higher for a number of months, allowing for excellent trading opportunities. But Maine potato futures were *delisted*—the market was closed down suddenly following some questionable dealings by one of the market's largest hedgers. In this case the market changed literally overnight, an extremely rare occurrence.

Value Line futures, the first stock index futures market, did not attract too much attention when introduced at the Kansas City Board of Trade. Based on early experience with the Value Line contract, traders did not expect S&P futures to attract much interest either. But the traders were wrong. S&P futures have become the premier stock index futures market, while all other stock index vehicles trail far behind. The Value Line contract, once reasonably active but notorious for poor order executions, has virtually lost all of its appeal to traders. Its personality has changed, but the process has taken time.

Currently, there are hints of a market that may replace S&P futures as the preeminent speculative market. The TOPIX Index, based on the Nikkei stock index, may over the next few years replace S&P futures as the volume and speculative leader. In fact, there have been forecasts by some of Japan's leading trading houses that by the year 2000 Japan will be the world center of futures trading. And they may be right. The astute trader would do well to keep close watch on such trends, taking advantage of them whenever and wherever possible. While individual market personalities are relatively static in most cases, some changes do occur dramatically. But the seemingly unchanging nature of the individual markets should not fool you into thinking that the personality of the futures market as a whole is unchangeable. This is not the case. New trading vehicles are always on the horizon—trading vehicles that may supplant the current speculative leaders. A knowledge of which trading methods and techniques have performed well in the past will lead you more quickly to systems that will work well in tomorrow's futures markets. This is a strategic consideration that has not been given much attention, but should be used by every trader who seeks to maximize his or her success and profits.

Market Trends in System Performance

Any trend-following system's performance will, by definition, be a function of trend. A trend-following system will perform well in strong trends, up and down, but it will lose money in sideways markets. As a point of information consider Figure 4.6, which shows some extremely interesting results of my test on the popular 4-day, 9-day, and 18-day moving average system. The parameters of this system in its basic form are simple. A buy signal is generated when the 4-day and 9-day MAs cross above the 18-day MA, and a sell signal is generated when the 4-day and 9-day MAs cross below the 18-day MA. This test-examined system results in nine different market categories as follows:

- **Bull:** a market that remained in a stable uptrend for the major portion of its contract life (i.e., through last complete month prior to delivery)
- **Bear:** a market that remained in a stable downtrend for the major portion of its contract life
- **Bull/Bear:** a market that had a stable bull move followed by a stable bear move
- **Bear/Bull:** a market that had a stable bear move followed by a stable bull move

- **Bull/Bear/Bull**: a market that had three distinct and stable trends as noted
- **Bear/Bull/Bear**: a market that had three distinct and stable trends as noted
- **Choppy Bull**: a bull market characterized by considerable up and down volatility or numerous price swings but still trended higher
- **Choppy Bear**: a bear market characterized by considerable up and down volatility or numerous price swings but still trended lower
- **Whipsaw**: a market showing virtually no trend

Markets were selected using specific mathematical criteria based on the above definitions. A complete test of the 4-day, 9-day and 18-day MA signals was completed to determine what effect, if any, trend had on the accuracy and profitability of the signals. Figure 4.6 shows the results.

Analysis of Trend Results

The test results clearly verify objectively what has been suspected all along: trend-following timing signals perform better in trending markets. As you can see, the Whipsaw market category showed the worst results, confirming the importance of strong trends in the success of trend-following systems. Another interesting fact is that the results in bear trends as noted by the Sell Signals category were considerably better (almost 400 percent better) than the Buy Signals category. This also confirms the importance of trend. Since bear markets decline faster than bull markets rise, signals will be more valid since there will be less time for signals to turn prematurely bullish.

To provide alternatives to the limitations of trend-following systems, I have included several different types of systems in this book. The moving average based systems I will discuss are trend-following systems. The seasonal system is based on historical patterns regardless of trend, the OOPS system is a counter-trend day-trade system, and the Quantum system is based on market breakouts and trends. Having access to several different types of systems will allow you to evaluate their performance in different types of markets so that you may decide which are best for you.

Figure 4.6   Results of 4-day, 9-day, 18-Day MA Trend Test

2 MA TO 1 MA (CLOSE/CLOSE)   LEVEL 3   MA 04 09 18

	BUY SIGNALS				SELL SIGNALS				TOTAL			
	NUM	% PROF	AVG $	TOT $	NUM	% PROF	AVG $	TOT $	NUM	% PROF	AVG $	TOT $
BULL	1305	20.00	-506.38	-660824.69	1335	51.84	872.87	1165287.00	2640	36.10	191.08	504462.56
BEAR	1766	49.32	673.97	1190238.00	1751	21.42	-506.43	-886763.94	3517	35.43	86.29	303474.37
BUBE	1602	38.83	234.35	375424.75	1629	34.56	312.12	508444.81	3231	36.68	273.56	883869.56
BEBU	1591	36.64	50.91	81000.44	1620	36.85	226.87	367535.00	3211	36.75	139.69	448535.44
BUBEBU	465	28.39	-139.72	-64970.98	472	40.68	456.98	215693.81	937	34.58	160.86	150722.81
BEBUBE	394	39.85	311.19	122610.31	381	31.23	35.89	13673.91	775	35.61	175.85	136284.25
CHOPBU	1065	23.66	-719.00	-765740.19	1088	47.06	1018.10	1107690.00	2153	35.49	158.82	341949.37
CHOPBE	792	46.59	320.89	254148.25	785	24.71	-361.87	-284065.25	1577	35.70	-18.97	-29916.98
WHIP	1030	36.89	5.78	5956.50	1028	35.12	-80.12	-82361.81	2058	36.01	-37.13	-76405.31
MA 04 09 18 10010		36.23	53.73	537842.69	10089	35.73	210.64	2125133.00	20099	35.98	132.49	2662976.00

Chapter

===== 5 =====

How To Develop and Test Systems

Each trader has his or her unique style for developing and testing systems. While my approach may not be the best for you, I think you will benefit from my extensive experience. I like to follow several steps in system development.

First Comes the Idea

I begin with an idea about the markets—an idea usually based on an observation or a direct experience with the market. Often quite simple, the idea is usually an outgrowth of something I've read or something that has happened to me while trading. In fact some of my best systems and indicators have been derived from very simple concepts.

Perhaps a real time example will help explain my thought process. For many years traders have been fascinated by closing price patterns. It seems logical that if a market closes lower eight, nine or even ten days in a row, that the next day is likely to bring a recovery. Furthermore, it would seem logical that markets also exhibit closing price patterns of other types.

To test the validity of my ideas about closing price patterns, I consulted the available literature. In *The New Commodity Trading Systems and Methods*, Perry J. Kaufman reported results on numerous closing price pattern analyses. I repeated the Kaufman studies using a historical data base that spanned over 25 years in most markets only to find that they did not hold up under rigorous and lengthy testing. This is not unusual. As I've pointed out, there is often an inverse relationship between the number of observations in a system test and the accuracy of the system or indicator—the more cases the lower the percentage accuracy. I found that only several patterns had been correct 60 percent of the time or more since the 1960s. The Kaufman results were based on limited historical data and did not, in my opinion, represent an adequate statistical test. And yet I still felt that there must be some validity to my idea unless, of course, the market was a random event.

The Next Step: Refine the Idea

Since my initial investigation of the idea yielded a dead end, I decided to refine the technique examining the closing price patterns within the constraints of clearly defined uptrends or downtrends. I reasoned that in an uptrend the probability of more than several days of successively lower closing prices would be minimal. Hence, a few days of lower closes should be followed by a higher closing price. I tested this idea and again found that there was no valid relationship for futures trading. I was still convinced that my idea had face validity, but how to turn it into a potentially money-making system was the question.

Change the Time Frame

I found some ideas that do not work well in the daily time frame, but work well on an intraday basis. Hence, I changed the time frame and tested my idea on hourly and half-hourly data. The positive results did not surprise me. However, now that there were positive results as a function of changing the time frame, I needed to investigate the same approach in different time frames and with different pattern types on the various time frames. I decided to test the following:

- Buy after three, four, five or six successive higher closes
- Sell and reverse after three, four, five or six successive lower closes
- Test the above on 10-minute, 30-minute and 60-minute data
- Test the most active markets such as Swiss franc, Japanese yen, crude oil, T-bonds and S&P futures

Figures 5.1 through 5.4 show the various results of these tests.

Refine the Basic Approach

Now that the basic model has proven potentially positive it's time to refine it by applying stop losses, slippage and commission deductions and by improving time frames.

Test It in Real Time

Naturally, the real time portion of the test is the most important. It's one thing for a system to test well on historical data, but it's far more important for the system to perform according to expectations in real time. Although it is best to be prepared for the worst case scenario, you may be pleasantly surprised to find that some systems actually perform better in real time than in hypothetical back-testing. By using the system in real time, you gain insights that would not ordinarily occur in hypothetical testing. Real time application of the system will give you hints about refined entry and exit techniques within the basic parameters of your system.

A Case for Systematic Entry and *Unsystematic* Exit

Although some purists will vehemently disagree with what I am about to say, my words come from the hard knocks of experience. I've found that when it comes to system trading a good case could be made for systematic market entry based purely on signals generated by the system and for less mechanical exit of positions. That's right, I'm suggesting a hybrid approach to systems trading!

Figure 5.1   Three Consecutive Closes System Test: 10-Minute S&P Futures

```
Total net profit        $ -56500.00   Open position P/L      $   1000.00
Gross profit            $ 259775.00   Gross loss             $-316275.00

Total # of trades             925     Percent profitable            33%
Number winning trades         306     Number losing trades          619

Largest winning trade   $  6900.00    Largest losing trade   $ -3000.00
Average winning trade   $   848.94    Average losing trade   $  -510.95
Ratio avg win/avg loss        1.66    Avg trade(win & loss)  $   -61.08

Max consecutive winners         5     Max consecutive losers          16
Avg # bars in winners          15     Avg # bars in losers             7

Max intraday drawdown   $ -60075.00
Profit factor                 0.82    Max # contracts held             1
Account size required   $  60075.00   Return on account            -94%
```

Performance Summary: Long Trades

```
Total net profit        $ -25450.00   Open position P/L      $      0.00
Gross profit            $ 127125.00   Gross loss             $-152575.00

Total # of trades             464     Percent profitable            33%
Number winning trades         154     Number losing trades          310

Largest winning trade   $  6525.00    Largest losing trade   $ -2350.00
Average winning trade   $   825.49    Average losing trade   $  -492.18
Ratio avg win/avg loss        1.68    Avg trade(win & loss)  $   -54.85

Max consecutive winners         4     Max consecutive losers          15
Avg # bars in winners          16     Avg # bars in losers             7

Max intraday drawdown   $ -34675.00
Profit factor                 0.83    Max # contracts held             1
Account size required   $  37675.00   Return on account            -68%
```

Performance Summary: Short Trades

```
Total net profit        $ -31050.00   Open position P/L      $   1000.00
Gross profit            $ 132650.00   Gross loss             $-163700.00

Total # of trades             461     Percent profitable            33%
Number winning trades         152     Number losing trades          309

Largest winning trade   $  6900.00    Largest losing trade   $ -3000.00
Average winning trade   $   872.70    Average losing trade   $  -529.77
Ratio avg win/avg loss        1.65    Avg trade(win & loss)  $   -67.35

Max consecutive winners         4     Max consecutive losers          15
Avg # bars in winners          14     Avg # bars in losers             7

Max intraday drawdown   $ -32725.00
Profit factor                 0.81    Max # contracts held             1
Account size required   $  32725.00   Return on account            -95%
```

Reprinted with permission of Omega Research, Inc.

Figure 5.2   Three Consecutive Closes System Test: 30-Minute S&P Futures

```
                        Performance Summary:  All Trades

Total net profit         $  26400.00   Open position P/L      $      0.00
Gross profit             $ 175875.00   Gross loss             $-149475.00

Total # of trades              367     Percent profitable           38%
Number winning trades          138     Number losing trades         229

Largest winning trade    $   8450.00   Largest losing trade   $  -2625.00
Average winning trade    $   1274.46   Average losing trade   $   -652.73
Ratio avg win/avg loss         1.95    Avg trade(win & loss)  $     71.93

Max consecutive winners          7     Max consecutive losers        10
Avg # bars in winners           10     Avg # bars in losers           4

Max intraday drawdown    $ -12300.00
Profit factor                  1.18    Max # contracts held           1
Account size required    $  12300.00   Return on account            215%
```

```
                        Performance Summary:  Long Trades

Total net profit         $  14475.00   Open position P/L      $      0.00
Gross profit             $  97125.00   Gross loss             $ -82650.00

Total # of trades              192     Percent profitable           37%
Number winning trades           71     Number losing trades         121

Largest winning trade    $   8450.00   Largest losing trade   $  -2625.00
Average winning trade    $   1367.96   Average losing trade   $   -683.06
Ratio avg win/avg loss         2.00    Avg trade(win & loss)  $     75.39

Max consecutive winners          4     Max consecutive losers        11
Avg # bars in winners           11     Avg # bars in losers           4

Max intraday drawdown    $ -12475.00
Profit factor                  1.18    Max # contracts held           1
Account size required    $  12475.00   Return on account            116%
```

```
                        Performance Summary:  Short Trades

Total net profit         $  11925.00   Open position P/L      $      0.00
Gross profit             $  78750.00   Gross loss             $ -66825.00

Total # of trades              175     Percent profitable           38%
Number winning trades           67     Number losing trades         108

Largest winning trade    $   5100.00   Largest losing trade   $  -1850.00
Average winning trade    $   1175.37   Average losing trade   $   -618.75
Ratio avg win/avg loss         1.90    Avg trade(win & loss)  $     68.14

Max consecutive winners          4     Max consecutive losers         9
Avg # bars in winners            9     Avg # bars in losers           4

Max intraday drawdown    $ -10650.00
Profit factor                  1.18    Max # contracts held           1
Account size required    $  10650.00   Return on account            112%
```

Figure 5.3   Five Consecutive Closes System Test: 30-Minute S&P Futures

---

Performance Summary: All Trades

Total net profit	$ 3775.00	Open position P/L	$ 0.00	
Gross profit	$ 51575.00	Gross loss	$ -47800.00	
Total # of trades	108	Percent profitable	37%	
Number winning trades	40	Number losing trades	68	
Largest winning trade	$ 8125.00	Largest losing trade	$ -2025.00	
Average winning trade	$ 1289.38	Average losing trade	$ -702.94	
Ratio avg win/avg loss	1.83	Avg trade(win & loss)	$ 34.95	
Max consecutive winners	3	Max consecutive losers	6	
Avg # bars in winners	11	Avg # bars in losers	5	
Max intraday drawdown	$ -11850.00			
Profit factor	1.08	Max # contracts held	1	
Account size required	$ 11850.00	Return on account	32%	

Performance Summary: Long Trades

Total net profit	$ 14325.00	Open position P/L	$ 0.00
Gross profit	$ 36950.00	Gross loss	$ -22625.00
Total # of trades	58	Percent profitable	43%
Number winning trades	25	Number losing trades	33
Largest winning trade	$ 8125.00	Largest losing trade	$ -2025.00
Average winning trade	$ 1478.00	Average losing trade	$ -685.61
Ratio avg win/avg loss	2.16	Avg trade(win & loss)	$ 246.98
Max consecutive winners	3	Max consecutive losers	6
Avg # bars in winners	11	Avg # bars in losers	6
Max intraday drawdown	$ -4450.00		
Profit factor	1.63	Max # contracts held	1
Account size required	$ 4450.00	Return on account	322%

Performance Summary: Short Trades

Total net profit	$ -10550.00	Open position P/L	$ 0.00
Gross profit	$ 14625.00	Gross loss	$ -25175.00
Total # of trades	50	Percent profitable	30%
Number winning trades	15	Number losing trades	35
Largest winning trade	$ 3750.00	Largest losing trade	$ -1075.00
Average winning trade	$ 975.00	Average losing trade	$ -719.29
Ratio avg win/avg loss	1.36	Avg trade(win & loss)	$ -211.00
Max consecutive winners	2	Max consecutive losers	6
Avg # bars in winners	10	Avg # bars in losers	5
Max intraday drawdown	$ -12975.00		
Profit factor	0.58	Max # contracts held	1
Account size required	$ 15975.00	Return on account	-66%

Figure 5.4   Six Consecutive Closes System Test: 30-Minute
S&P Futures

```
                    Performance Summary:  All Trades

Total net profit        $   22675.00   Open position P/L     $      0.00
Gross profit            $   49950.00   Gross loss            $ -27275.00

Total # of trades              37      Percent profitable          41%
Number winning trades          15      Number losing trades        22

Largest winning trade   $   12600.00   Largest losing trade  $  -2075.00
Average winning trade   $    3330.00   Average losing trade  $  -1239.77
Ratio avg win/avg loss          2.69   Avg trade(win & loss) $    612.84

Max consecutive winners         3      Max consecutive losers       5
Avg # bars in winners          39      Avg # bars in losers        15

Max intraday drawdown   $   -8625.00
Profit factor                   1.83   Max # contracts held         1
Account size required   $   11625.00   Return on account          195%
```

```
                    Performance Summary:  Long Trades

Total net profit        $   10775.00   Open position P/L     $      0.00
Gross profit            $   33825.00   Gross loss            $ -23050.00

Total # of trades              26      Percent profitable          31%
Number winning trades           8      Number losing trades        18

Largest winning trade   $   12600.00   Largest losing trade  $  -2075.00
Average winning trade   $    4228.13   Average losing trade  $  -1280.56
Ratio avg win/avg loss          3.30   Avg trade(win & loss) $    414.42

Max consecutive winners         2      Max consecutive losers       7
Avg # bars in winners          43      Avg # bars in losers        16

Max intraday drawdown   $  -10975.00
Profit factor                   1.47   Max # contracts held         1
Account size required   $   13975.00   Return on account           77%
```

```
                    Performance Summary:  Short Trades

Total net profit        $   11900.00   Open position P/L     $      0.00
Gross profit            $   16125.00   Gross loss            $  -4225.00

Total # of trades              11      Percent profitable          64%
Number winning trades           7      Number losing trades         4

Largest winning trade   $    4775.00   Largest losing trade  $  -1825.00
Average winning trade   $    2303.57   Average losing trade  $  -1056.25
Ratio avg win/avg loss          2.18   Avg trade(win & loss) $   1081.82

Max consecutive winners         5      Max consecutive losers       2
Avg # bars in winners          34      Avg # bars in losers        14

Max intraday drawdown   $   -2925.00
Profit factor                   3.82   Max # contracts held         1
Account size required   $    5925.00   Return on account          201%
```

Reprinted with permission of Omega Research, Inc.

Those who take exception to my suggestion will claim that by not using the system exactly as tested, you will not be trading the system you tested and the results will, therefore, be totally meaningless; your back-testing will be for naught. They'll claim that you might as well trade no system at all. But these are generally the same individuals who will stick doggedly to the system when it is clear that the fundamental situation has changed dramatically, that unprecedented events are affecting the market, or when market conditions are not at all similar to those that existed when the system was tested. I believe that in such extraordinary cases, extraordinary measures are necessary. I am not suggesting that you make an exit decision based on visceral factors. I am suggesting that you may want to exit based on technical indicators that were not part of the original system.

I offer this alternative method of exit because I firmly believe that the experience of a trader counts for something. I am absolutely certain given my years of market experience that traders learn much more than their systems, indicators and methods. They learn the internal language of the ticker, the intuitive message of the market that cannot be easily defined in purely mechanical or operational terms. To ignore such valuable knowledge would be a waste of valuable resources. I do not claim that traders become intuitive about the markets by a learning process, and I do not consider the terms *learning* and *intuition* to be mutually exclusive. Take what you have learned from thousands of hours of market experience, what you have learned from your losses and what you've learned from not following your instincts, and use this knowledge—but use it at the right time. Your feelings won't always be right. You will, at times get out too soon, but you'll learn from this experience as well. If you fear losing your position in the market, the answer is simple. When you enter a market, do so with twice the position you usually take. Exit one position strictly by the trading rules, and exit the second system on other indicators if a situation calls for it. See how your results compare.

An Example

Perhaps an example will help illustrate my point of view. Let's assume you have entered a long trade in S&P futures based on an exponential moving average system. As is often the case with good positions, your feelings upon entry are tentative—you're not convinced that this will be a profitable trade, but you are committed to the system and you follow the signal. Soon the market moves in your favor and you're rewarded. To your great pleasure the market soon begins to move strongly in your favor, and your moving average system is not even close to a possible reversal signal since, as you know, moving averages (and most timing signals) are lagging indicators. The higher and faster the market moves, the more the indicators lag. Naturally, you're subject to the trader's perennial fear—what if the market turns sharply lower now, and by the time you exit your trade you've given up too much potential profit? You're somewhat comforted by the fact that your system has a trailing stop loss, yet you fear that by the time your trailing stop loss is triggered the slippage will be significant and you'll give back too much profit?

What you're experiencing is not unique. Most (if not all) traders are victims of the same dilemma. What to do? Get out now and cut your profit short, or stay with the system religiously and take the risk of giving back too much profit.

Then, without warning fantastically bullish news develops. The market skyrockets. Your S&P position gains 900 points within hours after the market opens; it's gained more in several hours than it has in the last three weeks, and your open profit has more than doubled within hours after the opening. But you also know, given your experience with the markets, that bullish news is often associated with market tops. You know that such dramatic up moves are inspired by emotion and that this could easily be a *blowoff* top. But you're "locked into" a system. Again the dilemma tugs at your trading conscience, and this time harder than before. What if you get out too soon? What if this is just the start of another leg to the upside? What if this bullish news is just the beginning of something much more bullish? What if you lose your position and can't get back in? What if you break the rules now and learn a bad behavior?

Balancing the logic of following your trading system are the lessons of experience. Is there a happy medium? Can you exit the trade early using another indicator? While dyed-in-the-wool systems followers would object, I recommend you use another timing method to exit the trade if you've decided that a top is imminent. Another alternative, as previously recommended, would be to exit part of your position. This procedure represents a happy medium between system following and using your market experience to your advantage. Whether this method works for you can only be determined by trying it.

Combining Systems

Yet another important aspect of system development and testing is the hybridization of systems. For too many years traders have given equal weight to entry and exit signals. In other words, they consider the inverse of a buy signal to be a sell signal. This may not, however, be the most effective approach.

My experience has taught me that buy signals, sell signals and exit signals are not all equal sides of the same methodology. Market tops have distinctly different characteristics than do market bottoms, and downtrends have different characteristics than do sideways or uptrends. Markets top more dramatically than they bottom, and markets drop faster than they rise. A dual moving average crossover buy signal based on a 9-period and 18-period moving average will not necessarily work best as a sell signal when used in reverse. It may very well be that the best combination for buy signals is a 9-day and an 18-day moving average crossover, and for sell signals the best combination may be a 7-day and 16-day moving average crossover. It may also be true that when a reversal of the 9-day and 18-day MA parameters occurs, the system may be best off going flat, if a 7-day and 16-day sell signal has not already occurred. Remember that my examples are hypothetical; you can easily develop combinations of your own. When you do, use a more sensitive indicator on the sell side since sell signals and bear markets tend to develop more quickly and decline more quickly than bull markets rise.

Part
3

Market Timing

Chapter

6

Aspects of
Market Timing

Market timing based on technical indicators is nothing more than educated guesswork based on a preconceived notion of market behavior. And market timing based on a fundamental approach, although based on a different understanding of market trends, is also educated guesswork. While the purely technical trader attempts to discern future market activity based on the behavior of prices and other hard market data, the fundamental trader is charged with the same task, albeit from the perspective of an economic orientation. Both types of traders attempt to time market entry based on expectations that markets will move either as they have in the past under similar conditions, or on the basis of a logical relationship between their indicators and price trends.

To validate their timing indicators, technicians perform market tests based on the relationship between their operationally defined rules and historical price behavior. It is assumed, whether right or wrong, that the future will be much like the past or at least sufficiently similar to the past to allow traders to profit from their previously researched timing relationships. There is, however, no guarantee that the future will mirror the past no matter how logical, rational or seemingly valid a technical market theory may be. In the long run and short run prices will move based on factors that may not have any logical connection to technical timing indicators reacting rather to constantly changing multiple stimuli.

The fundamental trader takes refuge in an econometric understanding of price trends. In this view prices move up and down as a function of the two quintessential economic variables—supply and demand. Subsumed under these categories are numerous variables that affect one side of the equation or another. The logic is simple enough—when demand is high and supply is either unchanged or lower, prices move higher. If demand increases faster than supply, prices are also expected to rise. But if supply is higher than demand or if demand is declining relative to supply, prices decline. The fundamental trader, based on a structural or theoretical framework of supply, demand, price and their interrelationships, considers numerous variables—all related to supply and demand—to reach timing and trend decisions.

Experience teaches that neither approach is as effective as theory would have us believe. Market life is such that a given amount of randomness or disorder enters into price trends, making timing a less-than-perfect proposition. Whether timing is based on fundamentals, technicals or on a combination of both, it has not reached the level of development that allows a high degree of accuracy. In testing timing signals we find that an accuracy rate of 60 percent or more for an extended period of time is remarkable, the exception rather than the rule. We also find that the larger the number of observations in our sample, the more accuracy regresses to the mean.

The Timing Dilemma

To compensate for the inherent weakness in timing signal accuracy, traders have developed risk management principles. By limiting risk exposure through the use of money management stop losses, the inaccuracy of trading signals can be limited as long as the dollar amount of profitable trades exceeds losing trades by a significant amount. While this is both an effective as well as a necessary aspect of successful trading, it is also important for traders to understand the nature of technical timing tools. An understanding of the types of timing signals as well as their assets and liabilities will prove invaluable in your trading since it will:

- allow you to know what can be expected from certain types of signals.
- help you understand which types of signals to use in different types of markets.
- help you to determine which signals will be most consistent with the type of trading best suited to your personality and finances.

Characteristics of Timing Signals

I divide timing indicators into three categories based on their contiguity to market turns. While these are not rigid divisions, there are sufficiently significant distinctions among the three categories to permit differential applications as well as different results. Here are my definitions along with some examples.

Lagging Indicators

As the name implies, lagging indicators lag behind market turns. By virtue of their construction, they can only change direction after prices have turned. In other words, lagging indicators follow trend changes. As a result, lagging indicators work best in trending markets. Most timing indicators are lagging, or trend-following indicators. While trend-following indicators do well in markets with well-established trends, they deteriorate rapidly in sideways markets, often losing substantial funds. And trend-following timing signals are severely limited by virtue of their time-delayed character. By the time most trend-following signals have changed direction, a large percentage of their accrued gains have dissipated.

Moving averages, oscillators, stochastics and some chart formations are lagging indicators. If you use these indicators, you must be prepared for the following limitations:

Delayed Reaction Time   These indicators turn bullish and bearish after markets change trend. While there will be occasions when lagging indicators turn quickly following a trend change, they are often late in their turns and, as a consequence, the risk exposure is frequently quite great.

Best in Bear Markets   My research strongly suggests that trend-following, or lagging indicators, tend to produce their largest profits with their highest degree of accuracy in bear markets. Given the fact that most traders are either afraid to sell short or have an unconscious bias against selling short, they frequently avoid taking some of the best signals from their trend-following systems.

Numerous Successive Losing Trades   Common with lagging indicators, continuing losses are further exacerbated by slippage and mounting commission costs. This is, as explained earlier, most frequent in sideways or whipsaw markets. This single most annoying, frustrating and dysfunctional aspect of lagging indicators causes many traders to abandon trend-following systems based on such indicators.

But these limitations should not dissuade you from using lagging indicators provided, of course, that you understand how to minimize these negative aspects. While I will be more specific when I explain some of the strategic indicators, here are some suggestions:

- Use lagging indicators only for market entry while using other, more sensitive indicators for market exit. In the case of moving averages, for example, one set of moving averages can be used for entry and another, faster set of moving averages (i.e., fewer time periods) for market exit.
- Use lagging indicators with other indicators that are not based on the same principles as lagging indicators. A good combination would be stochastics along with cycles or seasonals, or moving averages with cycles and seasonals.
- Use time displaced lagging indicators to find turns earlier in their inception.
- Use weighted, exponential or triangular moving averages to compensate for their time lag.
- Use trend-following indicators to define the trend and use other indicators such as retracements to support and resistance to enter and exit trades.

Tip

The last two methods are particularly promising. I have been doing considerable research with triangular MAs and find them to be especially useful. Weighted MAs also have considerable potential in overcoming the time lag limitations. And the use of support and resistance methods within trends as defined by trend-following indicators is an excellent procedure as well.

Time Current Indicators

Some time indicators seem to be very sensitive to current market activity. In other words, they allow the trader to make a reasonably accurate determination of current market activity and anticipated trend. Among these indicators are trading volume, tick volume, price gaps, Market Profile®, the New York Stock Exchange Tick Indicator, Accumulation/Distribution, certain applications of George Lane's Stochastics and several others. While these indicators seem to provide an excellent picture of current events such as who is in *control* of the markets—buyers or sellers, and where prices might go over the short term, these indicators have their limitations. Here are some of my thoughts regarding the assets and liabilities of time current indicators:

- They tend to be useful for very short-term swings only. Since they are not, for the most part, based on intentionally lagged calculations (excluding stochastics), they are most responsive to current conditions. However, their quick response time can also be detrimental when spurious developments affect the markets.
- Given their nature they are best applied to extremely short-term trading. This is not, of course, feasible for many traders. But for those who have the ability to trade for the short term, time current indicators can be very effective.
- Because time current indicators change so rapidly, they frequently signal very small moves that, if followed by the trader, lead to substantial commissions and very small profits. On the other hand, losses can be extremely small as well.
- Some time current indicators such as the Market Profile® are

difficult to interpret and require considerable subjective evaluation. Hence, they may be unsuitable for traders with a penchant for strictly mechanical decision-making models.

Tip

Some of the best trading systems I know combine lagging indicators with time current indicators. They enter positions based on lagging indicators and use time current indicators to either limit losses, or confirm market entry or market exit.

Leading Indicators

The search for leading indicators is the futures trader's dream. The need to predict what will happen tomorrow, later today or in the distant future stems from the primeval insecurity of humankind. The drawings of Arguinacian cave dwellers thousands of years ago show a marked preoccupation with the future. Indeed, the need to prepare for tomorrow was even more important in ancient times than it is today. Life spans were considerably shorter, danger was omnipresent, hunger and disease were constant threats, and life was a never-ending struggle. To know what might come tomorrow was, and is, a quintessential ingredient in the struggle for survival. Hence, to predict the future is a deep-seated need in the life, mind and behavior of virtually every human being.

The search for tomorrow has fostered the development of diverse methodologies and myths. The physical sciences seek to make tomorrow better by understanding today in reductionist, analytical, mathematical terms. Social science attempts to improve society's lot so that life will be easier and happier tomorrow, while psychological science directs human behavior to relieve the stresses and strains that impede growth and the joys of tomorrow. Economic science examines yesterday to make tomorrow less disruptive, more comfortable and more efficient. And the list of tomorrows goes on.

As you know, there is really no significant difference among any of today's markets. The stock market is really a futures market as are the bond, real estate, coin, stamp, wine, antique, rare book and baseball card markets. To call them anything less than futures markets is to avoid paying service to their primary goal, which is profit. While each of these markets entails various degrees of aesthetics, the ultimate goal is that of appreciation in every sense of the word!

The search for effective leading indicators, therefore, occupies most traders' minds and pocketbooks. Forecasting, predicting, calling market turns, providing recommendations, writing research reports that predict short-run and long-run events, and developing software are important to every area of investment. But how valuable are leading indicators, and most important, how accurate are they?

Before digging more deeply into these issues, let's define the term *leading indicator*? Any indicator that purports to forecast the short-term, intermediate-term or long-term direction of prices, or of any other variable, is a leading indicator. Among some of the more popular leading indicators are cycles, seasonals, Fourier Analysis, Gann analysis, Fibonacci analysis, Elliott Wave analysis and Astrology.

There are some distinct limitations when these methods are used without the assistance of other timing indicators, but there are some advantages as well. Here is a synopsis of the good and the bad:

- Leading indicators often forecast a market's direction as well as the probable timing of the turn; however there is frequently a window of error in their forecasts that results in premature or delayed entry. In the case of premature entry, the problem is that a futures contract has a limited life. And in futures options, time value is lost with each passing day.
- A forecast leads to an expectation, and an expectation is a crutch that leads to impaired judgment. Rather than attend to the reality of the present and the importance of the current trend, the trader who is tied to a forecast either by vanity or ego is prone to cling to expectations that may lead to considerable losses.
- Forecasts, unless reevaluated frequently, tend to be unreliable, particularly if one is fitting many different variables into an organized methodology.
- When combined with other indicators, leading indicators

can be very powerful trading tools. Later I will discuss a specific method for doing so.

The use of leading indicators and the search for better leading indicators is a preoccupation of many traders and systems developers. However, their efforts may be wasted. My research—which covers many different indicators and a vast amount of historical price data, and spans nearly two decades—strongly suggests that leading indicators do not, in and of themselves, provide any great advantage to those who use them. As you will see later, however, the combination of short-term timing and leading indicators such as cycles, sentiment and seasonals *can* prove very beneficial.

Chapter

=== 7 ===

Revisiting Moving Averages

The moving average in its many forms represents the single most popular group of technical indicators used by stock and futures traders. Popularized by Richard Donchian in the 1950s, moving averages and indictors derived from the basic moving average concept have withstood the test of time both in terms of performance and popularity. Oscillators, weighted moving averages, exponential moving averages, geometric moving averages, stochastics, RSI, DMI and others are all variations on the moving average theme. However, moving averages have distinct limitations, the most common of which is their tendency to give numerous false signals. Since moving averages are lagging indicators, they will always be subject to the limitations inherent in such indicators. However, several refinements of the moving average concept have served me well and can also help you. The objectives of this chapter are as follows:

- To reexamine moving averages and moving average derived indicators

- To compare the traditional use of these indicators with several of my refinements
- To introduce several alternate approaches to moving averages that have the potential to enhance your performance

An Overview of Moving Averages

Moving averages and variations on this theme are the most popular trading indicators among futures traders. It is by virtue of their popularity alone that we should suspect their utility. By its very nature the moving average is a lagging indicator regardless of how it is manipulated. Moving average signals occur after tops and after bottoms. Unless a bottom holds and is followed by a sustained rise in prices, the original moving average buy signal will be reversed to a sell signal, then to another buy and another sell. The resulting whipsaw will prove costly in numerous consecutive losses and commission dollars.

Similarly, a moving average sell signal that is not followed by a sustained decline in price will usually result in a succession of buy and sell signals that accumulate losses. The next result of both moving average based buy and sell signals is often a low level of accuracy. But moving average systems base their success on catching large price swings that, in total, far surpass the smaller whipsaw and commission losses. But unless a market trends persistently higher or lower, moving average systems will not work well.

To minimize these limitations of moving average (MA) systems, traders have, over the years, attempted various refinements of MAs. In addition to the simple moving average, traders have refined and expanded on Richard Donchian's original ideas. The exponential moving average, for example, is a more responsive moving average designed to turn more quickly than do simple MAs. The logic is that signals will develop earlier in a trend change thereby resulting in less lag time before a position is reversed. And the shortened response time will, it is hoped, result in smaller losses and larger profits.

Weighted moving averages are designed to achieve the same end result as are exponential MAs. Weighted MAs give more consideration to more recent price behavior assuming that the behavior of prices in recent days is more important than that of several weeks ago. Accordingly, the last X number of prices are multiplied by a constant to increase their value. As illustrated later, weighted moving averages have not been given sufficient attention. My research shows that they have considerable potential in today's markets.

The triangular moving average, also called the geometric moving average, is a form of weighted MA that gives more weight to the center of the price data and less weight to the extremes. It is the least known and least used of all moving averages. Its claim to fame is that by giving more consideration to the midpoint of the data, it more closely resembles the so-called normal data distribution. Ideally, the triangular MA should perform better if the data being used is normally distributed.

Another adaptation of the moving average method uses multiple moving averages as opposed to one moving average. In the traditional approach a buy signal was generated when price crossed above MA and a sell or reverse signal when price crossed below MA. This technique was discarded in favor of a dual MA approach that utilized a longer and shorter MA. When the shorter MA crossed above the longer MA (i.e., a 9-day and a 36-day MA combination), a buy signal was generated; when the shorter MA crossed below the longer MA, a sell or reverse signal was generated. Eventually, a triple MA combination replaced this approach. The triple MA method, popularized in the 1970s by Joe Van Nice of Commodity Trend Service, was originally published in Iowa under the Victoria Feed Company name. The service is now published in North Palm Beach, Florida.

The triple MA method uses a longer, a shorter and a midrange MA such as 4-day, 9-day and 18-day. The concept is simple. When the two shorter term MAs cross above the longer MA, a buy or reverse to long signal is generated; when the two shorter term MAs fall below the longer MA, a sell or reverse to short signal is generated. My research clearly demonstrated that there are many moving average combinations that yield profitable trading results in the long run. I've also demonstrated that the combination of three moving averages produces better overall results on a per trade basis than does the two or one MA approach.

Figure 7.1 Results of Dual MA Signals in All Markets 1968 to 1990

	BUY SIGNALS				SELL SIGNALS				TOTAL			
	NUM	PROFIT	AVG $	TOT $	NUM	PROFIT	AVG $	TOT $	NUM	PROFIT	AVG $	TOT $
MA 09 11	15212	5496.23	54.64	831257.25	15213	6782.80	81.28	1236448.00	30425	12279.03	67.96	2067705.00
MA 09 15	8525	6773.76	144.56	1232375.00	8526	8260.70	193.75	1651913.00	17051	15034.46	169.16	2884288.00
MA 09 19	6356	6178.07	189.23	1202728.00	6367	8333.70	259.85	1654468.00	12723	14511.77	224.57	2857196.00
MA 09 23	5220	6320.77	188.25	982639.06	5247	8372.19	265.19	1391475.00	10467	14692.96	226.82	2374114.00
MA 09 27	4524	6207.39	243.41	1101165.00	4540	8207.83	331.73	1506052.00	9064	14415.22	287.65	2607217.00
MA 09 31	4032	6367.27	311.18	1254661.00	4042	8180.23	387.27	1565340.00	8074	14547.50	349.27	2820002.00
MA 09 35	3599	5638.10	332.96	1198340.00	3594	7309.43	400.48	1439319.00	7193	12947.52	366.70	2637659.00
MA 09 39	3257	5038.38	310.99	1012892.13	3258	7090.05	401.84	1309202.00	6515	12128.43	356.42	2322094.00
MA 09 43	3007	4649.11	327.61	985115.25	3005	6152.92	429.24	1289858.00	6012	10802.04	378.41	2274973.00
MA 09 47	2812	4228.42	348.89	981073.50	2811	5954.67	447.85	1258915.00	5623	10183.09	398.36	2239989.00
MA 09 51	2597	4369.77	372.56	967541.37	2607	5990.46	490.51	1278771.00	5204	10360.22	431.65	2246312.00
MA 11 15	9441	6391.30	120.48	1137497.00	9459	8206.76	165.45	1564944.00	18900	14598.06	142.99	2702442.00
MA 11 19	6469	5719.45	148.67	961751.81	6475	7916.19	216.55	1402147.00	12944	13635.63	182.63	2363899.00
MA 11 23	5162	6423.75	181.37	936231.06	5185	8466.95	254.22	1318116.00	10347	14890.70	217.87	2254347.00
MA 11 27	4384	5721.68	213.03	933911.19	4402	7593.47	295.18	1299378.00	8786	13315.15	254.19	2233289.00
MA 11 31	3844	5695.00	288.24	1107996.00	3857	7445.95	363.87	1403439.00	7701	13140.95	326.12	2511434.00
MA 11 35	3423	5432.95	312.68	1070308.00	3423	7055.40	384.86	1317391.00	6846	12488.36	348.77	2387699.00
MA 11 39	3099	4155.09	302.80	938374.75	3097	6201.58	397.97	1232501.00	6196	10356.68	350.37	2170875.00
MA 11 43	2839	5023.39	383.79	1089593.00	2836	6404.97	492.88	1397818.00	5675	11428.37	438.31	2487411.00
MA 11 47	2626	4383.19	368.73	968295.25	2625	5668.33	480.12	1260303.00	5251	10051.52	424.41	2228598.00
MA 11 51	2436	4372.58	393.12	957648.94	2442	5976.19	524.00	1279610.00	4878	10348.77	458.64	2237259.00
MA 13 15	12276	6932.46	89.38	1097217.00	12301	8564.28	122.62	1508397.00	24577	15496.75	106.02	2605614.00
MA 13 19	6854	6168.25	151.19	1036258.25	6869	7802.86	208.02	1428913.00	13723	13971.12	179.64	2465171.00
MA 13 23	5209	4973.61	150.37	783288.56	5219	7127.75	229.57	1198151.00	10428	12101.35	190.01	1981439.00
MA 13 27	4342	4870.03	199.01	864087.25	4354	6928.00	282.71	1230901.00	8696	11798.04	240.91	2094988.00
MA 13 31	3774	5244.61	281.94	1064025.00	3793	7188.50	360.52	1367455.00	7567	12433.11	321.33	2431480.00
MA 13 35	3342	4980.25	307.81	1028703.56	3349	6537.64	379.75	1271794.00	6691	11517.88	343.82	2300497.00
MA 13 39	3003	4725.07	322.69	969050.06	2988	6577.17	409.51	1223613.00	5991	11302.24	365.99	2192664.00
MA 13 43	2722	4304.07	356.11	969338.63	2721	5974.27	463.33	1260726.00	5443	10278.34	409.71	2230065.00
MA 13 47	2518	4605.51	393.51	990861.31	2506	5713.27	494.49	1239180.00	5024	10318.78	443.88	2230041.00
MA 13 51	2317	4220.66	383.13	887719.50	2320	5622.68	519.36	1204909.00	4637	9843.34	451.29	2092628.00
MA 15 19	7838	5296.51	97.30	762608.62	7831	6811.45	145.58	1140000.00	15669	12107.96	121.43	1902609.00
MA 15 23	5422	5204.39	135.08	732411.00	5402	7153.67	206.38	1114883.00	10824	12358.07	170.67	1847294.00
MA 15 27	4388	4752.08	176.68	775256.81	4393	6828.33	264.69	1162765.00	8781	11580.41	220.71	1938022.00
MA 15 31	3704	5151.09	285.24	1056540.00	3714	7049.39	362.89	1347757.00	7418	12200.48	324.12	2404297.00
MA 15 35	3269	4950.12	303.89	993415.50	3272	6532.55	382.14	1250361.00	6541	11482.67	343.03	2243777.00
MA 15 39	2919	5073.05	347.21	1013506.06	2906	6679.48	432.26	1256137.00	5825	11752.54	389.64	2269643.00
MA 15 43	2656	4710.23	337.94	897557.00	2650	6205.42	438.58	1162227.00	5306	10915.65	388.20	2059784.00
MA 15 47	2441	4777.73	371.49	906807.56	2420	6141.18	497.75	1204544.00	4861	10918.91	434.34	2111351.00
MA 15 51	2248	4247.19	381.73	858135.12	2242	5738.02	520.75	1167513.00	4490	9985.21	451.15	2025648.00
MA 17 19	10460	4245.31	54.61	571229.37	10448	6028.43	93.42	976097.94	20908	10273.73	74.01	1547327.00
MA 17 23	5871	5236.89	113.04	663673.12	5857	7233.80	181.44	1062678.00	11728	12470.70	147.20	1726351.00
MA 17 27	4492	4882.61	196.06	880688.50	4496	6953.34	283.89	1276367.00	8988	11835.95	239.99	2157056.00
MA 17 31	3726	4050.82	260.97	972392.25	3735	6052.84	341.94	1277137.00	7461	10103.67	301.51	2249530.00
MA 17 35	3231	4405.27	292.33	944529.81	3237	6098.09	370.09	1197934.00	6468	10503.36	331.25	2142514.00
MA 17 39	2875	4795.61	329.22	946509.12	2871	6373.31	418.85	1202511.00	5746	11168.92	374.00	2149020.00

Figure 7.1   Results of Dual MA Signals in All Markets 1968 to 1990 (Continued)

MA 17 43	4832 87	2591	364 10	943393 44	2573	6357 18	472 13	1214795 00	5164	11200 04	417 93	2158189 00
MA 17 47	5012 07	2370	405 57	961192 50	2351	6565 25	536 67	1261716 00	4721	11577 75	470 86	2222909 00
MA 17 51	4582 80	2203	399 44	961842 06	2189	5900 74	525 05	1149333 00	4362	10482 81	457 78	2010575 00
MA 19 23	5058 80	6792	369 65	676855 19	6789	7117 62	158 03	1072848 00	1358	12176 42	128 83	1749703 00
MA 19 27	4616 44	4726	200 31	946676 56	4724	6823 21	282 34	1333771 00	9450	11439 65	241 32	2280448 00
MA 19 31	4641 66	3835	255 02	978002 44	3835	6615 34	343 53	1317453 00	7670	11257 01	299 28	2295456 00
MA 19 35	5053 98	3259	319 62	1041630 63	3257	7023 46	401 60	1308008 00	6516	12077 45	360 60	2349639 00
MA 19 39	5187 52	2863	380 99	1090775 00	2851	6710 41	479 26	1363369 00	5714	11897 93	430 02	2457144 00
MA 19 43	5232 48	2566	420 21	1078260 00	2545	6925 86	533 23	1357090 00	5111	12158 72	476 49	2654540 00
MA 19 47	5153 03	2340	381 62	892986 75	2323	6818 15	514 20	1394475 00	4663	11971 18	447 67	2087452 00
MA 19 51	4681 50	2147	399 59	857913 62	2124	5860 06	546 31	1603769 00	4271	10089 56	472 55	2018275 00
MA 21 23	3928 04	9201	103 32	950651 94	9201	6182 93	151 14	1389769 00	18396	10010 97	127 22	2340430 00
MA 21 27	5140 00	5190	267 31	950674 19	5130	6750 59	260 91	1389454 00	10270	11416 61	224 74	2308128 00
MA 21 31	4590 02	3975	325 50	1062667 00	3966	6589 00	351 45	1393845 00	7941	11182 01	309 35	2414425 00
MA 21 35	5109 50	3293	393 38	1073176 00	3295	7141 31	407 06	1342850 00	6588	12250 81	366 49	2506697 00
MA 21 39	5222 41	2859	388 05	1124663 00	2856	6833 50	483 91	1382034 00	5715	12055 91	438 62	2290120 00
MA 21 43	5374 13	2569	367 23	996904 75	2551	7133 20	506 94	1293215 00	5120	12507 33	447 29	2018310 00
MA 21 47	4675 22	2331	367 23	852340 94	2294	6257 82	506 31	1161469 00	4615	10932 84	436 36	2018310 00
MA 21 51	4349 87	2107	386 38	814103 69	2083	5450 05	518 39	1079911 00	4190	9799 93	452 01	1893915 00
MA 23 27	4695 81	5960	174 99	1042946 31	5943	6943 89	237 63	1412206 00	11903	11639 71	206 26	2455152 00
MA 23 31	4521 92	4191	225 48	945000 87	4168	6493 53	303 17	1663627 00	8359	11015 45	264 82	2208628 00
MA 23 35	5234 49	2909	294 03	958042 87	3368	7397 42	472 72	1255331 00	5828	12231 77	328 34	2259734 00
MA 23 39	5236 93	2599	358 21	1402007 75	2936	6821 10	468 09	1186623 00	5087	10865 78	411 17	2091627 00
MA 23 43	4360 08	2594	305 99	945030 81	2276	5750 22	515 18	1287552 00	4580	10110 30	440 72	2018483 00
MA 23 47	3914 25	2117	357 58	759996 19	2083	5239 41	514 78	1721166 00	4200	9153 66	435 51	1829163 00
MA 25 27	4734 82	8210	120 24	987133 63	8190	6643 05	161 72	1325002 00	16400	11377 87	140 98	2312136 00
MA 25 31	4253 16	4641	207 48	962632 31	4615	6291 71	280 55	1247722 00	9256	10544 87	243 88	2257354 00
MA 25 35	4863 66	3552	277 56	985876 56	3537	7030 10	363 31	1285044 00	7089	11893 82	320 34	2270921 00
MA 25 39	4359 06	2983	330 79	986755 25	2979	6156 04	426 31	1699986 00	5962	10515 09	378 52	2256741 00
MA 25 43	4201 54	2580	332 25	986740 44	2576	5514 57	446 25	1149542 00	5156	9787 11	389 19	2006682 00
MA 25 47	2305 41	2305	352 05	851647 81	2274	5203 82	506 49	1517947 00	4579	9098 22	437 58	2006393 00
MA 25 51	3916 22	2108	352 05	742124 62	2064	5020 65	488 30	1708787 00	10807	7326 89	220 36	2381378 00
MA 27 31	3818 75	7510	186 59	1010940 44	5380	5825 46	359 40	1566091 00	7619	11047 80	315 06	2400460 00
MA 27 35	4442 34	3618	270 92	1043456 37	3065	6130 44	436 46	1337755 00	6121	10129 62	389 02	2381211 00
MA 27 39	4200 21	2638	331 02	873233 94	2637	5625 73	447 76	1180750 00	5275	9825 95	389 38	2053398 00
MA 27 43	3878 20	2822	353 57	820098 06	2072	5058 02	487 09	1118067 00	4615	9124 73	420 16	1939055 00
MA 27 47	3802 25	2110	342 27	722187 06	7480	6081 82	195 90	1099255 19	4182	8860 47	414 02	1731442 00
MA 27 51	3632 90	7510	146 00	1090047 00	7480	6734 87	355 80	1497204 00	14999	9714 79	170 96	2564247 00
MA 29 31	4423 00	4222	293 19	1151389 00	4208	6114 82	387 05	1257147 00	6404	11157 87	314 42	2650593 00
MA 29 35	3948 43	2604	295 32	958602 06	3248	5597 09	411 48	1037300 00	5385	9691 81	341 20	2157749 00
MA 29 39	4094 71	2604	270 67	753442 00	2091	5479 38	478 51	1057772 31	4201	9461 36	378 25	1759231 00
MA 29 43	4006 80	2338	310 72	726459 06	2316	5080 66	446 31	1050772 00	10024	9498 30	413 00	1735023 00
MA 29 47	4193 39	2121	348 65	739800 44	2080	5007 05	478 03	1412345 00	5632	11297 25	243 87	2444574 00
MA 29 51	4082 77	5017	203 03	834274 03	3516	6209 98	333 05	1171006 00	7020	10294 77	285 65	2005280 00
MA 31 35	3902 62	2820	271 01	834274 03	2812	5817 67	282 07	1075145 00	5632	9720 28	310 98	1751467 00
MA 31 39	3878 08	2404	208 09	673321 87	2386	5640 88	416 82	944534 81	4740	9522 96	343 64	1674698 00
MA 31 43	3995 00	2142	325 03	651512 44	2107	5170 07	464 39	978473 69	4249	9165 07	394 14	1674698 00
MA 31 47	3953 26	6897	143 67	690211 94	0912	6413 25	198 83	1374324 00	13909	10366 61	261 60	2365199 00
MA 33 35	4104 23	3906	213 13	832467 06	3904	6542 84	310 09	1210009 00	7810	10437 12	298 83	2049076 00
MA 33 39	3764 73	2514	235 42	703804 62	2977	5540 47	362 53	1092246 00	5607	9305 20	332 46	1763141 00
MA 33 43	3896 22	2473	263 18	650945 56	2456	5476 61	492 21	987829 19	4929	9375 82	332 46	1783675 00
MA 33 47	3378 88	2174	204 71	640075 94	2145	4501 50	418 75	987823 19	4319	7860 33	356 33	1538983 00

Figure 7.2   Results of Triple MA Test in All Markets 1968 to 1990

MA			BUY SIGNALS NUM	% PROF	AVG $	TOT $	SELL SIGNALS NUM	% PROF	AVG $	TOT $	TOTAL NUM	% PROF	AVG $	TOT $
09	11	14	14605	40.88	18.24	266374.31	14698	39.73	122.40	1798994.00	29303	40.30	70.48	2065368.00
09	11	19	10116	36.92	38.18	386258.00	10209	36.77	191.42	1954251.00	20325	36.85	115.15	2340509.00
09	11	24	8165	36.67	81.97	669244.81	8224	35.59	254.20	2090533.00	16389	36.13	168.39	2759778.00
09	11	29	6910	35.80	98.48	680490.12	6949	35.26	291.14	2023157.00	13859	35.53	195.08	2703647.00
09	11	34	6138	35.14	150.37	922994.00	6185	34.07	368.18	2277205.00	12323	34.60	259.69	3200199.00
09	11	39	5521	34.47	100.49	554824.37	5553	33.15	342.89	1904048.00	11074	33.81	222.04	2458872.00
09	11	44	5017	34.60	161.49	810171.25	5040	33.74	419.70	2115286.00	10057	34.17	290.89	2925458.00
09	11	49	4599	34.20	151.16	695187.75	4604	32.19	412.98	1901380.00	9203	33.20	282.14	2596568.00
09	11	54	4230	33.81	202.71	857483.00	4234	31.65	489.53	2072677.00	8464	32.73	346.19	2930160.00
09	16	19	9327	38.38	75.90	707905.37	9404	36.86	233.32	2194121.00	18731	37.62	154.93	2902027.00
09	16	24	7394	37.37	81.92	605687.19	7444	36.16	279.79	2082736.00	14838	36.76	181.19	2688424.00
09	16	29	6253	36.14	100.75	629987.62	6290	35.04	326.86	2055953.00	12543	35.64	214.14	2685940.00
09	16	34	5530	35.46	95.05	525654.00	5556	34.00	339.45	1885985.00	11086	34.73	217.54	2411639.00
09	16	39	4926	35.30	107.25	528333.62	4952	33.24	345.63	1711635.00	9878	34.27	226.75	2239868.00
09	16	44	4440	34.82	178.53	792678.69	4463	33.63	445.73	1989297.00	8903	34.22	312.48	2781976.00
09	16	49	4039	35.28	208.35	841518.94	4032	32.66	475.37	1916700.00	8071	33.97	341.74	2758219.00
09	16	54	3728	34.82	247.66	923259.50	3726	32.39	542.45	2021160.00	7454	33.61	395.01	2944420.00
09	21	24	7063	38.27	98.42	695112.12	7106	35.80	299.49	2128167.00	14169	37.03	199.26	2823279.00
09	21	29	5958	36.24	91.68	546238.62	5994	35.05	329.72	1976324.00	11952	35.64	211.06	2522562.00
09	21	34	5214	35.37	182.83	953254.12	5233	33.07	421.68	2206673.00	10447	34.15	302.47	3159927.00
09	21	39	4601	35.32	265.47	1221446.00	4618	33.07	517.88	2391548.00	9219	34.69	391.91	3612994.00
09	21	44	4118	35.28	270.46	1113769.00	4134	34.03	562.88	2326939.00	8252	34.66	416.95	3440708.00
09	21	49	3714	35.62	274.04	1017792.56	3699	32.47	566.36	2094960.00	7413	34.05	419.90	3112753.00
09	21	54	3430	34.26	242.33	831186.00	3423	33.16	569.10	1948018.00	6853	33.71	405.55	2779204.00
09	26	29	5885	36.16	152.33	896454.56	5920	33.99	366.98	2172523.00	11805	35.07	259.97	3068978.00
09	26	34	5005	35.24	238.20	1192183.00	5018	33.44	476.22	2389655.00	10023	34.72	357.36	3581838.00
09	26	39	4345	35.97	227.49	988456.12	4360	33.92	494.91	2157815.00	8705	34.70	361.43	3146271.00
09	26	44	3878	35.89	238.50	924906.81	3888	33.92	508.37	1976535.00	7766	34.91	373.61	2901442.00
09	26	49	3533	34.50	198.64	701801.56	3517	33.86	510.12	1794090.00	7050	34.18	354.03	2495891.00
09	26	54	3230	34.61	254.18	821001.75	3223	32.89	602.90	1943158.00	6453	33.75	428.35	2764159.00
09	31	34	4945	36.97	250.65	1239442.00	4992	34.70	468.89	2340677.00	9937	35.83	360.28	3580119.00
09	31	39	4164	37.13	296.02	1232615.00	4187	34.70	572.64	2397625.00	8351	35.91	434.71	3630240.00
09	31	44	3703	35.40	289.78	1073005.00	3705	34.36	576.16	2134664.00	7408	34.88	433.01	3207708.00
09	31	49	3354	35.33	245.88	824671.06	3336	33.42	590.96	1971459.00	6690	34.38	417.96	2796130.00
09	31	54	3055	35.09	235.04	718057.75	3044	33.18	609.13	1854190.00	6099	34.14	421.75	2572248.00
09	36	39	4207	35.94	284.73	1197849.00	4221	34.94	556.80	2350250.00	8428	35.44	420.99	3548099.00
09	36	44	3628	35.83	290.53	1054038.25	3638	34.42	576.05	2095677.00	7266	34.63	433.49	3149735.00
09	36	49	3272	35.03	246.47	806438.25	3252	33.61	589.63	1917474.00	6524	33.92	417.52	2723912.00
09	36	54	2965	34.94	304.19	901923.00	2947	32.98	504.99	1488209.00	5912	33.96	434.85	2929912.00
09	41	44	3708	35.68	305.20	1131682.00	3701	34.70	565.32	2092267.00	7409	34.91	434.91	3222282.00
09	41	49	3374	35.03	281.50	949781.00	3242	34.36	547.74	1478565.00	6616	34.65	290.76	1892575.00
09	41	54	2956	35.18	304.19	899190.00	2929	32.67	547.89	1479073.00	5906	33.63	332.18	1956216.00
09	46	49	2896	33.96	265.75	769612.00	2896	32.62	477.45	1381699.00	5993	33.51	299.03	1971782.00
09	46	54	2680	33.06	291.00	779880.00	2680	32.14	470.50	1360558.00	5360	33.51	292.89	1725974.00
14	16	19	11599	35.96	78.53	910602.69	11638	39.43	202.83	2360559.00	23237	40.24	140.50	3271860.00
14	16	24	8262	30.11	59.20	489116.62	8317	37.16	238.22	1981279.00	16579	37.24	149.01	2470595.00

Figure 7.2 Results of Triple MA Test in All Markets 1968 to 1990 (Continued)

MA	14	16	29	6794	36.74	77.51	526625.75	6823	35.66	290.15	1979696.00	13617	36.20	184.06	2506321.00
MA	14	16	34	5842	35.98	79.23	462855.62	5867	34.46	318.42	1868162.00	11709	35.22	199.08	2331018.00
MA	14	16	39	5188	35.35	123.17	639008.69	5225	33.68	371.22	1939619.00	10413	34.51	247.64	2578628.00
MA	14	16	44	4653	35.05	165.92	772036.56	4674	33.48	438.09	2047643.00	9327	34.27	302.31	2819679.00
MA	14	16	49	4219	35.32	199.57	841990.75	4219	33.09	461.82	1948431.00	8438	34.20	330.70	2790422.00
MA	14	16	54	3884	34.89	248.54	965322.94	3868	32.37	528.83	2045507.00	7752	33.63	388.39	3010830.00
MA	14	21	24	7755	39.43	89.93	697428.75	7795	37.68	280.17	2183927.00	15550	38.55	185.30	2881356.00
MA	14	21	29	6325	37.14	70.68	447067.69	6362	35.73	300.86	1914091.00	12687	36.43	186.11	2361159.00
MA	14	21	34	5440	35.48	173.09	941587.12	5462	34.16	413.56	2258891.00	10902	34.82	293.57	3200478.00
MA	14	21	39	4796	36.76	254.82	1222141.00	4826	33.67	497.65	2401665.00	9622	35.21	376.62	3623806.00
MA	14	21	44	4298	35.32	249.55	1072574.00	4314	34.28	535.57	2310461.00	8612	34.80	392.83	3383035.00
MA	14	21	49	3848	35.55	268.33	1032541.00	3841	32.83	560.88	2154356.00	7689	34.19	414.47	3186897.00
MA	14	21	54	3545	34.05	245.33	869710.25	3528	33.36	549.33	1938032.00	7073	33.71	396.97	2807742.00
MA	14	26	29	6108	37.13	119.76	731477.19	6142	34.94	326.94	2008053.00	12250	36.03	223.64	2739531.00
MA	14	26	34	5206	35.84	221.70	1154177.00	5216	34.68	457.65	2387100.00	10422	35.26	339.79	3541277.00
MA	14	26	39	4572	36.55	195.86	895493.50	4594	33.85	454.04	2085864.00	9166	35.20	325.26	2981357.00
MA	14	26	44	4057	35.84	215.06	872512.88	4072	34.18	488.48	1989097.00	8129	35.01	352.02	2861610.00
MA	14	26	49	3665	34.71	168.53	617666.37	3646	34.20	465.20	1696102.00	7311	34.45	316.48	2313768.00
MA	14	26	54	3337	34.28	253.39	845562.87	3324	33.18	587.64	1953307.00	6661	33.73	420.19	2798870.00
MA	14	31	34	5109	37.17	240.08	1226561.00	5155	35.50	461.61	2379618.00	10264	36.33	351.34	3606179.00
MA	14	31	39	4378	37.23	203.43	890608.00	4411	35.41	467.68	2062928.00	8789	36.32	336.05	2953536.00
MA	14	31	44	3835	35.83	217.60	834489.31	3843	34.95	505.98	1944477.00	7678	35.39	361.94	2778966.00
MA	14	31	49	3467	35.51	181.89	630597.37	3450	33.42	512.27	1767348.00	6917	34.47	346.67	2397945.00
MA	14	31	54	3145	34.75	229.09	720494.12	3130	33.42	600.30	1878934.00	6275	34.09	414.25	2599428.00
MA	14	36	39	4313	37.17	152.62	658267.31	4328	35.26	412.09	1783539.00	8641	36.21	282.58	2441806.00
MA	14	36	44	3738	36.38	202.50	756926.81	3745	33.51	489.66	1833763.00	7483	34.95	346.21	2590690.00
MA	14	36	49	3338	35.98	207.16	691485.12	3324	33.15	547.63	1820318.00	6662	34.57	377.03	2511803.00
MA	14	36	54	3036	35.08	145.09	440501.06	3008	33.78	500.41	1505219.00	6044	34.43	321.93	1945720.00
MA	14	41	44	3753	36.88	218.00	818156.06	3743	34.22	467.47	1749740.00	7496	35.55	342.57	2567896.00
MA	14	41	49	3280	35.76	137.78	451918.00	3257	33.07	470.16	1531310.00	6537	34.42	303.39	1983228.00
MA	14	41	54	2984	35.49	158.24	472178.31	2952	33.60	507.19	1497225.00	5936	34.55	331.77	1969403.00
MA	14	46	49	3345	36.05	159.71	534232.50	3311	33.59	443.11	1467129.00	6656	34.83	300.69	2001361.00
MA	14	46	54	2962	35.25	101.83	301630.81	2943	34.05	466.19	1371987.00	5905	34.65	283.42	1673618.00
MA	19	21	24	9856	41.91	72.47	714216.00	9907	40.71	222.70	2206261.00	19763	41.31	147.77	2920477.00
MA	19	21	29	7124	38.49	81.61	581396.31	7167	37.38	286.38	2052458.00	14291	37.93	184.30	2633854.00
MA	19	21	34	5886	36.43	173.56	1021550.75	5898	34.67	393.17	2318896.00	11784	35.55	283.47	3340447.00
MA	19	21	39	5085	36.74	253.07	1286846.00	5112	34.47	485.55	2482129.00	10197	35.60	369.62	3768975.00
MA	19	21	44	4547	35.69	250.87	1140724.00	4579	34.46	514.23	2354662.00	9126	35.08	383.01	3495386.00
MA	19	21	49	4046	35.76	267.03	1080389.00	4057	33.05	530.02	2150306.00	8103	34.41	398.70	3230695.00
MA	19	21	54	3695	34.40	236.17	872662.25	3678	32.95	526.85	1937749.00	7373	33.68	381.18	2810411.00
MA	19	26	29	6795	38.66	96.76	657490.50	6837	36.71	296.60	2027862.00	13632	37.68	196.99	2685352.00
MA	19	26	34	5573	37.07	211.47	1178541.00	5580	35.20	436.73	2436971.00	11153	36.13	324.17	3615512.00
MA	19	26	39	4788	36.86	216.37	1035963.00	4818	34.45	477.86	2302311.00	9606	35.65	347.52	3338274.00
MA	19	26	44	4266	36.33	215.81	920662.62	4293	34.29	466.48	2002598.00	8559	35.31	341.54	2923261.00
MA	19	26	49	3793	35.12	186.50	707387.69	3801	34.94	458.77	1743784.00	7594	35.03	322.78	2451172.00
MA	19	26	54	3465	34.26	234.75	813417.63	3454	33.24	537.60	1856876.00	6919	33.75	385.94	2670294.00
MA	19	31	34	5360	38.23	266.43	1428077.00	5406	36.66	484.84	2621033.00	10766	37.44	376.10	4049110.00
MA	19	31	39	4604	37.92	230.03	1059042.00	4638	36.24	481.03	2231001.00	9242	37.08	355.99	3290042.00
MA	19	31	44	4060	36.31	153.24	622146.19	4086	35.56	432.37	1766683.00	8146	35.93	293.25	2388829.00
MA	19	31	49	3635	35.85	146.75	533430.19	3641	33.92	423.37	1541473.00	7276	34.88	285.17	2074903.00
MA	19	31	54	3301	35.08	149.88	494758.37	3290	32.92	485.16	1596169.00	6591	34.00	317.24	2090928.00
MA	19	36	39	4518	38.05	144.29	651919.31	4534	36.81	411.56	1866000.00	9052	37.43	278.16	2517919.00
MA	19	36	44	3915	37.24	187.01	732136.81	3929	33.93	471.16	1851185.00	7844	35.58	329.34	2583322.00
MA	19	36	49	3498	36.71	179.20	626848.87	3498	33.62	481.32	1683672.00	6996	35.16	330.26	2310521.00
MA	19	36	54	3147	35.84	93.60	294548.31	3120	33.72	444.78	1387707.00	6267	34.79	268.43	1682255.00
MA	19	41	44	3875	36.18	188.38	729958.94	3874	35.13	469.68	1819529.00	7749	35.66	329.01	2549488.00
MA	19	41	49	3418	37.04	83.12	284110.25	3411	33.54	379.94	1295971.00	6829	35.29	231.38	1580082.00

Figures 7.1 and 7.2 show the results of my extensive study of dual and triple moving averages. These results reflect all signals in all active futures markets back to 1969 using the active contract month. The results are shown in dollars per trade and do not reflect commissions or slippage. To get a more accurate representation of the results, adjust the average trade figure by subtracting about $100 per trade. A close examination of the results shows there are many moving average combinations that generate more heat than light. Although not shown in the tabular listings, the dollar drawdown as well as the number of consecutive losers for all of these MA combinations, whether dual or triple, were significant. It is doubtful that most traders would have been able to withstand the drawdown before abandoning their positions. And therein rests one of the main drawbacks of MA systems— while they do exceptionally well when a significant trend begins, they create numerous losses and generate a vast amount of commission in the interim. In many cases the overall profitability of an MA combination in a given market rests on several large moves. Since most traders rarely ride a position to its fullest extent (they're often scared out well before the end of the move), they will not show the same results as these studies indicate.

The future of MA systems using three simple MAs is doubtful. I maintain that with the advent of more sophisticated computerized approaches to futures analysis the markets will become more efficient, meaning that price aberrations will not last too long. A market that moves out of phase with its underlying fundamentals will often be spotted quickly by computerized trading methods and the price swing will be essentially neutralized quickly by a horde of traders who rush in to take advantage of the deviation. Hence, price moves will likely occur more quickly. It seems as if the pendulum of market behavior is slowly but surely swinging faster and faster, making smaller and smaller arcs as the gravity of normality weighs on it more heavily than ever before.

I am not discounting the value of moving averages. I am suggesting, based on considerable research and personal experience, that traditional moving average systems based on simple or exponential moving averages may not be the best performers in today's markets. To maximize the performance of moving average systems, it is necessary to weight them more heavily for recent price activity since that is likely to be more important. While my theory may sound right, it must be back-tested.

Tip

Moving average systems are not right for every trader. Because they are subject to numerous whipsaws, fairly lengthy strings of losses and significant drawdown, they will severely test the the trader's resolve. Be prepared for the worst. When MA systems work in your favor they're marvelous, but when they lose repeatedly they'll make you question why you ever began trading futures.

Comparing Simple and Weighted Moving Average System Results

To test my theory I compared several simple and weighted moving combinations in several active markets. The tests were performed on Omega Research, Trade Station.

Test One

The first test was on Swiss franc futures (Figure 7.3), one of the more active markets during the 1980s and 1990s. The system was simple: I used a 5-day and 25-day weighted moving average of closing prices. A buy or reverse to long position was signaled when the 5-day WMA closed above the 25-day WMA. A sell or reverse to short side signal was generated when the 5-day WMA closed below the 25-day WMA. In addition, I deducted $100 per trade for slippage and commission.

Slippage refers to the difference between the price you are actually filled at and the price as back-tested. Since a back-test is hypothetical the fill price is assumed. Actual market conditions are significantly different at times. Although some traders may disagree, I consider the $100 figure somewhat high given today's discount commissions. Slippage of $50 is roughly eight ticks in the Swiss franc, which I consider to be unacceptable and not within the norm of my experience. Even five points slippage on the average would be more than necessary.

Figure 7.3   Performance of Swiss Franc 5/25 WMA—Daily Data, $3,000 Stop Loss, $2,500 Trailing Stop Loss

Performance Summary: All Trades

Total net profit	$ 66675.00	Open position P/L	$ 825.00
Gross profit	$ 208725.00	Gross loss	$-142050.00
Total # of trades	234	Percent profitable	37%
Number winning trades	86	Number losing trades	148
Largest winning trade	$ 11850.00	Largest losing trade	$ -2862.50
Average winning trade	$ 2427.03	Average losing trade	$ -959.80
Ratio avg win/avg loss	2.53	Avg trade(win & loss)	$ 284.94
Max consecutive winners	5	Max consecutive losers	10
Avg # bars in winners	29	Avg # bars in losers	8
Max intraday drawdown	$ -12350.00		
Profit factor	1.47	Max # contracts held	1
Account size required	$ 15350.00	Return on account	434%

Performance Summary: Long Trades

Total net profit	$ 31862.50	Open position P/L	$ 825.00
Gross profit	$ 101925.00	Gross loss	$ -70062.50
Total # of trades	117	Percent profitable	35%
Number winning trades	41	Number losing trades	76
Largest winning trade	$ 11850.00	Largest losing trade	$ -2787.50
Average winning trade	$ 2485.98	Average losing trade	$ -921.88
Ratio avg win/avg loss	2.70	Avg trade(win & loss)	$ 272.33
Max consecutive winners	4	Max consecutive losers	10
Avg # bars in winners	28	Avg # bars in losers	8
Max intraday drawdown	$ -19787.50		
Profit factor	1.45	Max # contracts held	1
Account size required	$ 22787.50	Return on account	140%

Performance Summary: Short Trades

Total net profit	$ 34812.50	Open position P/L	$ 0.00
Gross profit	$ 106800.00	Gross loss	$ -71987.50
Total # of trades	117	Percent profitable	38%
Number winning trades	45	Number losing trades	72
Largest winning trade	$ 9812.50	Largest losing trade	$ -2862.50
Average winning trade	$ 2373.33	Average losing trade	$ -999.83
Ratio avg win/avg loss	2.37	Avg trade(win & loss)	$ 297.54
Max consecutive winners	3	Max consecutive losers	10
Avg # bars in winners	30	Avg # bars in losers	8
Max intraday drawdown	$ -18862.50		
Profit factor	1.48	Max # contracts held	1
Account size required	$ 18862.50	Return on account	185%

Reprinted with permission of Omega Research, Inc.

The $50 commission figure is also too high by 1991 standards. Quality discount service can be found for as little as $21 per trade, although the norm is about $25 to $29. Hence, the average profit figure for this trading method could easily be raised to $300. Note that I tested for the worst case scenario, as a trader must do.

I also used a $3,000 initial stop loss and a $2,500 trailing stop loss. In other words, I was willing to risk $3,000 on each trade initially and $2,500 retracement in open profits. You may feel that the initial stop loss was much too liberal. Many traders, in fact too many traders, are unwilling to accept losses larger than $1,500 per trade. This is, perhaps, why they get stopped out so often. It's been my experience that wide stops are absolutely necessary if you want to give your position a good chance to perform.

In examining the performance listing, you will note that the average trade, wins and losses minus slippage and commission was +$284.94. The percentage of profitable trade, however, was only 37 percent. There are a few other factors to consider as well. First and foremost is the maximum number of consecutive losers, which was ten. This is an important figure since it lets you know how bad things have been in the past. In addition, the maximum drawdown was in excess of $12,000, which tells you what you would have had to sit through. The long trades and short trades were about evenly distributed, which is an indication that you would have had to take every trade rather than being selective about which side of the market you wanted to trade.

By way of contrast examine the same market using a 5 and 25 simple MA combination (Figure 7.4). The average trade here was $249.18, significantly less than the average trade for the 2/25 WMA combination cited previously. Although the actual dollar figure per trade seems small, multiplied by 234 trades the net profit figure using the WMA is $21,000 larger for the WMA. As you can see by an examination of the performance summaries, the differences were significant.

Test Two

Another popular market during the 1980s and 1990s has been the Japanese yen. I tested the same MA combination using $2,500 initial stop loss and $2,500 trailing stop loss. The results, as illustrated in Figure 7.5, were even better than the results for

Figure 7.4   Performance of Swiss Franc 5/25 SMA—Same Parameters as Figure 7.3

Performance Summary: All Trades

Total net profit	$ 45350.00	Open position P/L	$ -800.00
Gross profit	$ 167987.50	Gross loss	$-122637.50
Total # of trades	182	Percent profitable	39%
Number winning trades	71	Number losing trades	111
Largest winning trade	$ 10687.50	Largest losing trade	$ -3187.50
Average winning trade	$ 2366.02	Average losing trade	$ -1104.84
Ratio avg win/avg loss	2.14	Avg trade(win & loss)	$ 249.18
Max consecutive winners	5	Max consecutive losers	8
Avg # bars in winners	31	Avg # bars in losers	9
Max intraday drawdown	$ -14762.50		
Profit factor	1.37	Max # contracts held	1
Account size required	$ 17762.50	Return on account	255%

Performance Summary: Long Trades

Total net profit	$ 21225.00	Open position P/L	$ -800.00
Gross profit	$ 87287.50	Gross loss	$ -66062.50
Total # of trades	91	Percent profitable	40%
Number winning trades	36	Number losing trades	55
Largest winning trade	$ 10687.50	Largest losing trade	$ -2650.00
Average winning trade	$ 2424.65	Average losing trade	$ -1201.14
Ratio avg win/avg loss	2.02	Avg trade(win & loss)	$ 233.24
Max consecutive winners	6	Max consecutive losers	8
Avg # bars in winners	29	Avg # bars in losers	7
Max intraday drawdown	$ -20425.00		
Profit factor	1.32	Max # contracts held	1
Account size required	$ 23425.00	Return on account	91%

Performance Summary: Short Trades

Total net profit	$ 24125.00	Open position P/L	$ 0.00
Gross profit	$ 80700.00	Gross loss	$ -56575.00
Total # of trades	91	Percent profitable	38%
Number winning trades	35	Number losing trades	56
Largest winning trade	$ 9937.50	Largest losing trade	$ -3187.50
Average winning trade	$ 2305.71	Average losing trade	$ -1010.27
Ratio avg win/avg loss	2.28	Avg trade(win & loss)	$ 265.11
Max consecutive winners	4	Max consecutive losers	8
Avg # bars in winners	33	Avg # bars in losers	10
Max intraday drawdown	$ -14425.00		
Profit factor	1.43	Max # contracts held	1
Account size required	$ 17425.00	Return on account	138%

Reprinted with permission of Omega Research, Inc.

Swiss franc in spite of the fact that the percentage of profitable trades was only 33 percent. The remaining results are self-explanatory. Although the results were very impressive, a test of the SMA combination should be examined to see which is superior. As an examination of the SMA results (Figure 7.6) shows, this test outperformed the WMA test by a substantial margin.

While the WMA is often superior to the SMA, this is not always true. A deeper examination of the results indicates that using the WMA would produce smaller drawdown by about $3,000, a higher percentage return on account and a larger average winning trade on short positions. Hence, it's not a clear-cut victory for the SMA.

Test Three

Yet another test of the WMA was performed on coffee futures. The results here are spectacular, returning an average of over $773 per trade with 47 percent accuracy. Since coffee futures have been among the most volatile of the futures markets, I caution you to be particularly careful if you decide to trade coffee. Note also that the initial stop loss of $1,400 and the trailing stop loss of $1,200 are very reasonable considering the volatility of this market. Do note, however, that the MAs here are a little longer than those used for the currencies.

Tip

Coffee futures are among the most seasonal of all markets. There is a strong tendency for prices to bottom in the late July to early August time frame and to move higher through year end. A good way to time market entry into a seasonal trade for coffee is to use the 7/31 WMA combination for timing.

Now examine the results for coffee using a simple MA combination of 7 and 31 days. The results show that the WMA results were clearly superior by a large margin. The net profit for the WMA was nearly three times greater than it was for the SMA, and the accuracy figure was considerably higher with almost the same drawdown. Figure 7.8 illustrates these results. While the differences won't always be this pronounced, the results are a

Figure 7.5   Performance of Japanese Yen 5/25 WMA

Performance Summary: All Trades

Total net profit	$ 85637.50	Open position P/L	$	625.00
Gross profit	$ 194537.50	Gross loss	$-108900.00	
Total # of trades	198	Percent profitable	33%	
Number winning trades	65	Number losing trades	133	
Largest winning trade	$ 13125.00	Largest losing trade	$ -2837.50	
Average winning trade	$ 2992.88	Average losing trade	$ -818.80	
Ratio avg win/avg loss	3.66	Avg trade(win & loss)	$ 432.51	
Max consecutive winners	6	Max consecutive losers	9	
Avg # bars in winners	34	Avg # bars in losers	8	
Max intraday drawdown	$ -11612.50			
Profit factor	1.79	Max # contracts held	1	
Account size required	$ 11612.50	Return on account	737%	

Performance Summary: Long Trades

Total net profit	$ 54462.50	Open position P/L	$	625.00
Gross profit	$ 107537.50	Gross loss	$ -53075.00	
Total # of trades	99	Percent profitable	32%	
Number winning trades	32	Number losing trades	67	
Largest winning trade	$ 13125.00	Largest losing trade	$ -2837.50	
Average winning trade	$ 3360.55	Average losing trade	$ -792.16	
Ratio avg win/avg loss	4.24	Avg trade(win & loss)	$ 550.13	
Max consecutive winners	4	Max consecutive losers	9	
Avg # bars in winners	34	Avg # bars in losers	7	
Max intraday drawdown	$ -8200.00			
Profit factor	2.03	Max # contracts held	1	
Account size required	$ 11200.00	Return on account	486%	

Performance Summary: Short Trades

Total net profit	$ 31175.00	Open position P/L	$	0.00
Gross profit	$ 87000.00	Gross loss	$ -55825.00	
Total # of trades	99	Percent profitable	33%	
Number winning trades	33	Number losing trades	66	
Largest winning trade	$ 10500.00	Largest losing trade	$ -2662.50	
Average winning trade	$ 2636.36	Average losing trade	$ -845.83	
Ratio avg win/avg loss	3.12	Avg trade(win & loss)	$ 314.90	
Max consecutive winners	5	Max consecutive losers	11	
Avg # bars in winners	35	Avg # bars in losers	9	
Max intraday drawdown	$ -16862.50			
Profit factor	1.56	Max # contracts held	1	
Account size required	$ 19862.50	Return on account	157%	

Reprinted with permission of Omega Research, Inc.

Figure 7.6   Performance of Japanese Yen 5/25 SMA

```
                     Performance Summary:  All Trades

Total net profit       $  94112.50   Open position P/L      $     600.00
Gross profit           $ 179387.50   Gross loss             $  -85275.00

Total # of trades            158     Percent profitable           41%
Number winning trades         65     Number losing trades         93

Largest winning trade  $  13087.50   Largest losing trade   $   -2925.00
Average winning trade  $   2759.81   Average losing trade   $    -916.94
Ratio avg win/avg loss        3.01   Avg trade(win & loss)  $     595.65

Max consecutive winners        4     Max consecutive losers         7
Avg # bars in winners         34     Avg # bars in losers          10

Max intraday drawdown  $ -14762.50
Profit factor                 2.10   Max # contracts held           1
Account size required  $  14762.50   Return on account            638%
```

```
                     Performance Summary:  Long Trades

Total net profit       $  52175.00   Open position P/L      $     600.00
Gross profit           $  96112.50   Gross loss             $  -43937.50

Total # of trades             79     Percent profitable           41%
Number winning trades         32     Number losing trades         47

Largest winning trade  $  13087.50   Largest losing trade   $   -2925.00
Average winning trade  $   3003.52   Average losing trade   $    -934.84
Ratio avg win/avg loss        3.21   Avg trade(win & loss)  $     660.44

Max consecutive winners        6     Max consecutive losers        10
Avg # bars in winners         34     Avg # bars in losers           8

Max intraday drawdown  $ -14912.50
Profit factor                 2.19   Max # contracts held           1
Account size required  $  14912.50   Return on account            350%
```

```
                     Performance Summary:  Short Trades

Total net profit       $  41937.50   Open position P/L      $       0.00
Gross profit           $  83275.00   Gross loss             $  -41337.50

Total # of trades             79     Percent profitable           42%
Number winning trades         33     Number losing trades         46

Largest winning trade  $   9850.00   Largest losing trade   $   -2362.50
Average winning trade  $   2523.48   Average losing trade   $    -898.64
Ratio avg win/avg loss        2.81   Avg trade(win & loss)  $     530.85

Max consecutive winners        3     Max consecutive losers         7
Avg # bars in winners         35     Avg # bars in losers          11

Max intraday drawdown  $  -8212.50
Profit factor                 2.01   Max # contracts held           1
Account size required  $   8212.50   Return on account            511%
```

Reprinted with permission of Omega Research, Inc.

strong statement for using a WMA instead of an SMA in some cases. Note that the WMA combination showed only 8 consecutive losers compared to the 13 consecutive losers using the SMA.

Test Four

Another test examined the 7/31 WMA combination on crude oil futures. This market has not only been one of the most volatile in the 1980s and 1990s but also been among the most active. The results are very good at $318 per trade with 39 percent winners, a reasonably small drawdown and a reasonable number of consecutive losing trades. The initial stop loss of $1,400 and the $1,200 trailing are also most reasonable in today's markets. These results are shown in Figure 7.9.

Now compare these results to the same combination using simple MAs, shown in Figure 7.10. The results indicate that using the WMA here was superior as well. The total profits using the WMA combination were twice that of the SMA with similar accuracy. Again the WMA results were clearly superior to the SMA performance.

Test Five

A final test was performed on Gold Futures. The results are shown in Figure 7.11. The profit per trade after slippage and commission was $416.34 with a maximum intraday drawdown of slightly over $12,000. A comparison of results using the 5/25 SMA as shown in Figure 7.12 suggests initially that, at $455.99 per trade profit, this was the superior system. In fact, a closer examination of the results shows nearly three times the drawdown at almost $33,000 for this approach. Clearly, in this case the educated decision is to sacrifice the higher dollar per trade profit for the smaller drawdown.

Finally, the WMA approach shows a large percentage return on account. Although this figure should not concern you, it is something that you'll want to look at when comparing the results of two different methods in the same market. As you can see from the foregoing examples, a cursory examination of system test results is insufficient. The individual trader must examine overall test results using a number of factors, then accept or reject a system based on his or her specific needs and abilities in the

Figure 7.7   Performance of Coffee 7/31 WMA

```
                    Performance Summary:  All Trades

Total net profit        $ 163120.00   Open position P/L      $      0.00
Gross profit            $ 300420.00   Gross loss             $-137300.00

Total # of trades            211      Percent profitable          47%
Number winning trades        100      Number losing trades        111

Largest winning trade   $  23700.00   Largest losing trade   $ -11730.00
Average winning trade   $   3004.20   Average losing trade   $  -1236.94
Ratio avg win/avg loss         2.43   Avg trade(win & loss)  $    773.08

Max consecutive winners        8      Max consecutive losers        8
Avg # bars in winners          2      Avg # bars in losers          1

Max intraday drawdown   $ -11800.00
Profit factor                  2.19   Max # contracts held          1
Account size required   $  11800.00   Return on account          1382%

                    Performance Summary:  Long Trades

Total net profit        $ 101850.00   Open position P/L      $      0.00
Gross profit            $ 165930.00   Gross loss             $ -64080.00

Total # of trades            105      Percent profitable          50%
Number winning trades         52      Number losing trades         53

Largest winning trade   $  23700.00   Largest losing trade   $  -6230.00
Average winning trade   $   3190.96   Average losing trade   $  -1209.06
Ratio avg win/avg loss         2.64   Avg trade(win & loss)  $    970.00

Max consecutive winners        5      Max consecutive losers        8
Avg # bars in winners          2      Avg # bars in losers          1

Max intraday drawdown   $  -7330.00
Profit factor                  2.59   Max # contracts held          1
Account size required   $   7330.00   Return on account          1389%

                    Performance Summary:  Short Trades

Total net profit        $  61270.00   Open position P/L      $      0.00
Gross profit            $ 134490.00   Gross loss             $ -73220.00

Total # of trades            106      Percent profitable          45%
Number winning trades         48      Number losing trades         58

Largest winning trade   $  18760.00   Largest losing trade   $ -11730.00
Average winning trade   $   2801.88   Average losing trade   $  -1262.41
Ratio avg win/avg loss         2.22   Avg trade(win & loss)  $    578.02

Max consecutive winners        5      Max consecutive losers        7
Avg # bars in winners          2      Avg # bars in losers          1

Max intraday drawdown   $ -12350.00
Profit factor                  1.84   Max # contracts held          1
Account size required   $  12350.00   Return on account           496%
```

Reprinted with permission of Omega Research, Inc.

Figure 7.8   Performance of Coffee 7/31 SMA

Performance Summary: All Trades

Total net profit	$ 59540.00	Open position P/L	$ 0.00
Gross profit	$ 195010.00	Gross loss	$-135470.00
Total # of trades	164	Percent profitable	35%
Number winning trades	58	Number losing trades	106
Largest winning trade	$ 22160.00	Largest losing trade	$ -12690.00
Average winning trade	$ 3362.24	Average losing trade	$ -1278.02
Ratio avg win/avg loss	2.63	Avg trade(win & loss)	$ 363.05
Max consecutive winners	4	Max consecutive losers	13
Avg # bars in winners	2	Avg # bars in losers	1
Max intraday drawdown	$ -31010.00		
Profit factor	1.44	Max # contracts held	1
Account size required	$ 31010.00	Return on account	192%

Performance Summary: Long Trades

Total net profit	$ 34260.00	Open position P/L	$ 0.00
Gross profit	$ 103150.00	Gross loss	$ -68890.00
Total # of trades	82	Percent profitable	43%
Number winning trades	35	Number losing trades	47
Largest winning trade	$ 17740.00	Largest losing trade	$ -12690.00
Average winning trade	$ 2947.14	Average losing trade	$ -1465.74
Ratio avg win/avg loss	2.01	Avg trade(win & loss)	$ 417.80
Max consecutive winners	5	Max consecutive losers	10
Avg # bars in winners	3	Avg # bars in losers	1
Max intraday drawdown	$ -29390.00		
Profit factor	1.50	Max # contracts held	1
Account size required	$ 29390.00	Return on account	117%

Performance Summary: Short Trades

Total net profit	$ 25280.00	Open position P/L	$ 0.00
Gross profit	$ 91860.00	Gross loss	$ -66580.00
Total # of trades	82	Percent profitable	28%
Number winning trades	23	Number losing trades	59
Largest winning trade	$ 22160.00	Largest losing trade	$ -3600.00
Average winning trade	$ 3993.91	Average losing trade	$ -1128.47
Ratio avg win/avg loss	3.54	Avg trade(win & loss)	$ 308.29
Max consecutive winners	3	Max consecutive losers	11
Avg # bars in winners	2	Avg # bars in losers	1
Max intraday drawdown	$ -13350.00		
Profit factor	1.38	Max # contracts held	1
Account size required	$ 13350.00	Return on account	189%

Reprinted with permission of Omega Research, Inc.

Figure 7.9 Performance of Crude Oil Futures 5/25 WMA

```
                    Performance Summary:  All Trades

Total net profit      $  26130.00   Open position P/L     $      0.00
Gross profit          $  60600.00   Gross loss            $ -34470.00

Total # of trades          82       Percent profitable         39%
Number winning trades      32       Number losing trades       50

Largest winning trade $   6970.00   Largest losing trade  $  -1780.00
Average winning trade $   1893.75   Average losing trade  $   -689.40
Ratio avg win/avg loss     2.75     Avg trade(win & loss) $    318.66

Max consecutive winners     4       Max consecutive losers      8
Avg # bars in winners      30       Avg # bars in losers        7

Max intraday drawdown $  -6490.00
Profit factor              1.76     Max # contracts held        1
Account size required $   9490.00   Return on account         275%
```

```
                    Performance Summary:  Long Trades

Total net profit      $  15030.00   Open position P/L     $      0.00
Gross profit          $  34020.00   Gross loss            $ -18990.00

Total # of trades          41       Percent profitable         37%
Number winning trades      15       Number losing trades       26

Largest winning trade $   6970.00   Largest losing trade  $  -1780.00
Average winning trade $   2268.00   Average losing trade  $   -730.38
Ratio avg win/avg loss     3.11     Avg trade(win & loss) $    366.59

Max consecutive winners     3       Max consecutive losers      4
Avg # bars in winners      38       Avg # bars in losers        6

Max intraday drawdown $  -4730.00
Profit factor              1.79     Max # contracts held        1
Account size required $   7730.00   Return on account         194%
```

```
                    Performance Summary:  Short Trades

Total net profit      $  11100.00   Open position P/L     $      0.00
Gross profit          $  26580.00   Gross loss            $ -15480.00

Total # of trades          41       Percent profitable         41%
Number winning trades      17       Number losing trades       24

Largest winning trade $   3980.00   Largest losing trade  $  -1410.00
Average winning trade $   1563.53   Average losing trade  $   -645.00
Ratio avg win/avg loss     2.42     Avg trade(win & loss) $    270.73

Max consecutive winners     4       Max consecutive losers     10
Avg # bars in winners      23       Avg # bars in losers        8

Max intraday drawdown $  -6090.00
Profit factor              1.72     Max # contracts held        1
Account size required $   9090.00   Return on account         122%
```

Reprinted with permission of Omega Research, Inc.

Figure 7.10   Performance of Crude Oil 5/25 SMA

```
               Performance Summary:  All Trades

Total net profit      $   13310.00    Open position P/L      $        0.00
Gross profit          $   46580.00    Gross loss             $   -33270.00

Total # of trades            69       Percent profitable              39%
Number winning trades        27       Number losing trades            42

Largest winning trade $    6630.00    Largest losing trade   $    -1420.00
Average winning trade $    1725.19    Average losing trade   $     -792.14
Ratio avg win/avg loss       2.18     Avg trade(win & loss)  $      192.90

Max consecutive winners       4       Max consecutive losers          11
Avg # bars in winners        30       Avg # bars in losers             7

Max intraday drawdown $   -7600.00
Profit factor                1.40     Max # contracts held             1
Account size required $   10600.00    Return on account             126%
```
```
               Performance Summary:  Long Trades

Total net profit      $   14640.00    Open position P/L      $        0.00
Gross profit          $   30730.00    Gross loss             $   -16090.00

Total # of trades            34       Percent profitable              44%
Number winning trades        15       Number losing trades            19

Largest winning trade $    6630.00    Largest losing trade   $    -1420.00
Average winning trade $    2048.67    Average losing trade   $     -846.84
Ratio avg win/avg loss       2.42     Avg trade(win & loss)  $      430.59

Max consecutive winners       3       Max consecutive losers           5
Avg # bars in winners        38       Avg # bars in losers             7

Max intraday drawdown $   -5230.00
Profit factor                1.91     Max # contracts held             1
Account size required $    5230.00    Return on account             280%
```
```
               Performance Summary:  Short Trades

Total net profit      $   -1330.00    Open position P/L      $        0.00
Gross profit          $   15850.00    Gross loss             $   -17180.00

Total # of trades            35       Percent profitable              34%
Number winning trades        12       Number losing trades            23

Largest winning trade $    3810.00    Largest losing trade   $    -1300.00
Average winning trade $    1320.83    Average losing trade   $     -746.96
Ratio avg win/avg loss       1.77     Avg trade(win & loss)  $      -38.00

Max consecutive winners       3       Max consecutive losers           8
Avg # bars in winners        21       Avg # bars in losers             6

Max intraday drawdown $   -5980.00
Profit factor                0.92     Max # contracts held             1
Account size required $    5980.00    Return on account             -22%
```

Reprinted with permission of Omega Research, Inc.

marketplace. What's right for one trader in terms of risk to reward ratio is not right for another. And this is yet another reason to avoid *canned* trading systems in preference to your own trading system and timing indicator development.

Tip

You might want to test the same WMA combinations for entries and different indicators or WMA combinations for exits. Bear market characteristics are distinctly different than bull market characteristics. By using one set of WMAs for entry and another for exits you can significantly improve results.

Short-Term Trading with a Weighted MA System

The WMA method can also be applied to short-term trading. Figure 7.13 shows the test results of 25-minute crude oil using a 7-period and 37-period combination with $75 slippage and commissions, a $1,500 initial stop loss and an $870 trailing stop loss. The results are favorable. The maximum number of consecutive losers is five with about $5,000 in drawdown. The performance evaluation period covers about one year of intraday data and 126 trades, which constitutes a statistically valid test. The 25-minute time increment allows for an equal number of time slots in crude oil futures based on the length of their trading day. This permits the system or timing method to be adapted to day trading.

At present there are several other markets that lend themselves to intraday application of WMA systems. Among these are S&P futures, yen, Swiss franc and T-bond futures. In fact, most active markets will show favorable results on short-term trading using an intraday data analysis. Remember, however, not to optimize results too tightly!

Conclusions about Weighted Moving Average Systems

WMA systems do not work in all markets. They are particularly difficult in markets that show low volatility and are not

Figure 7.11   Performance of Gold Futures 5/25 WMA

Performance Summary: All Trades

Total net profit	$ 99090.00	Open position P/L	$ 970.00
Gross profit	$ 217520.00	Gross loss	$-118430.00
Total # of trades	238	Percent profitable	36%
Number winning trades	86	Number losing trades	152
Largest winning trade	$ 22810.00	Largest losing trade	$ -6680.00
Average winning trade	$ 2529.30	Average losing trade	$ -779.14
Ratio avg win/avg loss	3.25	Avg trade(win & loss)	$ 416.34
Max consecutive winners	4	Max consecutive losers	9
Avg # bars in winners	32	Avg # bars in losers	8
Max intraday drawdown	$ -12330.00		
Profit factor	1.84	Max # contracts held	1
Account size required	$ 15330.00	Return on account	646%

Performance Summary: Long Trades

Total net profit	$ 32600.00	Open position P/L	$ 0.00
Gross profit	$ 97740.00	Gross loss	$ -65140.00
Total # of trades	119	Percent profitable	35%
Number winning trades	42	Number losing trades	77
Largest winning trade	$ 22810.00	Largest losing trade	$ -4000.00
Average winning trade	$ 2327.14	Average losing trade	$ -845.97
Ratio avg win/avg loss	2.75	Avg trade(win & loss)	$ 273.95
Max consecutive winners	5	Max consecutive losers	8
Avg # bars in winners	30	Avg # bars in losers	7
Max intraday drawdown	$ -13020.00		
Profit factor	1.50	Max # contracts held	1
Account size required	$ 16020.00	Return on account	203%

Performance Summary: Short Trades

Total net profit	$ 66490.00	Open position P/L	$ 970.00
Gross profit	$ 119780.00	Gross loss	$ -53290.00
Total # of trades	119	Percent profitable	37%
Number winning trades	44	Number losing trades	75
Largest winning trade	$ 17600.00	Largest losing trade	$ -6680.00
Average winning trade	$ 2722.27	Average losing trade	$ -710.53
Ratio avg win/avg loss	3.83	Avg trade(win & loss)	$ 558.74
Max consecutive winners	6	Max consecutive losers	7
Avg # bars in winners	34	Avg # bars in losers	10
Max intraday drawdown	$ -11510.00		
Profit factor	2.25	Max # contracts held	1
Account size required	$ 14510.00	Return on account	458%

Reprinted with permission of Omega Research, Inc.

Figure 7.12   Performance of Gold Futures 5/25 SMA

```
                    Performance Summary:  All Trades

Total net profit        $   87550.00    Open position P/L     $    1410.00
Gross profit            $  193480.00    Gross loss            $-105930.00

Total # of trades              192      Percent profitable          42%
Number winning trades           80      Number losing trades        112

Largest winning trade   $   26990.00    Largest losing trade  $   -5020.00
Average winning trade   $    2418.50    Average losing trade  $    -945.80
Ratio avg win/avg loss        2.56      Avg trade(win & loss) $     455.99

Max consecutive winners          4      Max consecutive losers         9
Avg # bars in winners           32      Avg # bars in losers          11

Max intraday drawdown   $  -32980.00
Profit factor                 1.83      Max # contracts held           1
Account size required   $   35980.00    Return on account           243%
```

```
                    Performance Summary:  Long Trades

Total net profit        $   29420.00    Open position P/L     $       0.00
Gross profit            $   82840.00    Gross loss            $  -53420.00

Total # of trades               96      Percent profitable          40%
Number winning trades           38      Number losing trades        58

Largest winning trade   $   26990.00    Largest losing trade  $   -3730.00
Average winning trade   $    2180.00    Average losing trade  $    -921.03
Ratio avg win/avg loss        2.37      Avg trade(win & loss) $     306.46

Max consecutive winners          3      Max consecutive losers         6
Avg # bars in winners           28      Avg # bars in losers          11

Max intraday drawdown   $  -28720.00
Profit factor                 1.55      Max # contracts held           1
Account size required   $   31720.00    Return on account            93%
```

```
                    Performance Summary:  Short Trades

Total net profit        $   58130.00    Open position P/L     $    1410.00
Gross profit            $  110640.00    Gross loss            $  -52510.00

Total # of trades               96      Percent profitable          44%
Number winning trades           42      Number losing trades        54

Largest winning trade   $   18800.00    Largest losing trade  $   -5020.00
Average winning trade   $    2634.29    Average losing trade  $    -972.41
Ratio avg win/avg loss        2.71      Avg trade(win & loss) $     605.52

Max consecutive winners          7      Max consecutive losers         6
Avg # bars in winners           35      Avg # bars in losers          12

Max intraday drawdown   $  -13930.00
Profit factor                 2.11      Max # contracts held           1
Account size required   $   16930.00    Return on account           343%
```

Reprinted with permission of Omega Research, Inc.

recommended for use in such markets. In addition, stock index futures, from my experience, seem to be resistant to performing well using weighted MAs. Yet there are other indicators that do appear to do well in stock index futures such as the MACD (moving average convergence divergence). In most cases WMAs perform better than simple MAs, and I encourage you to use them and to test them in other markets. Most of the successful WMA combinations are in the range from 5/23 to 9/37 days. I don't mean to suggest that there are no SMA combinations that may work as well as WMA combinations. However, if you discover a promising SMA or EMA combination in a given market, it's a good idea to test the same length WMA.

In addition, there are good possibilities for using WMAs in short-term trading on intraday data. My research in this area is still somewhat limited; however, with the relatively low cost of tick data and powerful analysis programs such as TradeStation, this research is easily performed.

Figure 7.13   Results of 7/37 WMA System in 25-Minute
Crude Oil Data

```
                        Performance Summary:  All Trades

Total net profit        $   31300.00   Open position P/L      $     -70.00
Gross profit            $   60380.00   Gross loss             $  -29080.00

Total # of trades            126       Percent profitable          46%
Number winning trades         58       Number losing trades         68

Largest winning trade   $    5255.00   Largest losing trade   $   -4285.00
Average winning trade   $    1041.03   Average losing trade   $    -427.65
Ratio avg win/avg loss        2.43     Avg trade(win & loss)  $     248.41

Max consecutive winners        5       Max consecutive losers        5
Avg # bars in winners         27       Avg # bars in losers         11

Max intraday drawdown   $   -5110.00
Profit factor                 2.08     Max # contracts held          1
Account size required   $    8110.00   Return on account           386%
```

```
                        Performance Summary:  Long Trades

Total net profit        $   21115.00   Open position P/L      $     -70.00
Gross profit            $   32720.00   Gross loss             $  -11605.00

Total # of trades             63       Percent profitable          48%
Number winning trades         30       Number losing trades         33

Largest winning trade   $    5255.00   Largest losing trade   $    -945.00
Average winning trade   $    1090.67   Average losing trade   $    -351.67
Ratio avg win/avg loss        3.10     Avg trade(win & loss)  $     335.16

Max consecutive winners        4       Max consecutive losers        5
Avg # bars in winners         31       Avg # bars in losers         10

Max intraday drawdown   $   -2510.00
Profit factor                 2.82     Max # contracts held          1
Account size required   $    5510.00   Return on account           383%
```

```
                        Performance Summary:  Short Trades

Total net profit        $   10185.00   Open position P/L      $       0.00
Gross profit            $   27660.00   Gross loss             $  -17475.00

Total # of trades             63       Percent profitable          44%
Number winning trades         28       Number losing trades         35

Largest winning trade   $    3855.00   Largest losing trade   $   -4285.00
Average winning trade   $     987.86   Average losing trade   $    -499.29
Ratio avg win/avg loss        1.98     Avg trade(win & loss)  $     161.67

Max consecutive winners        5       Max consecutive losers       10
Avg # bars in winners         22       Avg # bars in losers         11

Max intraday drawdown   $   -4735.00
Profit factor                 1.58     Max # contracts held          1
Account size required   $    7735.00   Return on account           132%
```

Reprinted with permission of Omega Research, Inc.

Chapter
8

Stochastics Revisited

Dr. George Lane of Investment Educators, Watseka, Illinois, is credited with popularizing and developing what is likely to be the single most popular technical indicator with the exception of moving averages—the stochastic indicator (SI), actually an oscillator or a variation on the MA theme. Like all indicators stochastics has its good and bad points, and numerous applications as well. George Lane has spent a virtual lifetime researching and studying stochastics. And my studies have revealed a variety of applications beyond those discovered by Dr. Lane. The SI can serve as a timing indicator, used as part of a free-standing system, or as a confirming indicator used with other timing indicators.

In my book *Short-Term Traders Manual* I discussed several SI applications. Since then there have been many advances in system-testing technology, the foremost of which are System Writer Plus (SWP) and TradeStation (TS), both developed by Bill Cruz and associates at Omega Research. The powerful capabilities of SWP and TS permit evaluation and optimization of trading indicators and systems. They have allowed me to develop and refine new timing techniques and indicators, and to more thoroughly test indicators I've introduced and used in the past. These programs have facilitated testing both on a tick-by-tick basis as well as on a daily basis.

My *Short-Term Traders Manual* helped fill a void in the literature available to short-term traders. I was contacted by traders throughout the world who were pleased with the indicators and concepts introduced. However, they had more questions than I could easily answer. In fact, some of their questions were impossible to answer given the limitations of my knowledge. Many questions pertained to my applications for stochastics, particularly to my Pop application for the SI. I was most amazed by the number of traders who were interested not only in the Pop technique but in virtually any application related to the SI. Now, over three years and a wealth of research later, I have answers that I did not have then, and will share some of them with you.

The purpose of this chapter is to:

- Reexamine the SI, its traditional applications, assets and limitations.
- Suggest several ways in which these limitations may be overcome.
- Introduce several alternative methods of SI application that I feel have the potential to improve your trading.
- Provide historical validation of their efficacy.

An Introduction to Stochastics

My never-ending search for profitable trading indicators, system and methods has been the stimulus for thousands of tests. The primary conclusion of my research has clearly been that the *perfect* trading system does not exist. Nevertheless, too many traders have spent too much time and money searching for the Holy Grail. Their search has been abetted by a cadre of unscrupulous operators who have sold, resold, packaged and repackaged "ultimate trading systems" in response to public demand. But *the perfect trading system does not exist, and never will exist.* Every so often, however, a system, method or indicator with excellent potential is developed. Unfortunately, the trading public in their eternal search for the ultimate indicator latches on to such promising indicators and attributes to them qualities far above and beyond those intended by the original developers of these systems. And so it has been with stochastics.

While George Lane, the man most closely associated with stochastics, has suggested numerous methods for SI application to futures trading, too many analysts have perpetuated the myth that stochastics cures all ills. Although the stochastic indicator (SI) is far from perfect, it's definitely one of the better tools available to traders. Dr. Lane claims that the stochastic indicator is not a panacea; it is merely an indicator with considerable potential, limited only by the discipline and acuity of the trader (personal communication, 1989).

In this chapter I'll share my latest thoughts and methods of stochastic application. First I will introduce stochastics—discussing its basic construction, application, assets and limitations. Then I'll explain my stochastic methodology, which has been refined to the point of application as a self-contained trading system when used within specific parameters. But remember that this stochastic technique has some distinct limitations. My use of stochastics reflects my *personal adaptation* of the basic indicator.

My first contact with stochastics was through Dr. George Lane's work at Investment Educators. My studies and initial applications of stochastics to futures trading convinced me that this approach did have some potentially profitable applications—all I needed to do was to find them! I knew that there were some definite advantages to using stochastics in conjunction with other timing indicators, and as an adjunct to cyclical and seasonal methodologies, but I needed to find more profitable applications. Before I discuss some of my findings I'll provide a brief explanation of stochastics and its logic.

Basic Theory and Application

The stochastic indicator consists of two values—%K and %D. The formula for stochastics is shown in Figure 8.1. In its most basic form the SI tells you when a market is *overbought* (i.e., overpriced) and likely to turn down, or *oversold* (i.e., underpriced) and likely to turn up. Figure 8.2 shows the SI versus price. A marked correlation between price and SI is readily apparent. SI and price top and bottom together. Additionally, the SI acts as a detrending indicator by removing trend from price, thereby highlighting tops and bottoms. SI approaches the 100 percent and 0 percent level as upper and lower limits.

However, it should not be assumed that the degree of oversold or overbought is necessarily an indication that a change in trend is imminent. *High or low SI percentages do not mean that a market will definitely change direction at any time in the near future. In fact, the greatest single liability of the SI is its tendency to remain in an overbought or oversold condition for a long time.*

The Pitfalls of Overbought and Oversold

The overbought/oversold concept has been used by traders for many years. I, too, have been guilty of using these terms without really understanding the erroneous message that they convey. While these terms may be convenient for describing our feelings about a market, they do not necessarily convey any factual information, and are often misleading.

Let's define the terms overbought and oversold. *Over* suggests that the market to which the term refers has gone too far in a given direction. The terms also strongly imply that the market must retrace its move, and suggest further that *what goes up must come down.* While prices will eventually reverse their trend, this simple epigram does not tell you *when* a market will go down or up after it has entered the so-called overbought or oversold condition. These terms force an undesirable mind-set on the trader. If you feel that a market is overbought, you will be disinclined to buy, fearing that price is too high; if you feel that a market is oversold, you will be disinclined to sell short, fearing that you are selling at the bottom. *Yet, markets often make their largest and quickest moves during the final stage of a strong bull or bear move.* This is, in fact, the most negative consequence of interpreting the SI in terms of overbought and oversold.

SI Used for Trend-Following

I consider SI to be a trend-following method since, in its traditional applications, it tends to give signals *after* tops and bottoms have been made. Figures 8.3 through 8.6 illustrate SI in weekly, daily and monthly time frames. And Figure 8.7 is a 30-minute price chart versus SI. The SI versus price relationships

Figure 8.1   Computing the Stochastic Indicator

According to the Commodity Quote Graphics (CQG) technique, the SI is calculated as follows:

1. Assume you want to run a ten-time-unit SI. Take the highest high and the lowest low of the ten-unit period. Subtract the two.

2. Take the low of the ten units and subtract it from the current close. Divide the difference by the figure arrived at in Step 1.

3. The next increment plot is calculated by dropping the oldest data point and recalculation (according to the above steps) using the most recent data, as you would do for a moving average. You have now calculated %K.

4. The second line (called %D) is a three-period smoothed moving average of the first figure (%K). This completes the calculation for *fast* stochastic.

5. Slow %K is the Fast %D, and Slow %D is a three-period smoothed moving average (MA) of Slow %K.

Figure 8.2   SI versus Price

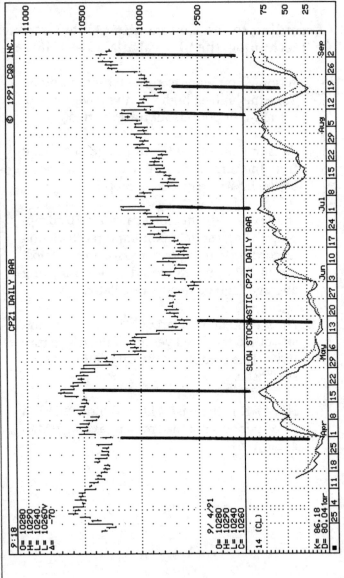

Note the close correlation between highs and lows in price and SI.

©1991 CQG Inc. Reprinted with permission.

discussed previously are applicable to virtually any time frame. As a consequence, the range of SI application extends from ultra-short-term analysis (i.e., intraday) all the way to monthly analysis. While time frames will vary according to individual needs, the goal in selecting a time frame and an appropriate stochastic length is to use those that provide the smoothest and clearest turns as well as the highest correlation with price.

Basic Approaches to SI Timing

Crossovers   The SI can be used in either a fast or slow mode. I recommend using slow SI, which is a moving average version of the fast mode. This method of SI timing uses the slow SI to buy and sell on crossovers of the SI lines. This approach, illustrated in Figure 8.8, entails a considerable amount of trading, which is a direct function of the length of the SI indicator. Shorter lengths of SI yield more trades and vice versa. This technique, which is subject to the limitations of all MA and oscillator applications as discussed earlier, generates numerous false signals and depends on a few large winning trades to compensate for many small losses, commissions and slippage.

Twenty-five Percent and 75 Percent Crossovers   Because the SI can stay in the overbought (OB) or oversold (OS) area for quite some time, I advise against sell decisions made simply on the basis of an OB condition or buy decisions made simply on the basis of an OS condition. *If you use the SI for the purpose of selling and buying on such extremes, you must wait for the cross to occur from OB back under 75 percent or for a cross above 25 percent from OS before you take a position.* In other words, wait for SI to rise to 75 percent or higher and then to fall below 75 percent; when it does sell or reverse your long position to short. Wait for SI to fall to 25 percent or lower and then to rise above 25 percent; when it does buy or reverse your short position to the long side. This is the traditional application of SI, and has good potential for trading in virtually all time frames.

Remember that the SI alone will not tell you where to put your stop or where to take your profit. You must use your other methods to do so, or you must rely on your own judgment for stop loss placement. As with any method or system you must be

Figure 8.3   The SI versus Daily Data—The Relationship Between Stochastics and Price Trends

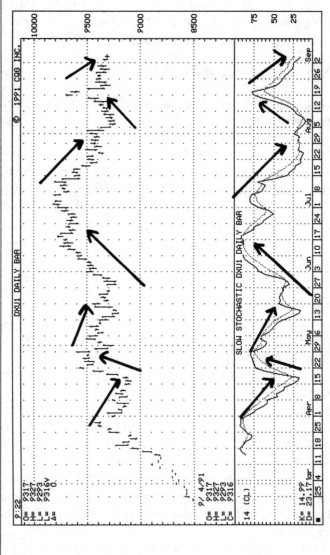

Note how closely the 14-period stochastic indicator correlates with highs, lows, up and down trends. Note also the tendency for stochastics to change direction at about the same time as do prices.

©1991 CQG Inc. Reprinted with permission.

Figure 8.4 The SI versus Weekly Prices

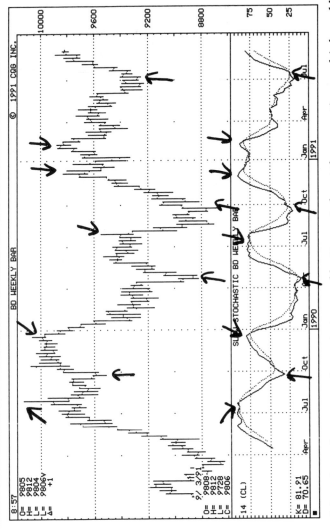

Note that weekly prices show a tendency to top and bottom at about the same time as high and low readings on the SI.

Figure 8.5   The SI versus Monthly Prices

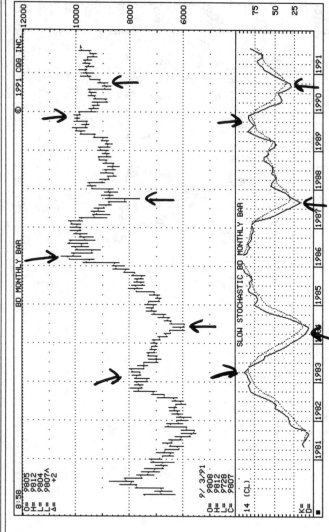

Note the tendency for monthly prices to top and bottom at about the same time as highs and lows in the SI and for trends to be similar.

©1991 CQG Inc. Reprinted with permission.

Figure 8.6   The SI versus Monthly Prices (Additional Example)

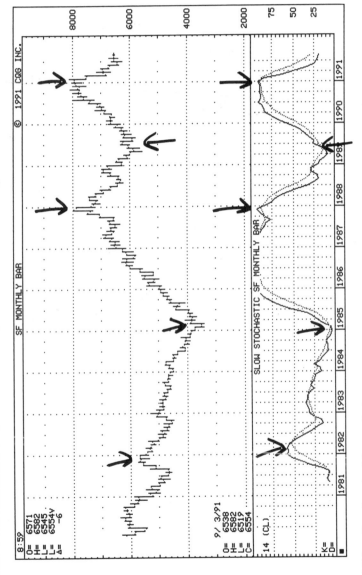

Figure 8.7   The SI versus Intraday Prices

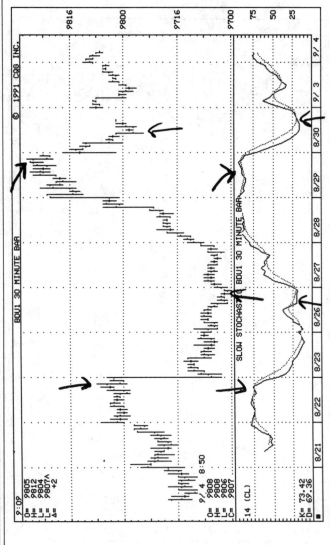

This chart clearly illustrates the relationship between SI and intraday prices (in this case 30-minute data). The relationships are similar to those exhibited by daily, weekly and monthly prices.

©1991 CQG Inc. Reprinted with permission.

prepared to take your losses when necessary. Please don't resort to excuses to avoid taking your loss and don't add to losing positions just because the SI is heading in a given direction. *The SI is not infallible.*

I have found this approach to be more fruitful than the crossover method previously described. Figure 8.9 shows a market example of this method, which can be used in virtually any time frame.

SI as an Aid to Spotting Cycle Turns   If you trade according to cyclical or seasonal indicators, the SI can also be very helpful. Assume that you are waiting for a cycle or seasonal to bottom. Consult the SI. It should be approaching the oversold area (25 percent or lower). Once it turns back above 25 percent, you have reasonable confirmation that the cycle or seasonal has turned higher. The reverse would hold true at anticipated cycle or seasonal tops. Assume you are waiting for a top. As the top approaches, the SI will become overbought by going above 75 percent. *This does not mean that a top has been made*—only that a top is likely. Once SI drops below 75 percent, there is good reason to believe that a top has been made.

Divergence in Price versus SI   Divergence is a very useful tool with virtually any indicator. Consider the following situation: price makes a new high but SI fails to achieve a new high. Although price has made a new high, SI has not, which suggests that the market is not as strong as it appears to be since the new price high was not accompanied by a new SI high. A downturn should, therefore, develop quite soon. The reverse would happen at market bottom divergences. For bullish divergence to occur, price must make a new low while SI does not. See Figure 8.10 for examples of bullish and bearish divergence.

The Stochastic Pop Indicator

Another, and I feel very powerful, application of the SI is to buy when the SI is high and to sell short when the SI is low. To explain the logic of this application, I'll first need to return to my pet peeves—overbought and oversold. As noted earlier, the use of overbought and oversold in connection with stochastics is not recommended. It can, in fact, be dangerous to your financial

Figure 8.8   Buy and Sell Signals on SI Crossovers

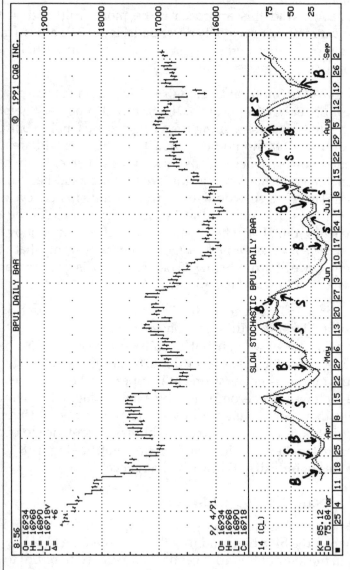

B=Buy Signals, S=Sell Signals

©1991 CQG Inc. Reprinted with permission.

Figure 8.9 Twenty-five Percent and 75 Percent Stochastic Crossover Signals

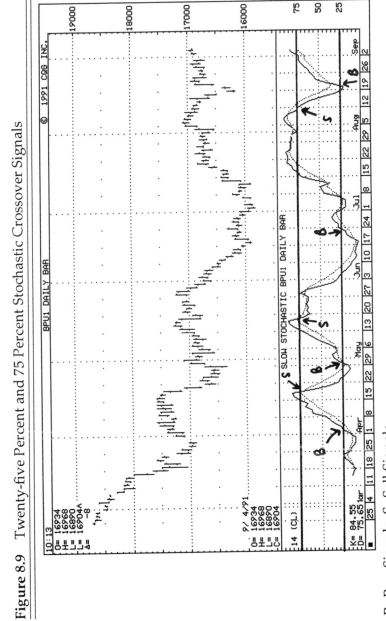

B=Buy Signals, S=Sell Signals

©1991 CQG Inc. Reprinted with permission.

Figure 8.10   Bullish and Bearish Divergence Between SI and Price

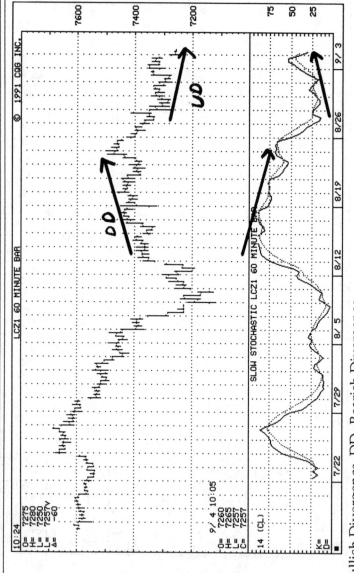

UD=Bullish Divergence, DD=Bearish Divergence

©1991 CQG Inc. Reprinted with permission.

health. Although the SI has an upper limit of 100 percent and a lower limit of 0 percent, futures prices have no upper limit and never reach their lower limit of zero. Logic will tell you that while the SI can reach an overbought condition (i.e., 75 percent or more), price may continue upward since it has no limit. And while SI can reach an oversold condition of 25 percent or lower, price can continue lower while SI can only approach zero as a limit. My observation of this fact led me to an amazing find. I discovered that many strong up and down moves occur while SI is in an extreme position. In other words, I found that when SI goes to 75 percent or higher, prices have a high probability of rising; when SI goes to 25 percent or lower, prices have a high probability of falling. Frequently, the magnitude and velocity of price movement once these extremes have been reached can be substantial. Figure 8.11 illustrates this condition. The decision to avoid buying when this market became overbought would have not been a good one, nor would the decision to avoid selling short when the market became oversold have been a good one. After many observations of this condition I decided to develop and test a trading system based on SI.

When I first introduced the SI Pop indicator in 1988, the application was quite simple. The ability to more thoroughly test and retest the SI Pop has allowed considerable improvement in results. Using TradeStation I modified the original SI Pop method. Before discussing the new parameters, I'll explain both the theory and rationale behind the SI Pop as well as its applications.

A Contrarian Application of Stochastics

We are captives of our own perceptions and interpretations. We view the world with preconceived notions within rigid frameworks called theories or systems. The same holds true for market indicators. We tend to view market indicators according to similar beliefs in terms of absolutes: the market is either bullish or bearish. When a market becomes oversold, we are afraid to go short. When prices are "too high," we are afraid to go long. When the market is "overbought," we are afraid to buy. When prices are too low, we are afraid to sell short, and so on. Our thinking colors and mediates our actions—perceptions and preconceptions often dissuade us from seeing things as they really are.

Figure 8.11   SI Can Remain Overbought or Oversold for a Long Time

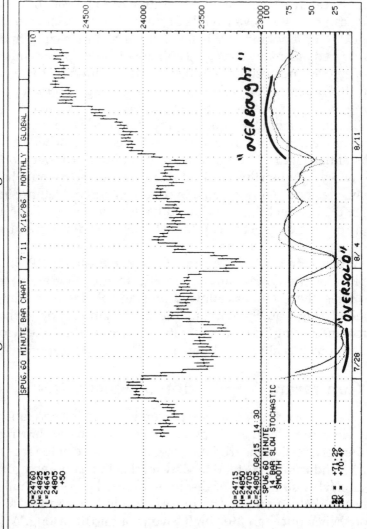

Consider, for example, the stochastic indicator discussed earlier in this chapter. One way of using the SI is to buy and sell on crossings of %K and %D. Another way is to sell short after a market has crossed from overbought (above 75 percent to below the critical 75 percent line), or to buy after a market has become oversold (under 25 percent) and crossed back above 25 percent. Both strategies have merit. However, as explained earlier, I have discovered a different approach that seems to fly in the face of traditional stochastic logic. Abandoning preconceived notions of stochastic application I asked myself: why not buy a market when it becomes "overbought" and sell a market when it becomes "oversold"? *Why not?*

I reasoned that just as a body in motion tends to stay in motion, so markets tend to continue in up or down trends. I observed that markets often made large moves up once SI reached 75 percent and large moves down once SI fell to 25 percent. I tested the theory and found that it worked! But there is some degree of danger in buying into a strong uptrend or in selling into a strong downtrend—you must exit your position at the slightest indication of a turn to avoid a quick reversal in trend.

In studying the markets I discovered that some of the largest moves, up and down, have happened *after* markets have become overbought or oversold. Although many traders are afraid to take positions once overbought or oversold levels have been hit, it is precisely these situations that appear to offer the greatest potential. See Figures 8.12 through 8.14 and my comments for illustrations of this technique. I called this technique the *Pop* since it was not unusual for the markets to "pop" up or down once they have reached an extreme level.

The Pop technique triggers long entry when a market becomes overbought on stochastic (75 percent and above). When a market becomes oversold on stochastic (25 percent or lower), Pop goes short. This approach is contrary to what many analysts advocate, yet it makes sense because it seeks to isolate strong moves. *When combined with the trading rules I've developed and refined during the last few years, the Pop method achieves its true potential.* The stochastic pop (SP) rules are as follows:

1. As soon as %K or %D rises above 75 percent on a closing basis, go long and stay long until the two lines reverse their

relationship. It doesn't take much for %D and %K to cross when the market is overbought—a crossover of the two values occurs almost as soon as a market shows even a slight amount of weakness. When this happens, don't sell short; just liquidate your long.

2. All entries and exits are *at the market.*

3. SI values are calculated on a closing basis. SP can be used on weekly, monthly, daily or intraday data; however, it appears that the best potential is on intraday data, preferably 30 or 60 minutes. Figures 8.12 through 8.14 will illustrate the mechanics and implementation of the SP method.

4. When either SI value falls below 25 percent, sell short and exit when the values reverse on a closing basis. See the accompanying illustrations for examples.

SP is best used for short-term moves in active markets, although it also has potential on daily and weekly data. Remember that you cannot enter or exit a Pop trade until your time segment has been completed. The Pop is not calculated on a tick-by-tick basis, but on the basis of the time segment you are tracking (i.e., hourly, half-hourly, five-minute).

I tested the SP signals very thoroughly. The test results are shown in Figures 8.15 through 8.17.

Summary of the SP Method

The SP was designed primarily for short-term trading. It is based on the tendency for markets to make their most reliable and often largest moves during the latter part of bull or bear trends. SP, therefore, buys when most traders consider a market to be overbought and sells short when most traders consider a market to be oversold. Positions can be exited quickly once the stochastic lines have reversed their relationship. While the SP can be used as a trading system, it can also be used as an indicator for adding to existing positions and/or for exiting positions established using other indicators.

Here are some suggestions for using the SP drawn from my experience:

1. Attempt to use the SP in short-term time frames. You can use the SP for monthly, weekly or daily trades; however, it performs best in 30-minute and 60-minute time frames.

Figure 8.12   Ideal Stochastic Pop Buy and Sell Signals

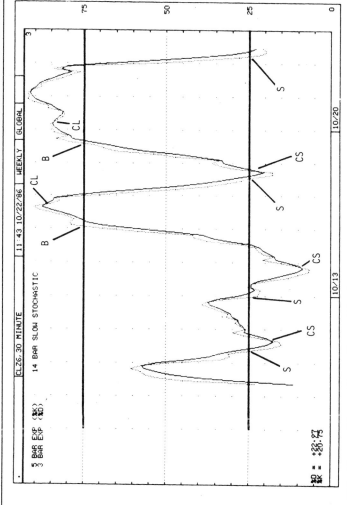

S=Sell Short, CS=Cover Short, Buy=Buy, CL=Exit Long

©1991 CQG Inc. Reprinted with permission.

Figure 8.13 An Example of SI Pop Signals

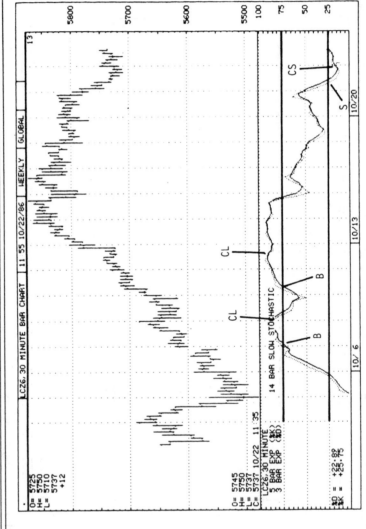

Figure 8.14   Another Example of SI Pop Signals

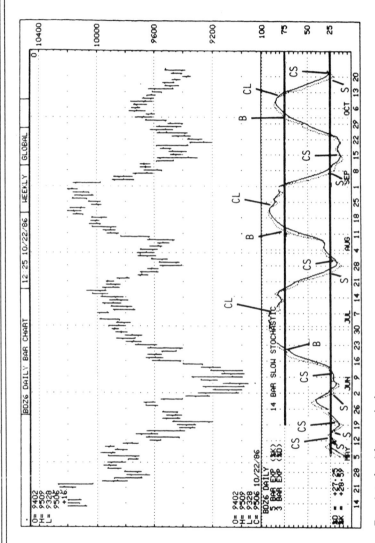

©1991 CQG Inc. Reprinted with permission.

2. Use the SP in active and volatile markets only. The cost of commissions and slippage makes the use of SP in quiet markets uneconomical. You need to use the SP in markets that have a history of making large moves during fairly brief periods of time and that also have sufficient liquidity to prevent poor price executions.

3. Don't overstay your SP position once the exit signal has developed. Although this is always a good idea, it is especially important when using the SP since markets that are severely overbought or oversold can reverse quickly. If you stay too long, you will let a small loss turn into a large one, or worse yet you'll let a profit turn into a loss, and that's not good practice.

4. Experiment with varying stochastic lengths and cutoff points. While I've used 14 periods, 75 percent and 25 percent in my research, they're not written in stone. I suggest you experiment with different values. And remember that the entry and exit levels need not be symmetrical. In other words you needn't use 75 percent and 25 percent as entry points, both a distance of 25 from their extremes; you can use 80 percent and 30 percent, or 90 percent and 20 percent. Whatever you do, I suggest you test your procedures thoroughly before using any of these methods or indicators.

Finally, I'd like to emphasize that the SP method works because it is based on a rational, reasonable and valid understanding of market behavior. It is a prime example of how a theory based on market observation can be transformed into a trading method. It is an example of strategic trading because it uses a strategy derived from market experience and study. In the chapters that follow I'll provide additional examples of indicators developed by using a strategic analysis of market behavior.

Figure 8.15   Fourteen-Day 80/20 Stochastic Indicator: Pop Results in Bull and Bear Markets

	BUY				SELL				TOTAL		
#	PROF	AVG $	TOT $	#	PROF	AVG $	TOT $	#	PROF	AVG $	TOT $
BULL	1026	2401.91	396.58	406888.75	487	-214.54	-202.79	-98760.06	1513	2187.37	203.65	308128.69
BEAR	612	-522.30	-157.54	-96411.88	1343	1559.80	132.66	178167.50	1955	1037.50	41.82	81755.63

Note: #=Total of Signals, Prof=Profit in Points, Avg=Average Profit/Loss Per Trade, Tot $=Total $Profit/loss

Figure 8.16 Fourteen-Day 75/25 Stochastic Indicator: Pop Results in Bull and Bear Markets

	BUY				SELL				TOTAL			
	#	PROF	AVG $	TOT $	#	PROF	AVG $	TOT $	#	PROF	AVG $	TOT $
BULL	1021	2732.91	462.46	472176.19	582	-144.21	-190.39	-110809.75	1603	2588.70	225.43	361366.44
BEAR	752	-859.70	-194.48	-146251.56	1360	2037.84	179.60	244249.37	2112	1178.14	46.40	97997.81

Note: #=Total of Signals, Prof=Profit in Points, Avg=Average Profit/Loss Per Trade, Tot $=Total $ Profit/loss

Figure 8.17   Fourteen-Day 65/35 Stochastic Indicator: Pop Results in Bull and Bear Markets

		BUY				SELL				TOTAL		
	#	PROF	AVG $	TOT $	#	PROF	AVG $	TOT $	#	PROF	AVG $	TOT $
BULL	936	2508.60	529.96	496042.06	724	-61.38	-174.66	-126455.69	1660	2447.22	222.64	369586.37
BEAR	921	-859.51	-129.15	-118951.00	1247	2685.27	254.85	317799.69	2168	1825.76	91.72	198848.69

Note: #=Total of Signals, Prof=Profit in Points, Avg=Average Profit/Loss Per Trade, Tot $=Total $ Profit/loss

Chapter
═══ 9 ═══

The Box Theory and Quantum Trading

---

*I just jog along with the trend, trailing my stop-loss
insurance behind me . . .
There are no good or bad stocks, there are only
rising and falling stocks* —Nicholas Darvas

Nicholas Darvas is virtually unknown to many stock and futures traders. His background as a professional dancer provides no clue to his skill as an investor. His best-selling book *How I Made $2,000,000 in the Stock Market* advanced several important technical concepts about the markets. Yet in spite of his popularity in the 1960s and 1970s Darvas and his work are known to few traders in the 1990s. This is, perhaps, because his original theory, the Box Theory, was exceptionally simple and lacked the sex appeal that so many traders today seem to require as a prerequisite to acceptance. A simple trading system does not seem to have the credibility of a complex computer-generated method. But as you can see, things have not changed; even in the 1960s simple was not considered effective, and technical trading was even more of a red herring. Although Darvas's great success attracted positive commentary and attention from many financial analysts and market advisors as well as a *Time* Magazine interview, Darvas is not known to many contemporary speculators and investors.

Basics of the Box Theory

Darvas's theory was based upon the tendency of stock prices to move through different levels or boxes. Stock XYZ, for example, might trade in the range from 11 to 14 for several years, bouncing back and forth between these extremes. In so doing it establishes a box or range. You might think of the box as support and resistance; however, in establishing a box the market does not necessarily establish clear-cut support and resistance trend lines in the traditional sense of technical chart analysis.

The market could continue to trade within its box for two weeks, two months or two years. However, when it leaves its box, either up or down, the investor must act in the direction of the move. Hence, if stock XYZ moves from the 11 to 14 box by rising to 15 to 16, this is an indication that the stock has jumped to a new level and that it is in an uptrend. The concept is simple in terms of support and resistance: a market will move within the bounds of support and resistance until it has either gathered the buying power to break into a new level or box or until it has been subjected to sufficient selling to result in its falling through the bottom of its box to a new and lower box or level.

Darvas preferred to see a stock break through its upper or lower *door* as he called it, and frequently bought on stop orders above a well-established box or sold on stop orders below a well-established box. He limited his risk by using very close stop loss orders and was not willing to wait too long before exiting a stock that did not perform soon after he entered it. In addition, he preferred to trade stocks that were active since they were often stocks that made large moves. He later acquired a penchant for higher-priced stocks since they helped him save on commissions and often made large moves.

Figure 9.1 illustrates a recent example applied to September 1991 Swiss franc futures. I've drawn in my selection of the boxes along with some notes that will assist you in understanding how the box theory works as applied to this chart. Prices tend to move through levels or quanta. In a strong bull market a stock or futures contract will move through its boxes or levels quickly, and in a weak bear market a stock will fall through its boxes quickly. Frequently, previous boxes will serve as support levels as prices fall and as resistance levels as prices rise. In some respects the rules for using the box theory are similar to those of traditional charting techniques. I've used some of the original concepts presented by Darvas in developing my own method, which I've termed Quantum Trading. *Quantum* refers to level. I've also adapted the concepts to futures trading primarily for position trades as opposed to short-term trades since this is where the method appears to have its greatest potential.

The Rules and Theory of Quantum Trading (QT)

The QT theory is simple: it is based on the assumption that as the price of a given market rises it will move through layers or quanta on the way to its final destination, and as the price of a given futures market falls it will decline through various levels or quanta. Illustrating this concept is Figure 9.2, which is a weekly price chart of gold futures. I've drawn the quanta on the chart as well as some explanatory notes that show what happens when prices move from one well-established quantum to another. As you can see, a market can spend a considerable amount of time in one quantum; however, it must remain within a given quantum for a minimum number of weeks before that quantum is established as a valid level. The minimum number that I've determined empirically is six weeks when working with weekly data and five days when working with daily data. Quantum trading can also be used with intraday data. In this case use a five-bar period for establishing the box. There is no limit to how large a quantum can be in terms of magnitude; it could be $20 or $100 depending on the amount of time spent in the given level.

Following are rules that apply to buying and selling on quantum penetrations:

1. QT works best in trending markets; however, if the correct

Figure 9.1   The Box Theory Applied to Swiss Franc Futures

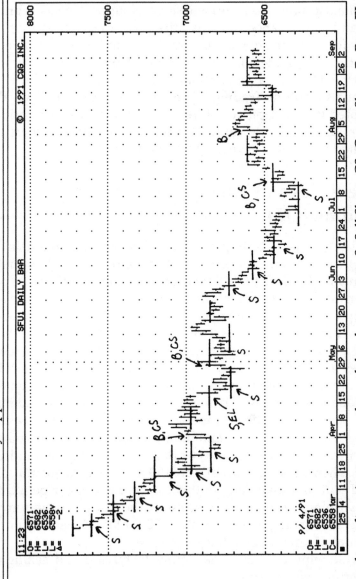

Note tendency for price to move through levels or quanta. S=Sell Short, CS=Cover Short, B=Buy, EL=Exit Long

©1991 CQG Inc. Reprinted with permission.

box size is used, it will also avoid many of the whipsaws so common in non-trending markets.

2. QT can be used in various time frames depending upon your orientation to the market.

3. QT will keep you in the market at all times; however, you may adapt the technique to exit at previous box support and resistance levels.

4. QT is still somewhat subjective insofar as determination of box size. You will need to use some judgment and market study to determine correct box size. As a rule of thumb use larger boxes for more volatile markets.

Examples of Quantum Trading

Since my current use of the QT concepts is not organized into a well-defined trading system with definitive rules, I suggest you study it and develop some applications on your own. Given the limitations of trend-following systems using moving averages, QT can offer some important solutions to the moving average dilemma. By waiting for prices to penetrate upper or lower boundaries of their quanta, you will avoid the whipsaw tendencies so common with moving average based systems.

Figures 9.3 and 9.4 provide specific examples of QT applications to various markets in several different time frames.

Conclusions Regarding Quantum Trading

I've reintroduced the quantum or box theory concept since it appears to offer considerable strategic value in today's markets. We know that the big money is made in following the major trend. After working with the QT concept I think you'll find, as I have, that it allows you to follow the major trends up and down while eliminating many of the limitations of lagging indicators. Hence, the QT is more of a breakout system, similar in some ways to the current volatility breakout systems. For those interested in quantifying the QT approach, I suggest using a methodology similar to that used in volatility breakout systems. In other words, use a range of prices as the base and buy or sell on breakouts above or beyond the given range. Such systems are relatively simple to program, strictly objective in their signals and equally simple to implement.

Figure 9.2   Gold Futures and QT

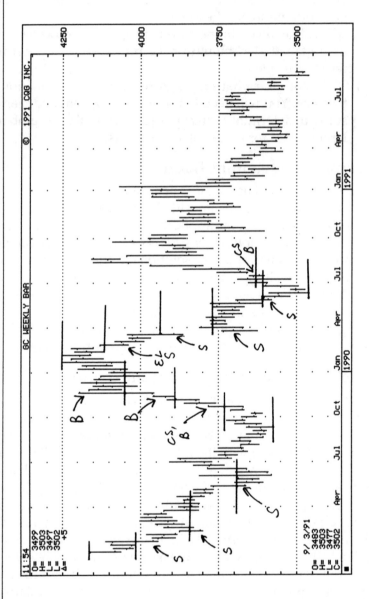

EAGLE SCOUTS OF TROOP 46
FIRST PRESBYTERIAN CHURCH, LAKE FOREST, ILLINOIS

1931 Ian McPherson	1970 Robert B. Herber	1988 Richard Wolfgra
1941 Paul Goeldner	1971 Baxter Martin	1989 Todd Bartine
1941 Ralph Kirkman	1972 John R. Karstrom	1989 Andrew Knight
1941 Andrew Martinson	1972 Robert M. Hume	1989 Paul Valenti
1942 William Burgess	1972 Mark Kammerer	1990 David Shih
1943 Joseph C. Emmma II	1973 Robert C. Watson	1990 Mark Hoffman
1943 Robert J. Swanson	1973 Kendrick C. Taylor, Jr.	1991 Mark Morrison
1945 John D. Ingram	1973 David S. Springer	1991 Kris Harris
1951 Malcom C. Douglas	1973 Wyn Hughes	1991 Chris Weil
1953 Gunnard Stark	1973 Alan F. Jackson	1991 Garrick Bunting
1955 Don Verbeke	1974 Steven P. Goodell	1992 Collin Webb
1955 Bill Frangquist	1974 Ken McPheeters	1992 Brett Nerstrom
1955 Richard Phillips	1974 Morgan Matthews	1992 Mark Plandowsk
1955 James B. Butterworth	1976 Dennis Kammerer	1992 Marc Taylor
1956 Robert R. Behrens	1976 Michael Kammerer	1992 Andrew Leamon
1957 Bill Williams	1977 Drew H. Adams	1992 Pontus Weibull
1957 Don Tiffany	1978 Karl K. Hartung	
1957 Carl Roderwald	1978 Thomas A. Hume	
1957 Bruce Douglas	1979 C. David Parker	
1958 Jack Renz	1979 N. Bruce Schleicher	
1961 Michael J. Hall	1980 John F. DelMissier	
1961 Robert D. Haslach	1980 Jay Siekmann	
1961 Robert Watt	1981 James Roadcap	
1961 Jeremy Wilson	1982 Pat W. Metzger	
1962 Jim Snodgrass	1983 William L. Loving, Jr.	
1962 Richard J. Bennett	1983 Robert J. Boutin	
1963 Chris Boerup	1983 Kurt H. Klingenberg	
1963 Fred A. Stripe	1983 Joseph F. Borkowski	
1963 Bruce R. Williams	1983 Bryan E. Keyt	
1963 Randy K. Griffis	1984 Craig L. Hartung	
1963 Robert A. Schwahn	1984 Michael J. Metzger	
1964 Richard C. Snodgrass	1984 Paul T. Revenaugh	
1964 Gerald F. Tichelbout	1985 Sanford Schleicher	
1965 George J. Anastos	1985 John H. Mallory	
1965 Mark A. Millard	1985 Eric Vratimos	
1965 John P. Herber	1986 Matthew Gross	
1965 Johann N. Bruhn	1986 Chip Tucker	
1966 Thomas S. Proehl	1986 Doug Tucker	
1966 Robert P. Elfering	1986 Paolo Camoletto	
1966 William Griffis	1987 Andy Keyt	
1966 Timothy W. Karstom	1987 Rob Knight	
1966 Fred Haslach III	1987 Charles Stephens	
1967 Bruce T. Cankar	1987 Gary Tucker	
1967 John B. Sollis	1988 Piero Camoletto	
1969 Fritz Neuschel	1988 John Schade	

COURT OF HONOR
BOY SCOUT TROOP 46
First Presbyterian Church
Lake Forest, Illinois
October 20, 1992

OPENING CEREMONY/COLOR GUARD	David Gustafson, SPL
INTRODUCTION	Tim Weil, TG
WELCOMING REMARKS	Mr. Dick Gustafson, CC
TROOP ACTIVITIES/HIGH ADVENTURE	
CAMP MAKAJAWAN	Mr. Hank Weil, SM
ADVANCEMENT	
RANK	Mr. Hank Weil, SM
MERIT BADGES	Dr. J.B. Schleicher
SPECIAL AWARDS	Mr. Hank Weil, SM
CLOSING	David Gustafson, SPL

EAGLE SCOUT CEREMONY
Honoring:

NILS PONTUS WEIBULL
ANDREW PRESTON LEAMON

PRESIDING	Mr. Bert Tucker
MEMBERS OF THE COURT	Mr. Dick Gustafson
	Mr. Jim Nerstrom
	Dr. J.B. Schleicher
	Mr. John Bacevicius
THE CHARGE TO THE CANDIDATE	Mr. Hank Weil

RECEPTION FOLLOWING IN THE YOUTH LOUNGE

Figure 9.3   Example of QT Application in Wheat

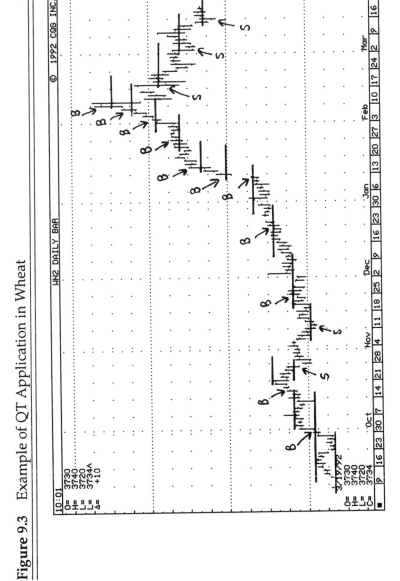

Figure 9.4 Example of QT Application in Swiss Franc

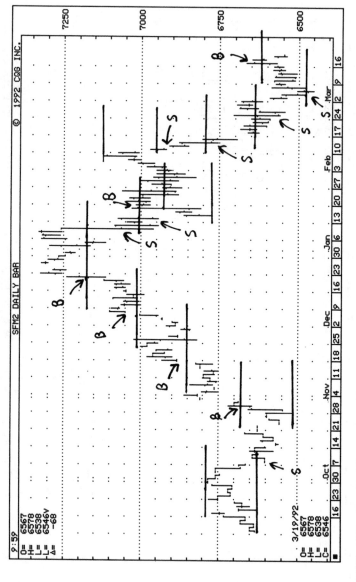

©1992 CQG Inc. Reprinted with permission.

Chapter
═══ 10 ═══

Consecutive Closes

One of the most intriguing and yet challenging approaches to futures trading is the use of patterns and pattern recognition. To most traders it seems logical that markets would follow patterns and that an intensive study of market behavior would reveal such patterns.

Pattern Categories

What exactly is a pattern? While there is no one response to this question, there are a number of different pattern categories.

Day of Week Patterns

Through the years day of week patterns have been important. Traders have assumed, right or wrong, that a strong price close on Friday should mean a higher opening and possibly even a higher close on Monday, and vice versa for a weak close on Friday. For many years traders believed important lows often come on Tuesdays, and markets tend to reverse trend on Thursdays. In *The New Commodity Trading Systems and Methods* Kaufman listed many day of week patterns, some reliable for trading purposes. His data sample was limited, and few patterns are statistically reliable. While there are a few day of week patterns whose reliability is slightly above chance, their use is questionable.

Closing Price Patterns

Studied extensively by futures traders, a closing price pattern is a specific pattern of up or closes that forecasts the direction of the next closing price. Where + equals a close higher than the day before and where - equals a close lower than the day before and where + means a higher close the next day and - means a lower close the next day, some patterns might look as follows:

$$+ + + + + - (+); \text{ or } - + - - - - (+); \text{ or } + + + + (+)$$

There are thousands of closing price patterns. In my book *Timing Signals* I listed most of these combinations by market, illustrating that the more days of data we study, the less reliable the price patterns become. In the study of statistics this phenomenon is called *regression to the mean*.

My studies also revealed that market trend did not make closing price patterns more reliable. One would assume that in a bull market certain patterns would be more reliable than in bear markets or trendless markets. A pattern of - - - - - - - - should be very rare in a bull market, and it is. However, the next day in this sequence does not have a probability greater than chance of being a + close. The same holds true in bear trends with down closes.

These findings were important since they rejected the notion that by studying simple closing price patterns one could predict the direction of the next close with any reasonable degree of accuracy. Although I had the feeling that there must be some value to this type of work, I was at a loss as to how it might be employed in a profitable system. I'll expand on this topic later.

More about Price Patterns

In *The Definitive Guide to Futures Trading*, Larry Williams discussed several price patterns based on more detailed parameters than the closing price patterns I studied. Figure 10.1 illustrates one of these patterns and the probable outcomes.

After years of study, I concluded that many price patterns were useless since they tended to regress to the mean. To prove the validity of price patterns, I turned to testing intraday data. I tested active markets using various lengths of intraday data—the results were favorable, particularly in stock index futures. I will discuss these following an overview of the basic rules.

The Basic Concept

As with all of the indicators discussed in this book, the consecutive closes (CC) indicator is easy to understand. Please note the following abbreviations that I will use in my discussion:

CC—consecutive closes
CCU—consecutive closes up
CCD—consecutive closes down
CCU or CCD preceded by a number indicates the number of consecutive closes up or down.

The algorithms I tested were three, four, five and six CCU and CCD. The trading rules are simple:

- A buy or reverse to long signal is generated on the close of trading of the nth consecutive up close.
- A sell or reverse to short position is generated on the close of the nth consecutive down close.
- The unit of time varies according to test. The results commentary that follows specifies the time unit used.

Sample Buy and Sell Signals

A buy signal, using a 4CC system, therefore, might appear as follows:

Closing Price	Change	Count
4550	+25	+1
4545	-05	-1
4560	+15	+1
4565	+05	+2
4590	+25	+3
4600	+10	+4 Buy on Close

A sell signal would occur on the fourth consecutive lower close. The position would be taken on the close of trading and held until stopped out or reversed by a 4CCD sell signal.

As you can see, the system is extremely simple and requires no computer or sophisticated mathematical formulae. It is simple

Figure 10.1   Williams's Price Patterns in Various Markets

Selling a key reversal top where the key reversal day is the highest high of the last eight days.

% of Time Correct

		S&P	VAL	BNDS	SLVR	S BNS	P BEL	S FRANC
D	1	35.23	43.18	42.11	29.73	51.79	55.84	46.67
A	2	51.14	39.77	44.74	43.24	53.57	54.55	50.00
Y	3	44.32	36.36	47.37	54.05	55.36	55.84	50.00
S	4	42.05	36.36	48.68	54.05	58.18	58.44	46.67
	5	42.05	37.50	47.37	54.05	56.36	63.64	50.00
A	6	44.32	44.32	44.74	56.76	54.55	58.44	53.33
F	7	37.50	42.05	46.05	51.35	54.55	51.95	56.67
T	8	37.50	39.77	43.42	51.35	50.91	51.95	53.33
E	9	34.09	37.50	43.42	48.65	56.36	57.14	46.67
R	10	31.82	42.05	43.42	48.65	58.18	53.25	46.67
	11	36.36	42.05	40.79	51.35	56.36	51.95	43.33
O	12	36.36	42.05	44.74	54.05	56.36	50.65	43.33
C	13	36.36	38.64	39.47	59.46	50.91	55.84	46.67
C	14	29.55	36.36	39.47	64.86	65.45	54.55	50.00
U	15	35.63	38.64	40.79	64.86	61.82	58.44	46.67
R	16	36.78	36.36	39.47	64.86	56.36	55.84	46.67
R	17	34.48	34.09	38.16	62.16	61.82	53.25	43.33
E	18	33.33	34.09	38.16	75.68	60.00	51.95	46.67
N	19	35.63	37.50	38.16	72.97	58.18	55.84	40.00
C	20	36.78	41.38	34.21	70.27	58.18	55.84	36.67
E	21	35.63	40.23	38.16	70.27	67.27	53.25	33.33

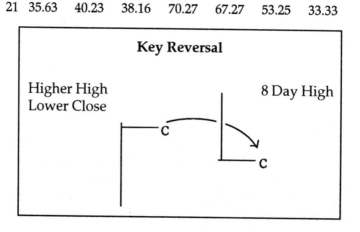

Key Reversal

Higher High
Lower Close

8 Day High

to implement and easy to track provided you have access to intraday data. Figure 10.2 illustrates sample buy, reverse to long, sell and reverse to short signals.

Tip

Consider a hybrid CC system where you enter on one CC combination and exit on another. We know that markets move up more slowly than they move down. Hence a 5CC entry signal and a 3CC exit/reverse combination might prove much more effective than a linear entry and exit signal.

Results of the CC Method

Test One: 60-Minute S&P Futures 4CC Performance Summary

Figure 10.3 illustrates the results of this test, which I consider impressive. The test covered about one year of tick-by-tick data and 84 trades. The accuracy rate was 46 percent with seven maximum consecutive losers. It was necessary to use a rather wide initial stop loss as well as a large trailing stop loss given the volatile nature of S&P futures. Admittedly, a large percentage of the net profit came from one large profit of over $12,000, but the system performance *even without this trade* is still very respectable at over $394 profit per trade.

Test Two: 30-Minute S&P Futures 4CC Performance Summary

Now examine the results of the 30-minute S&P method using 6CC as the indicator (see Figure 10.4). The results here are even more impressive than they were for the 60-minute test on an average trade basis. Note that nearly half of the net profits were the result of one large winner of nearly $13,000. However, *even if this winner is removed from the total figure*, the net profit per trade is still very high at over $286.

Figure 10.5 shows the performance of the 6CC indicator in 30-minute crude oil futures. The results are impressive, even after

Figure 10.2   Consecutive Closes—Sample Signals

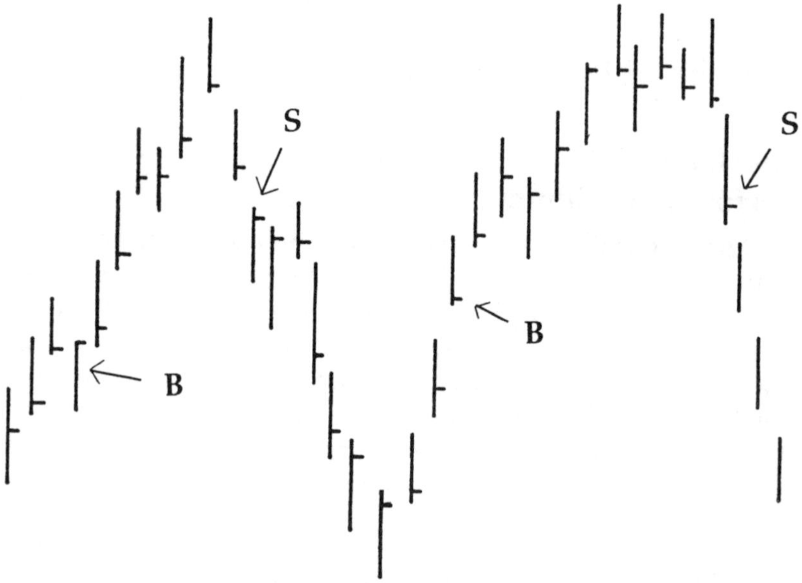

deducting $75 for slippage and commission. At $476.47 per trade after slippage and commission, this approach is well worthwhile. Even better results are possible in crude oil futures if you vary time length and CC length. I have not tested too many other CC periods or time frames and suggest you do so if you are interested in this approach. The ideal situation, of course, would be to find a combination of time frame and CC length that produces consistent profits without a high percentage of the net profit per trade attributable to only one or two trades.

Conclusions

The CC system appears to have considerable merit in application to short-term trading. I have not tested the system for day trading; however, in active markets it appears to be one of the better strategic systems available. As I indicated previously in this chapter, a hybrid system might actually work better than a simple CC system alone. Since the CC system is a reversing system, it is an "always in the market" system. Sell signals serve to exit longs and establish shorts and vice versa for buy signals. A hybrid system, on the other hand, would make use of a specific stop loss procedure related to market activity, which could allow the system to go flat or neutral. I've found that the addition of such a methodology can be very helpful with short-term trading systems and I suggest, therefore, that you research it accordingly.

One limitation regarding the use of a CC system has become apparent—in order to generate a signal the given market will need to be strong or weak for a given period of time. This is true by definition of the system. A buy signal may be generated only after a fairly strong rally. The typical trader will be concerned about buying into the market "too high" or selling into the market "too low." Although a perennial concern of traders, it is not valid. Effective trading means buying into strength and selling into weakness since this is what trend following is all about. While the short-term CC system is a strategic approach with considerable merit, it is a system that, for the aforementioned reasons, may be difficult to implement. Be aware of this inasmuch as it may, therefore, pose a psychological problem if you are the type of trader who likes to buy low and sell high as opposed to one who likes to buy high and sell higher.

Figure 10.3   Sixty-Minute 4CC, $75 Slippage and Commission, $2,500 Initial Stop Loss, $1,850 Trailing Stop Loss

Performance Summary: All Trades

Total net profit	$ 45400.00	Open position P/L	$ 0.00
Gross profit	$ 91350.00	Gross loss	$ -45950.00
Total # of trades	84	Percent profitable	46%
Number winning trades	39	Number losing trades	45
Largest winning trade	$ 12675.00	Largest losing trade	$ -1925.00
Average winning trade	$ 2342.31	Average losing trade	$ -1021.11
Ratio avg win/avg loss	2.29	Avg trade(win & loss)	$ 540.48
Max consecutive winners	5	Max consecutive losers	7
Avg # bars in winners	16	Avg # bars in losers	6
Max intraday drawdown	$ -10150.00		
Profit factor	1.99	Max # contracts held	1
Account size required	$ 10150.00	Return on account	447%

Performance Summary: Long Trades

Total net profit	$ 36800.00	Open position P/L	$ 0.00
Gross profit	$ 60450.00	Gross loss	$ -23650.00
Total # of trades	44	Percent profitable	50%
Number winning trades	22	Number losing trades	22
Largest winning trade	$ 12675.00	Largest losing trade	$ -1925.00
Average winning trade	$ 2747.73	Average losing trade	$ -1075.00
Ratio avg win/avg loss	2.56	Avg trade(win & loss)	$ 836.36
Max consecutive winners	5	Max consecutive losers	5
Avg # bars in winners	20	Avg # bars in losers	6
Max intraday drawdown	$ -10125.00		
Profit factor	2.56	Max # contracts held	1
Account size required	$ 10125.00	Return on account	363%

Performance Summary: Short Trades

Total net profit	$ 8600.00	Open position P/L	$ 0.00
Gross profit	$ 30900.00	Gross loss	$ -22300.00
Total # of trades	40	Percent profitable	42%
Number winning trades	17	Number losing trades	23
Largest winning trade	$ 5525.00	Largest losing trade	$ -1925.00
Average winning trade	$ 1817.65	Average losing trade	$ -969.57
Ratio avg win/avg loss	1.87	Avg trade(win & loss)	$ 215.00
Max consecutive winners	8	Max consecutive losers	9
Avg # bars in winners	11	Avg # bars in losers	6
Max intraday drawdown	$ -11825.00		
Profit factor	1.39	Max # contracts held	1
Account size required	$ 11825.00	Return on account	73%

Reprinted with permission of Omega Research, Inc.

Figure 10.4   Thirty-Minute S&P 6CC Results

```
                    Performance Summary:  All Trades

Total net profit      $   23075.00   Open position P/L     $      0.00
Gross profit          $   48450.00   Gross loss            $ -25375.00

Total # of trades            37      Percent profitable          38%
Number winning trades        14      Number losing trades         23

Largest winning trade $   12750.00   Largest losing trade  $ -1925.00
Average winning trade $    3460.71   Average losing trade  $ -1103.26
Ratio avg win/avg loss        3.14   Avg trade(win & loss) $   623.65

Max consecutive winners       3      Max consecutive losers        5
Avg # bars in winners        36      Avg # bars in losers         14

Max intraday drawdown $   -8450.00
Profit factor                 1.91   Max # contracts held          1
Account size required $   11450.00   Return on account          202%
```

```
                    Performance Summary:  Long Trades

Total net profit      $   14375.00   Open position P/L     $      0.00
Gross profit          $   35025.00   Gross loss            $ -20650.00

Total # of trades            26      Percent profitable          31%
Number winning trades         8      Number losing trades         18

Largest winning trade $   12750.00   Largest losing trade  $ -1925.00
Average winning trade $    4378.13   Average losing trade  $ -1147.22
Ratio avg win/avg loss        3.82   Avg trade(win & loss) $   552.88

Max consecutive winners       2      Max consecutive losers        7
Avg # bars in winners        40      Avg # bars in losers         14

Max intraday drawdown $   -9775.00
Profit factor                 1.70   Max # contracts held          1
Account size required $   12775.00   Return on account          113%
```

```
                    Performance Summary:  Short Trades

Total net profit      $    8700.00   Open position P/L     $      0.00
Gross profit          $   13425.00   Gross loss            $  -4725.00

Total # of trades            11      Percent profitable          55%
Number winning trades         6      Number losing trades          5

Largest winning trade $    4925.00   Largest losing trade  $ -1675.00
Average winning trade $    2237.50   Average losing trade  $  -945.00
Ratio avg win/avg loss        2.37   Avg trade(win & loss) $   790.91

Max consecutive winners       3      Max consecutive losers        2
Avg # bars in winners        29      Avg # bars in losers         12

Max intraday drawdown $   -2625.00
Profit factor                 2.84   Max # contracts held          1
Account size required $    5625.00   Return on account          155%
```

Reprinted with permission of Omega Research, Inc.

Figure 10.5   Thirty-Minute Crude Oil Futures 6CC Results

```
                    Performance Summary:  All Trades

Total net profit      $   16200.00   Open position P/L     $     150.00
Gross profit          $   33305.00   Gross loss            $  -17105.00

Total # of trades            34      Percent profitable           50%
Number winning trades        17      Number losing trades          17

Largest winning trade $    7145.00   Largest losing trade  $   -2225.00
Average winning trade $    1959.12   Average losing trade  $   -1006.18
Ratio avg win/avg loss       1.95    Avg trade(win & loss) $     476.47

Max consecutive winners       2      Max consecutive losers         3
Avg # bars in winners        56      Avg # bars in losers          38

Max intraday drawdown $   -4505.00
Profit factor                1.95    Max # contracts held           1
Account size required $    7505.00   Return on account           216%
- - - - - - - - - - - - - - - - - - - - - - - - - - - - - - - - - - - - -
                    Performance Summary:  Long Trades

Total net profit      $    1220.00   Open position P/L     $       0.00
Gross profit          $   14650.00   Gross loss            $  -13430.00

Total # of trades            18      Percent profitable           33%
Number winning trades         6      Number losing trades          12

Largest winning trade $    6405.00   Largest losing trade  $   -2225.00
Average winning trade $    2441.67   Average losing trade  $   -1119.17
Ratio avg win/avg loss       2.18    Avg trade(win & loss) $      67.78

Max consecutive winners       2      Max consecutive losers         5
Avg # bars in winners        63      Avg # bars in losers          36

Max intraday drawdown $   -9055.00
Profit factor                1.09    Max # contracts held           1
Account size required $   12055.00   Return on account            10%
- - - - - - - - - - - - - - - - - - - - - - - - - - - - - - - - - - - - -
                    Performance Summary:  Short Trades

Total net profit      $   14980.00   Open position P/L     $     150.00
Gross profit          $   18655.00   Gross loss            $   -3675.00

Total # of trades            16      Percent profitable           69%
Number winning trades        11      Number losing trades           5

Largest winning trade $    7145.00   Largest losing trade  $   -1665.00
Average winning trade $    1695.91   Average losing trade  $    -735.00
Ratio avg win/avg loss       2.31    Avg trade(win & loss) $     936.25

Max consecutive winners       3      Max consecutive losers         1
Avg # bars in winners        52      Avg # bars in losers          41

Max intraday drawdown $   -2465.00
Profit factor                5.08    Max # contracts held           1
Account size required $    5465.00   Return on account           274%
```

Reprinted with permission of Omega Research, Inc.

Chapter
═══ 11 ═══

On-Balance Volume
Reformulated

Perhaps the single most colorful figure in stock market forecasting is Joe Granville. He's been called a sinner and a saint, a wise man and a fool. No matter what you think of Joe, his work deserves attention. I suspect that much criticism directed at Joe was a function of jealousy as well as dislike of his tendency toward *braggadocio*. Although Joe will be remembered as all of the above, his contribution to the markets in the form of on-balance volume (OBV) will live forever. Thank you, Joe Granville.

On-balance volume is an ingenious technique that considers price and volume of trading to assess the balance of buying power and selling power. While OBV was originally developed for the stock market, it has considerable potential in futures trading. The difficulty in applying OBV to futures analysis is twofold:

1. There are many different contract months of each market, which leaves the question of whether one uses total volume or individual contract volume.
2. Futures markets can make *locked limit* price moves during which trading ceases, distorting OBV readings.

The purpose of this chapter is to:

1. Review the theory and application of OBV, showing its assets and liabilities.
2. Illustrate new applications of OBV.

The Theory of On-Balance Volume

On-balance volume was introduced in 1976 by Joe Granville in his now classic reference work *Granville's New Strategy of Daily Stock Market Timing for Maximum Profit*. The original application of OBV was in the stock market. In introducing OBV Granville illustrated a classic example of its application to American Motors stock over a long period of time. Both the theory and application of OBV were impressive. In its original form, OBV was a very logical indicator.

Here's how OBV works: When the price of a stock closes higher on one day (compared to the previous day), all of the trading volume for that day is assigned a positive value. If the stock is higher again the next day, the volume for this day is also assigned a positive value, and it is added to the volume of the first day. On the third day if the price is down, the volume is *selling volume*; it is assigned a negative value and subtracted from the running total.

The logic behind this operation is both rational and simple. The OBV figure provides an index of buying power and selling power. When the OBV is positive, there is reason to believe that stock is being accumulated in expectation of a continued rise. When the OBV turns negative, it suggests that the market is becoming weak and about to turn bearish.

Before discussing further details of OBV, I'd like to point out a major shortcoming of OBV: it assigns the same volume to a given day regardless of how much price has been up or down. If, for example, a stock trades 100,000 shares and rises $6, the 100,000 shares are added to the running total. But if the stock rises only $1/8$ point, it is also assigned the positive 100,000 shares positive volume. I consider the $1/8$ point up move to be objectively less positive than the $6 move. In fact, the $1/8$ point move could actually be negative if the stock closed near its low for the day after being considerably higher because the bulk of the volume might actually be considered selling volume.

Regardless of my concerns, Joe Granville was very successful with OBV and his indicator became quite the rage. Before going into my variation on the theme of OBV and its application to futures trading, I'll review the OBV rules. These rules, adapted from the summary of OBV offered by George Angell in his book *Winning in the Commodities Market* (1979), are:

1. Collect at least five or six weeks data. This will be necessary to get a good reading of what is happening in the market.
2. Look for up or down breakouts in OBV. These signal potential moves in the breakout's corresponding direction.
3. Look for clusters in the data. Movements in a given direction, termed clusters, signal accumulation or distribution and provide advance warning of a top or a bottom.

There is much more to the use of OBV than I've discussed herein. If you're interested in learning about OBV in its original form, I urge you to read Granville's book on the subject. Unfortunately, the rules for applying OBV are not sufficiently objective to allow a totally mechanical approach to market entry or exit. My experience has taught me that while market exit need not always be objective or mechanical, market entry should, more often than not, be a function of objective selection criteria. OBV does not allow such concise determinations. While it is certainly possible to determine and test specific aspects of OBV that are mechanical, I've developed an application of OBV that is more conducive to the needs of the futures trader.

The Problems with Using OBV in Futures

There are several problems with using OBV in the futures markets. First and foremost, trading volume is usually not available soon enough in the day to allow for prompt calculation. Although this situation has improved in recent years with increased speed of reporting by the exchanges, there are yet several other problems. As you know, futures contracts have a limited life. Volume early in the life of a contract is low. It increases as the contract becomes the lead month. As the contract comes up for delivery, volume declines and reaches zero when the contract month expires. This causes a problem for those following OBV since volume fluctuates as a function of factors other than just buying or selling pressures. One answer—and a good one—is to use total trading volume rather than contract month volume.

There's also the problem of limit moves. A locked limit move often means little or no trading volume. In spite of the fact that price is very strong or very weak, little or no trading activity will take place. This does not appropriately weight the OBV and may in fact yield a distorted view of the market. Some will argue that the volume will carry over into the next trading session (or to the next session during which trading takes place) and that this will compensate for the limited volume on the locked limit days. This may be true, but I have my doubts.

A Solution

One solution to the availability of actual volume data is to use tick volume. Tick volume does not represent actual trading volume, but rather represents price change volume. Assume that the price of a given commodity is $55.50. If the next price is $55.51, a tick value of +1 is assigned to it. If the next price is $55.52, tick volume is +1, and it is added to the existing total. The total tick volume is now +2. If the next tick is $55.52, the same as the previous tick, no tick volume is added or subtracted, and it is considered a neutral trade. If the next tick is lower than the previous, it is given a -1 tick volume value and subtracted from the running total. Each price change can only carry with it a tick value increase or decrease of 1 unit.

This approach has limitations—the most obvious is that tick volume does not consider the size of the transaction at the given price. A change in price from $55.55 to $55.56 would receive a tick volume assignment of +1 no matter how many contracts actually exchanged hands at this price. As shown later this problem is solved by using the Market Profile®. However, this technique is extremely difficult for most traders to understand and apply.

My Theory of Tick Volume

Markets tend to top and bottom with spikes in trading volume that are the result of many traders acting on news, reports, recommendations by advisors and/or from large buying or selling by commercial interests and fund managers. Trading volume peaks and troughs are closely correlated with market tops and bottoms. The actual final number of contracts exchanging hands at any given price is generally unavailable to the public until after the trading session is over. Estimates *are* possible to obtain, but this is a time-consuming process and difficult to maintain on a regular basis. Once the markets have closed, The Chicago Board of Trade releases these figures for CBOT futures contracts in their LDB (Liquidity Data Bank) Report.

Futures traders do not have access to this data during market hours. For the more advanced trader I strongly recommend using the Market Profile® concepts; however, for most traders tick volume is currently the only viable method for short-term market feedback. Tick volume provides a reasonable substitute for actual contract volume. As previously noted tick volume measures the *number* of price changes rather than the actual number of contracts traded—it is a cumulative total of price changes over a given period of time. Tick volume moves up and down with increases and decreases in activity. Tick volume:

1. Allows determination of when and where major activity is taking place.
2. Helps you differentiate whether the trading activity was primarily a function of selling pressure or buying pressure.
3. Facilitates determination of accumulation and distribution patterns (to be defined) in futures markets.
4. Provides an early warning system of when a market is losing its upward or downward momentum.
5. Helps you spot price levels at which significant trading activity took place in the past and at which it is likely to recur in the future.
6. Is frequently an important confirming indicator of new lows or highs in virtually any time frame, even though it does not always pinpoint unsupported highs or lows. Its most promising application is in the area of bullish and bearish divergence.

Price and Volume Relationships

Figure 11.1 is a half-hour T-bond futures chart with tick volume plotted as a histogram below price. The higher the vertical line, the higher the tick volume. Note that the first and last half-hours of each day typically have high tick volume. This is normal. However, note that there are spikes and troughs in tick volume during the day as well. The opening volume spikes are marked with Os and the closing volume spikes with Cs to differentiate them from one another. Of much greater significance are arrows A, B and D. Price was near a high at A, and A showed the lowest tick volume for the day. This suggested that price was *not supported by new buying and that a top should be expected.*

Point B showed a similar situation. Point D, however, showed a downtrend with low tick volume. This suggested that low prices did not bring in more selling and that a rally was likely due to a lack of participation on the sell side. Low volume on declining prices, however, is not a definitive way to discern market bottoms because declining prices tend to be accompanied by falling volume. This is because public participation on the short side is usually less pronounced than on the buy side. Generally, however, sharply declining volume with declining price tends to lead to a selling climax in volume. This occurs when price has been declining for a relatively long time on declining or steady volume subsequent to which several very high volume spikes occur, thereby indicating massive liquidation of longs and a probable bottom.

A rule of thumb is that expanding tick volume on the downside is a bearish indication, and contracting tick volume on the downside indicates that the downtrend should soon end. On the upside, expanding tick volume indicates a continued rally, while contracting tick volume suggests that the rally is likely to end soon. Figure 11.2 illustrates some of these relationships on the 30-minute T-bond futures chart.

Basic Relationships Between Price and OBV

To overcome the limitations of raw tick volume or actual volume, I have suggested using on-balance volume. Figure 11.3 shows the OBV plotted on its own. A rising OBV trend usually indicates a rising market, a market that is under accumulation. And a falling OBV indicates a declining market. This chart shows two distinct uptrends and one distinct downtrend. Now examine OBV again in Figure 11.4, which shows the same OBV plot but this time against price. A strong correlation between OBV trend and price trend is evident. You will observe that when price made a new high for the indicated trend at point A, this high was accompanied by a new high in OBV, which indicated buying support for the trend. At point B price made another new high,

Figure 11.1   Price versus Tick Volume

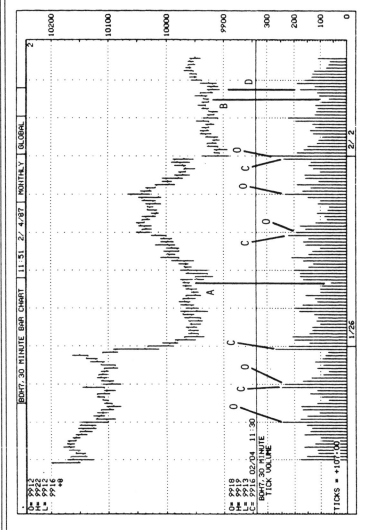

Figure 11.2   Another Example of Tick Volume versus Price

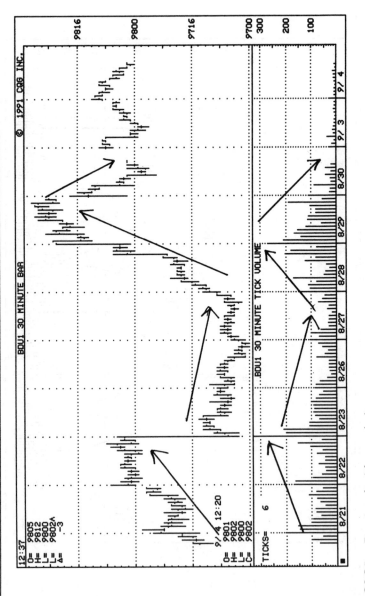

which was not supported by a new OBV high at point D. This was a bearish indication suggesting a decline in buying support.

OBV Trend Line Penetrations

There is yet another way to use OBV that makes its value more readily discernible as well as useful for trading purposes. The OBV trend line can serve as an excellent but subjective way to monitor price trend changes. To use OBV in this way simply monitor trend line penetrations of OBV for signals. Figure 11.5 is the daily soybean chart with an OBV line at bottom. I have marked buy and sell signals generated by trend line crossings.

Trendline penetrations are often subjective. Much depends upon how thin or thick the lines are drawn and how significantly the penetrations exceed the trend lines. Examine the daily cotton chart OBV trend line (Figure 11.6). As you can see, this market has clearer signals than did the soybean market by virtue of its more definitive trends. Although the OBV trend line analysis is a viable method, it is more subjective than most of the other techniques.

There are several additional aspects of OBV that can be employed in a short-term trading program, the most important of which is divergence. *Divergence* is defined as an indicator and price moving in different directions.

Divergence in OBV or tick volume can be applied as follows:

1. When price makes a new high for a given time frame but the new high is not confirmed by an OBV or tick indicator high, divergence is negative, suggesting a likely decline in price.
2. When price makes a new low for a given time period but OBV or tick indicator fail to make a new low, divergence is positive, suggesting that an up move in price is likely.

Figures 11.7 and 11.8 demonstrate divergence in a variety of conditions using OBV.

Mechanical Applications of OBV

Another way of using OBV is by a mechanical application of OBV plotted against a moving average of itself. This common technique slows an indicator to determine when it has changed

Figure 11.3   On-Balance Tick Volume Alone

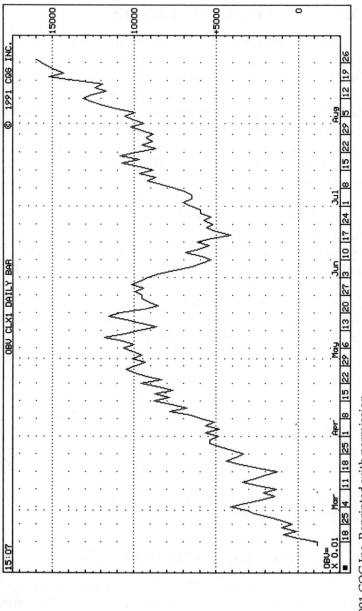

©1991 CQG Inc. Reprinted with permission.

Figure 11.4   On-Balance Tick Volume with Price

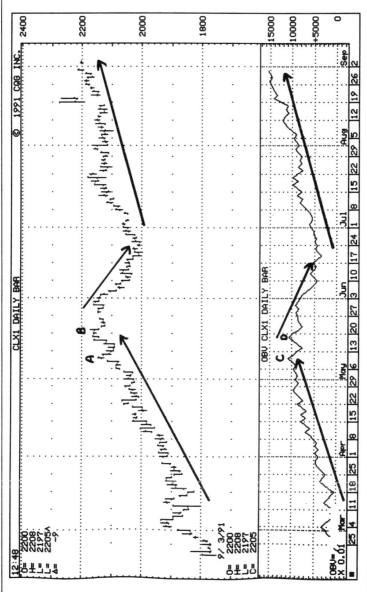

trend. It allows for a relatively mechanical application of trend lines. Figure 11.9 shows how this application works. Be aware, however, that some markets are more responsive to this technique than are others. It may be best to use a third order derivative of the OBV for this purpose. In other words, you may wish to take a moving average of the OBV and plot the moving average of the OBV against a moving average of itself. This will result in smoother signals that are likely to be considerably more reliable.

Conclusions

Perhaps the single most important application of tick OBV is its use as a divergence indicator. While I cannot offer a totally mechanical approach to using this method, I do have some helpful suggestions. They are as follows:

- A rising price accompanied by a falling OBV or an OBV losing its upward slope or momentum is a trend in danger of topping. OBV can isolate such situations much more clearly than can most methods. And OBV can be computed on an intraday basis to more carefully time the market turn. Higher prices must be accompanied by increased buying activity, which is expressed in terms of rising OBV. While it is reasonable and normal for prices in an uptrend to experience periodic downside corrections, tick volume on the decline should not be so large as to indicate massive selling. In short, higher prices must be accompanied by rising participation as expressed by rising tick volume.
- A falling trend should also be accompanied by increased selling. If prices decline on rising/falling tick volume, the market will soon reach a point from which an uptrend will begin. While it is reasonably normal for volume on declines to be lighter than volume on rallies, lower and lower OBV correlated with lower and lower prices will eventually reach a level from which a strong rally is likely. Intraday and daily timing indicators can be used in such cases as well.
- There are many derivatives of OBV that may be used along with OBV to mechanize the trade selection process. A recent addition to my work has been the use of momentum (MOM) and rate of change (ROC) indicators along with OBV.

Figure 11.5   Tick OBV versus Price and Trend Line Penetrations

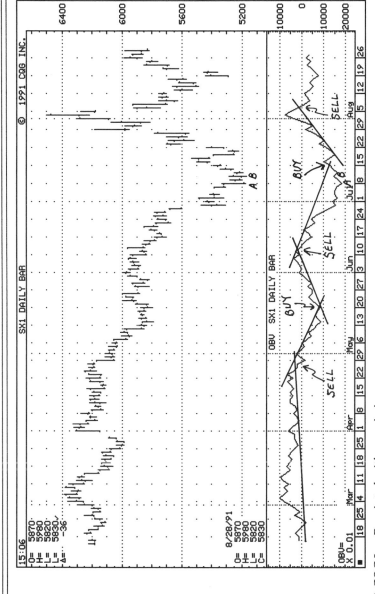

Figure 11.6   Tick OBV versus Price and Trend Line Penetrations

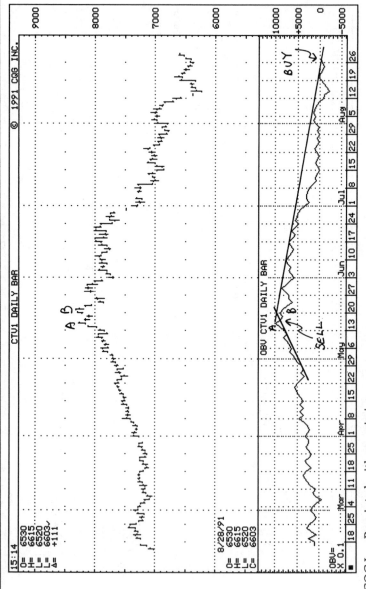

©1991 CQG Inc. Reprinted with permission.

Figure 11.7 Tick OBV versus Price Divergence

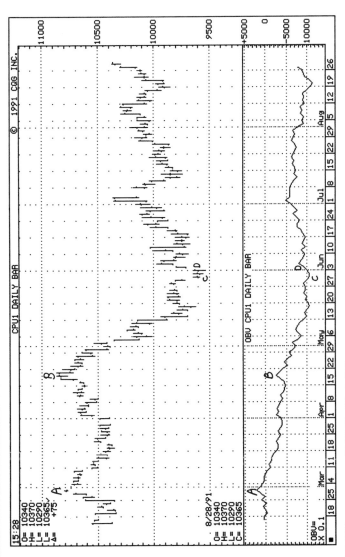

A-B=Bearish Divergence, C-D Bullish Divergence

©1991 CQG Inc. Reprinted with permission.

Figure 11.8   Tick OBV versus Price Divergence

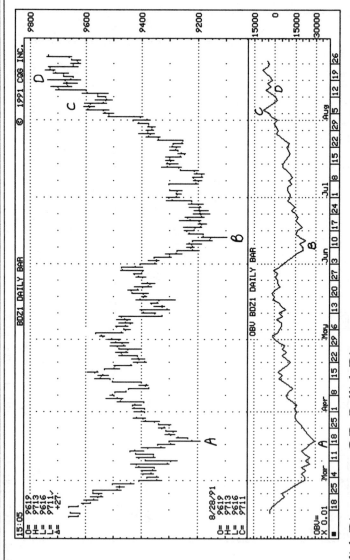

A-B=Bullish Divergence, C-D=Bullish Divergence

©1991 CQG Inc. Reprinted with permission.

Figure 11.9 OBV Plotted Against Its Own Moving Average and Price

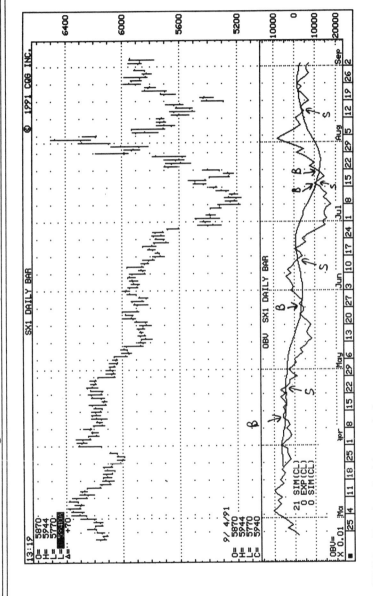

Chapter

=== 12 ===

Daily Seasonal Tendencies and Clusters

For years many stock and futures traders have heard the word *seasonality* applied to various stocks, futures markets and the stock market as a whole. Such terms as *pre-Christmas demand, tax selling, quarterly window dressing* and *pre-Fourth of July rally* are types of seasonal behavior. Throughout futures and stock trading history, experienced traders have come to expect certain price movements to occur on or near specific dates.

While it may seem too simple to assume that futures markets will trend in relatively predictable directions with a high frequency on or about certain times of the year, it may be a fact of market life that such tendencies do actually exist and will likely continue to exist for many years. If such tendencies are valid, it is our task, indeed, our obligation to find them and to use them to our advantage.

A study of market history and research reveals that *daily* seasonality is not unknown to traders. In fact, Arthur A. Merrill in his classic book *Behavior of Prices on Wall Street* gave many examples of highly consistent price behavior in the Dow Jones Industrial Average (DJIA) prior to important holidays, events, etc. Merrill demonstrated unequivocally that prices for the Dow Jones Industrial Average have had a marked propensity to move higher on the day before many legal and religious holidays. Figure 12.1 shows some of the relationships he discovered using historical data from January 1897 through December 1983.

Merrill's data base covered many cases; therefore, his test constituted a statistically valid analysis of seasonal price behavior in the DJIA. As you can see, some of these patterns are very reliable. In fact, several are so reliable that the odds of their being chance events are extremely low. In other words, these are particularly valid results that are most likely to be a true reflection of market behavior as opposed to a statistical aberration.

Merrill's studies distinctly show that pre-holiday behavior is a valid phenomenon in the Dow Jones Industrial Average. Although it may not be strictly valid to project from these findings and conclude that futures prices also exhibit reliable pre-holiday behavior, a thorough test of this hypothesis as applied to futures markets will lead to definitive conclusions.

My research on such daily seasonal tendencies in the futures markets indicates that there is compelling evidence supporting the validity of such patterns. This chapter will examine a variety of patterns related to seasonal tendencies by exact calendar date. In other words, I will demonstrate that daily seasonality exists in the futures markets and show how to use timing in conjunction with seasonality as a strategic combination.

I must alert you: there is considerably less futures data at our disposal than there is stock market data. Most contemporary market analyses study from 10 to 15 years of historical futures data; they examine the performance of their parameters over the period from roughly the mid to early 1970s through present time. To have the greatest degree of confidence in my seasonal studies, I have included as much data as possible. Futures contracts traded at the Chicago Mercantile Exchange and the International Monetary Market were studied back to their inception in the 1960s; a number of Chicago Board of Trade Markets were studied back to the 1920s (with a hiatus during the 1940s when exchanges were closed due to World War II). While this is still not as much data history as a strict statistician would prefer, it is sufficient to permit many good conclusions regarding the seasonal patterns and indicators I will examine in this chapter.

Pre-Holiday Behavior in the Futures Markets

A good starting point for our examination of daily futures seasonals is to study pre-holiday behavior in a fashion similar to Merrill's technique. In generating the statistical results that follow, I used the following technique:

- All active futures markets were examined by contract month and year; in other words, every delivery month for every futures market I have on file was studied for possibly reliable seasonal tendencies.
- The closing price direction on the market day prior to major legal holidays in the United States was recorded.
- The closing price direction on the market day after major legal holidays in the United States was recorded.

Figure 12.2 shows the results that were generated by my study.

Discussion of Results: Pre-Holiday and Post-Holiday Behavior

My studies confirmed the validity of pre-holiday behavior in the futures markets. Knowing this, the serious futures trader can use seasonal tendencies to establish high probability short-term trades. Later in this chapter I will show a number of timing techniques that will help you minimize the losses while fine tuning entry and exit.

If it could be demonstrated that other days during the year have also shown high probability seasonal moves, the trader would have yet another important weapon to facilitate profitable trading. To determine if there were other important seasonal dates that were not necessarily related to holidays, I studied every calendar date for every market using the same techniques described earlier. The results of my studies revealed the following information for each market (see also Figure 12.3):

- percent of time prices have closed up or down for each calendar date
- ranking of percent reliability for each date
- average percent size of up or down move for each date

I have provided a listing for the two most active contract months of most major futures markets in Appendix B. These will

Figures 12.1 Merrill's Pre-Holiday and Post-Holiday Results

PRE AND POST HOLIDAY BEHAVIOR

Percentage of Years in which the Dow Jones Industrial Average Posted an Increase for the Day

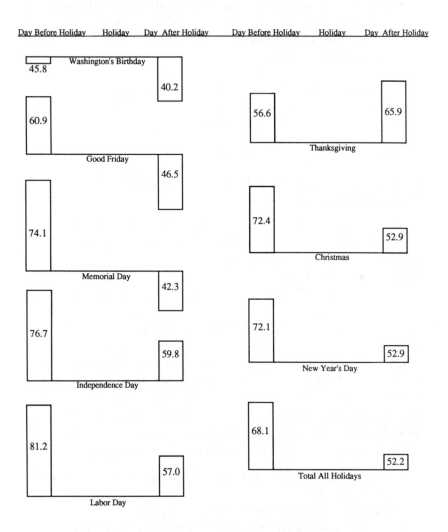

A. Merrill, *The Behavior of Prices on Wall Street* (Chappaqua, N.Y.: Analysis Press, 1984), 14. Reprinted with permission.

Figure 12.2   Pre-Holiday and Post-Holiday Behavior of Cattle, Copper and Wheat Futures in the United States

Day Before

New Year's Day
Feb Lv Cattle +64%, Mar Wheat +87%, Mar Copper +63%

Good Friday
Jun Lv Cattle -66%, Jly Wheat -75%, Mar Copper +71%

Memorial Day
Jun Lv Cattle +74%, Jly Wheat -62%, Sep Copper +55%

Independence Day
Oct Lv Cattle +66%, Jly Wheat 50%, Sep Copper +58%

Labor Day
Dec Lv Cattle +67%, Dec Wheat +69%, Dec Copper +61%

Thanksgiving
Dec Lv Cattle -69%, Dec Wheat -59%, Dec Copper +65%

Christmas
Feb Lv Cattle +72%, Dec Wheat +69%, Dec Copper +83%

Day After

New Year's Day
Feb Lv Cattle +61%, Mar Wheat -74%, Mar Copper +63%

Good Friday
Jun Lv Cattle -72%, Jly Wheat -53%, Mar Copper -53%

Memorial Day
Jun Lv Cattle +64%, Jly Wheat -65%, Sep Copper -52%

Independence Day
Oct Lv Cattle -54%, Jly Wheat 50%, Sep Copper +52%

Labor Day
Dec Lv Cattle +53%, Dec Wheat +69%, Dec Copper +60%

Thanksgiving
Dec Lv Cattle -55%, Dec Wheat -67%, Dec Copper +61%

Christmas
Feb Lv Cattle -73%, Dec Wheat +53%, Dec Copper +81%

help you apply the timing indicators discussed later. Remember that statistics change every year. You may keep the data current on your own, or you may wish to contact my office for up-to-date statistics (see Appendix B).

Each market and contract month has a separate listing that begins approximately six months prior to contract expiration and ends at approximately contract expiration. Due to space limitations I have not provided listings for all contract months of all markets; however, those provided will give a good idea of what my daily market probability studies have shown.

Explanation of Printouts/Precautions and Limitations

Figure 12.3 explains the data listed on each of the daily market probability study printouts (Appendix B). Please note the following additional explanatory notes:

- Percent of time up or down reading is based on the amount of data analyzed for each of the printouts. The data lengths are as follows:
  - Grains, soybean complex, meats, cotton, silver and copper early to mid 1960s through 1991
  - All others from start of futures trading through 1991
- Note that for markets such as S&P and T-bonds the number of years data history is limited and, as a consequence, percent readings are not as reliable as they might be for markets with longer histories. Remember this when you use the daily market probability statistics in your trading program(s).
- These figures do not constitute a trading system. They are merely historical listings that should be used in conjunction with timing indicators.
- Stop losses should be used regardless of how high a given percent reading may be. Risk management is an integral aspect of successful futures trading. The timing indicators I will discuss should help minimize risk and losses.
- + and - in the far left column are interpreted as: + equals up close 60 to 70 percent of the time; ++ equals up close 71 to 79 percent of the time; +++ equals up close 80 percent of the time or more; - equals down close 60 to 70 percent of the time; - - equals down close 71 to 79 percent of the time; - - - equals down close 80 percent of the time or more.

Figure 12.3   Example of Daily Market Probability Statistics

DAILY MARKET PROBABILITY STUDIES
EXPLANATION OF PRINTOUT

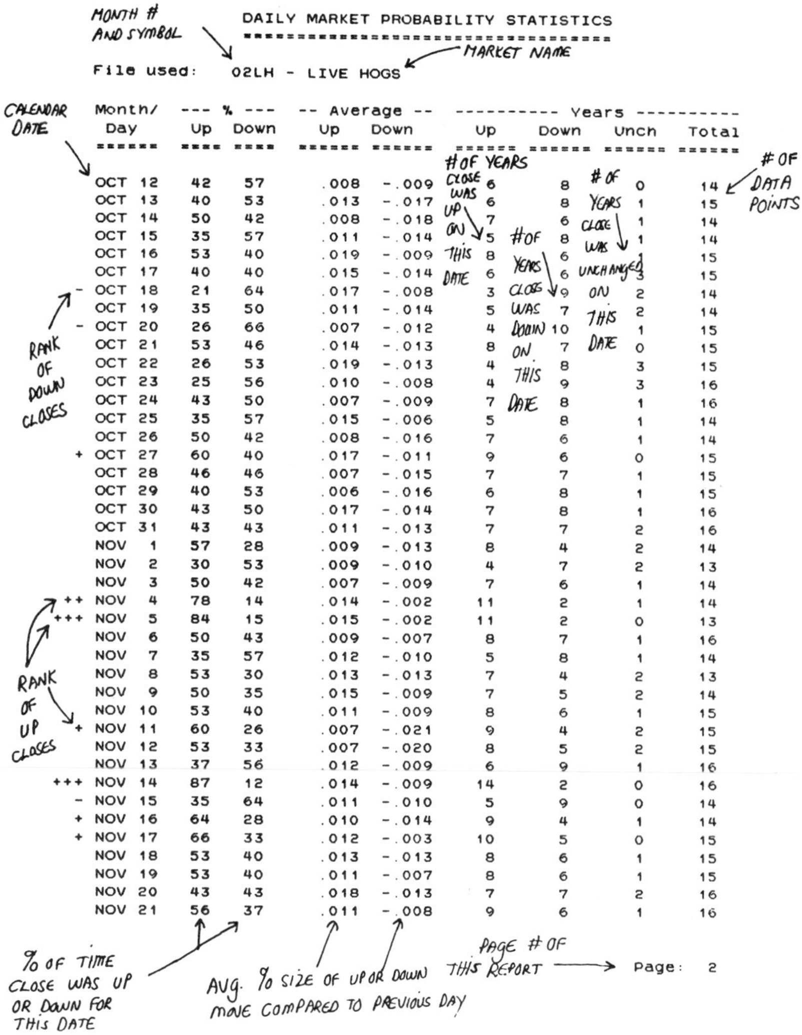

MONTH # AND SYMBOL →

DAILY MARKET PROBABILITY STATISTICS
■■■
MARKET NAME

File used: 02LH - LIVE HOGS

CALENDAR DATE	Month/ Day	--- % ---		-- Average --		---------- Years ----------			
		Up	Down	Up	Down	Up	Down	Unch	Total
	OCT 12	42	57	.008	-.009	6	8	0	14
	OCT 13	40	53	.013	-.017	6	8	1	15
	OCT 14	50	42	.008	-.018	7	6	1	14
	OCT 15	35	57	.011	-.014	5	8	1	14
	OCT 16	53	40	.019	-.009	8	6	1	15
	OCT 17	40	40	.015	-.014	6	6	3	15
−	OCT 18	21	64	.017	-.008	3	9	2	14
	OCT 19	35	50	.011	-.014	5	7	2	14
−	OCT 20	26	66	.007	-.012	4	10	1	15
	OCT 21	53	46	.014	-.013	8	7	0	15
	OCT 22	26	53	.019	-.013	4	8	3	15
	OCT 23	25	56	.010	-.008	4	9	3	16
	OCT 24	43	50	.007	-.009	7	8	1	16
	OCT 25	35	57	.015	-.006	5	8	1	14
	OCT 26	50	42	.008	-.016	7	6	1	14
+	OCT 27	60	40	.017	-.011	9	6	0	15
	OCT 28	46	46	.007	-.015	7	7	1	15
	OCT 29	40	53	.006	-.016	6	8	1	15
	OCT 30	43	50	.017	-.014	7	8	1	16
	OCT 31	43	43	.011	-.013	7	7	2	16
	NOV 1	57	28	.009	-.013	8	4	2	14
	NOV 2	30	53	.009	-.010	4	7	2	13
	NOV 3	50	42	.007	-.009	7	6	1	14
++	NOV 4	78	14	.014	-.002	11	2	1	14
+++	NOV 5	84	15	.015	-.002	11	2	0	13
	NOV 6	50	43	.009	-.007	8	7	1	16
	NOV 7	35	57	.012	-.010	5	8	1	14
	NOV 8	53	30	.013	-.013	7	4	2	13
	NOV 9	50	35	.015	-.009	7	5	2	14
	NOV 10	53	40	.011	-.009	8	6	1	15
+	NOV 11	60	26	.007	-.021	9	4	2	15
	NOV 12	53	33	.007	-.020	8	5	2	15
	NOV 13	37	56	.012	-.009	6	9	1	16
+++	NOV 14	87	12	.014	-.009	14	2	0	16
−	NOV 15	35	64	.011	-.010	5	9	0	14
+	NOV 16	64	28	.010	-.014	9	4	1	14
+	NOV 17	66	33	.012	-.003	10	5	0	15
	NOV 18	53	40	.013	-.013	8	6	1	15
	NOV 19	53	40	.011	-.007	8	6	1	15
	NOV 20	43	43	.018	-.013	7	7	2	16
	NOV 21	56	37	.011	-.008	9	6	1	16

Handwritten annotations:

OF YEARS CLOSE WAS UP ON THIS DATE — # OF YEARS CLOSE WAS UNCHANGED ON THIS DATE — # OF DATA POINTS

RANK OF DOWN CLOSES

RANK OF UP CLOSES

% OF TIME CLOSE WAS UP OR DOWN FOR THIS DATE

AVG. % SIZE OF UP OR DOWN MOVE COMPARED TO PREVIOUS DAY

PAGE # OF THIS REPORT → Page: 2

Suggestions for Using the Daily Market Probability Statistics

If you feel, as I do, that daily market probabilities constitute a valid approach to the isolation of repetitive patterns in the futures markets, consider the following suggested applications.

As a Filter to Your Trading Signals

Assume that your trading system has signaled a short sale. When you examine the daily listings for the given market, you notice that the next three trading days have shown a high percent of time up closing for the day. This might lead you to suspect the short signal as potentially invalid. You might wait for the system to give a second sell signal before taking action. As an alternative, you might pass on the trade entirely, particularly if the percent of time readings are very high (i.e., 80 percent or higher).

As a Confirming Indicator to Your Trading Signals

An adaptation of the previous application is to use the daily percent readings as a confirming indicator with your trading signals. Simply stated, this means that when your signals are to go long and are in agreement with strong percent up readings, you will go long. When your signals are to go short and are in agreement with strong percent of time down readings, you will go short. Finally, if there are no strong percent up or down readings, you will either take no action, or you will trade exclusively with your timing signals.

As a Trading System

The market probability readings can be developed into a trading system. This requires developing the following elements and incorporating them into an operational plan:

- Timing indicators
- Risk management considerations
- Precise entry and exit procedures

Consider the following approach as a further suggestion for developing a trading system based on the percent readings: Trades will only be made when percent reading for a given day is 75 percent or higher, up or down. Toward the end of the previous trading day you will begin to watch intraday timing indicators (i.e., moving averages, oscillators, stochastics). If and when these indicators turn in the same direction as the percent reading for the next day or several days, you will enter the market consistent with the direction of the expected move. You will exit when the timing indicators turn in the opposite direction, at the end of the day, on days prior to strong percent reading(s) in the opposite direction, or at a predetermined stop loss or price objective that is determined by another method of analysis.

As an Indicator of More Significant Seasonal Movement

By examining the daily percent readings over blocks of time (i.e., weekly or monthly), you can ascertain probable seasonal movement for the given block of time. December and February live hog futures, for example, show a large number of percent time up closes for the month of November. The conclusion is that November has often been a bullish month for live hog futures. This information should prove especially valuable to hedgers, producers and commercial interests, as well as position traders.

To Isolate Possible Seasonal Spread Situations

This application is also one particularly suited to hedgers, commercial interests and more experienced traders. By examining the percent of time up/down readings during similar periods of time for different contract months of the same market, or for the same contract months of different but related markets (i.e., July corn and July wheat), one can determine the historical tendency of prices on a relative basis. Assume that during a given month July corn futures show only a few plus readings with a majority of minus readings but that July wheat futures show few minus readings with a majority of plus readings. In such a situation the spread—long July wheat, short July corn—appears to have merit from a seasonal standpoint. There are many such situations both on an intra-market and inter-market basis.

Trade Only the Highest Readings

You may wish to scan the data for the highest percent up and down readings, trading the markets consistent with these readings. Look for the + + + or - - - notations in the left-hand margin for each of the listings. These figures note the largest percent of time readings and are likely to be the most reliable.

Trade Only High Percent of Time Strings or Clusters

One might reasonably argue that, taken by itself, any one day of high percent of time up or down reading could be a random or chance event. To minimize this possibility, one might ignore such days and, as a more reliable alternative, focus only on strings of days having high percent readings in the same direction. As an example, note the strings taken from actual statistics for the given markets (Figures 12.4 and 12.5).

Strings, or clusters of successive days of high readings in the same closing direction are more likely to be statistically valid than are single days.

Pre-Holiday or Pre-Report Behavior

This application can be evaluated by using the daily market probability studies. Examine markets for their percent readings on days before major holidays or other significant days (i.e., Labor Day, Christmas, Fourth of July, New Year's, Jewish New Year, election days, key government report days, etc.). Examples have been cited previously (Figure 12.2).

Graphic Representation of Daily Seasonal Tendencies

The daily seasonal tendencies could also be shown on a chart to visualize the trends. Figures 12.6 and 12.7 illustrate two daily seasonal tendency charts. By using these charts instead of the daily seasonal probability listings, you can get an idea of trend as well as probabilities.

Systematic Trading Using Daily Seasonal Probabilities

The daily seasonal probability statistics provide a base to which we can apply timing. The futures trader has a number of choices regarding the application of such data. These have been suggested earlier. The most specific applications are as follows:

Figures 12.4   High Probability Clusters of Daily Percent Readings

File used: 110J - ORANGE JUICE

Month/Day	--- % ---		-- Average --		--------- Years ---------			
	Up	Down	Up	Down	Up	Down	Unch	Total
	====	====	======	======	======	======	======	======
AUG 23	46	53	.010	-.010	6	7	0	13
AUG 24	50	50	.007	-.012	6	6	0	12
++ AUG 25	78	21	.009	-.007	11	3	0	14
- AUG 26	35	64	.006	-.009	5	9	0	14
AUG 27	46	53	.007	-.008	7	8	0	15
+ AUG 28	68	25	.010	-.009	11	4	1	16
AUG 29	46	40	.012	-.009	7	6	2	15
- AUG 30	38	61	.013	-.005	5	8	0	13
AUG 31	53	38	.008	-.010	7	5	1	13
++ SEP 1	70	30	.012	-.011	7	3	0	10
- SEP 2	27	63	.019	-.009	3	7	1	11
+ SEP 3	66	25	.010	-.013	8	3	1	12
SEP 4	46	46	.008	-.014	6	6	1	13
+++ SEP 5	84	7	.009	-.004	11	1	1	13
+ SEP 6	63	36	.010	-.005	7	4	0	11
+ SEP 7	60	40	.004	-.017	6	4	0	10
+++ SEP 8	85	14	.004	-.011	12	2	0	14
+ SEP 9	64	21	.011	-.010	9	3	2	14
SEP 10	53	33	.014	-.007	8	5	2	15
SEP 11	56	43	.010	-.014	9	7	0	16

Figures 12.5   High Probability Clusters of Daily Percent Readings

File used: 04LC - LIVE CATTLE

Month/ Day		--- % ---		-- Average --		---------- Years ----------			
		Up	Down	Up	Down	Up	Down	Unch	Total
	JAN 25	54	27	.013	-.007	6	3	2	11
-	JAN 26	33	66	.009	-.009	4	8	0	12
+++	JAN 27	81	18	.011	-.005	9	2	0	11
+	JAN 28	66	33	.012	-.008	8	4	0	12
++	JAN 29	71	28	.009	-.010	10	4	0	14
-	JAN 30	33	66	.011	-.011	5	10	0	15
-	JAN 31	30	69	.016	-.008	4	9	0	13
++	FEB 1	75	25	.011	-.013	9	3	0	12
	FEB 2	41	58	.011	-.005	5	7	0	12
	FEB 3	50	41	.008	-.003	6	5	1	12
	FEB 4	58	41	.009	-.016	7	5	0	12

- Trade only high percentage up and down readings by entering on the close of trading the day before the given percentage. Exit the trade on the close of trading the day of the high percentage reading.
- Improve your odds by trading only strings or clusters of high percentage readings.
- Use the high percentage strings with timing to reduce the error rate that is unavoidable with seasonals (and with all other technical and fundamental methods).

For using daily seasonal probabilities, I suggest the following procedure:

- Find a high probability move using either daily market probability listings or daily seasonal futures charts. The best seasonals are those that occur in clusters as opposed to single day moves unless these moves have very high percentages. (i.e., 80 percent or higher).
- Use a time window of about 30 percent of the length of the seasonal cluster. If, for example, the cluster is six days in length, then begin looking for buy or sell signals about two days before the start of the cluster. Continue to watch for signals until about 75 percent of the cluster has passed. If there are no signals, leave the market alone.
- It is preferable to use intraday signals for timing in such cases. Either 30-minute or 60-minute data can be used. The Consecutive Closes or moving average indicators discussed in Chapter 10 will serve this purpose well. Or you may use other short-term timing indicators such as stochastics or RSI. Daily timing could also be used.

Here's an example. Consider Figure 12.8, which shows the daily seasonal tendency in September T-bond futures. I have marked the strong cluster of bearish seasonal dates that begins on or about 22 August. Figure 12.9 shows the daily December wheat chart for the same period. Note the confluence of bullish timing indicators during the ideal time for a seasonal rally.

Here are some additional guidelines for using timing in conjunction with daily seasonals and clusters of seasonals:

- Use short-term timing to fine tune market entry.
- If you have a bullish seasonal and the timing indicator(s) you

Figures 12.6 Daily Seasonal Probability Chart—March Soybeans

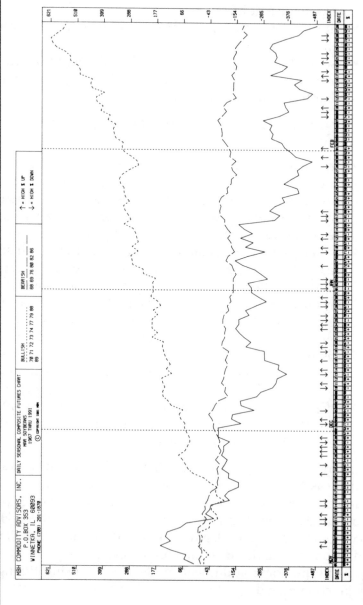

©1991 MBH

Figures 12.7   Daily Seasonal Probability Chart—December Live Hogs

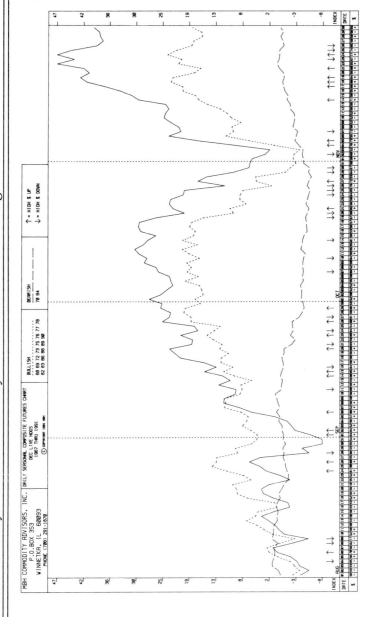

©1991 MBH

are using fail to turn bullish by 75 percent into the length of the cluster (i.e., number of days in cluster times 75 percent), don't enter the trade. If you have a bearish seasonal and signals do not turn bearish, forget the trade. This is how timing will help you avoid those years when the seasonal will probably not work or when it is late.

- Once the cluster is over you may wish to remain in the trade so long as it is in your favor. Use timing to exit the trade promptly once it changes trend.
- There are various other procedures that you may devise to maximize the seasonal timing procedure. Multiple positions, trailing stop losses and price objectives can be used to your advantage as well.

For your assistance I've provided a seasonal listing, the *Seasonal Cheat Sheet* (Figure 12.10). The cheat sheet is a highly condensed version of major seasonal moves covering virtually all markets and contract months. It will alert you to high probability moves by specific calendar date and market, and it will also give you an estimate of how strong the moves have been in the past. As in the case of all seasonals, you must keep the work up-to-date since the data will change every year. Rules for using the cheat sheet are indicated in Figure 12.10 as well.

Figure 12.8   Daily Seasonal Tendency Chart—December Wheat

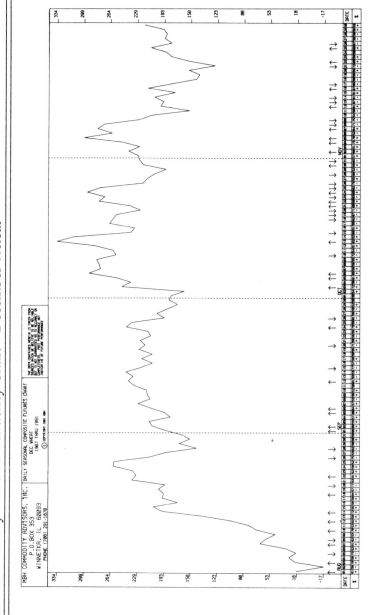

©1991 MBH

Figure 12.9   Daily December Wheat Chart

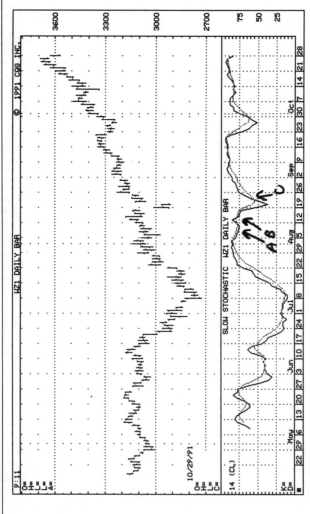

Note also Figure 12.8, which shows daily seasonal turning bullish in early August, at which time stochastic (points A & B) was bearish. When stochastic turned bullish at point C, a buy should have been entered since seasonals and timing were then bullish.

©1991 CGQ Inc. Reprinted with permission.

Figure 12.10 *The Seasonal Cheat Sheet*

Jake Bernstein's Seasonal "Cheat Sheet"

The Seasonal "Cheat Sheet" highlights what have been the best seasonal up and down moves based on daily seasonal price tendencies. By best I mean highest percentage repetition and longest string of uninterrupted or near uninterrupted moves in a given direction. Don't automatically assume that because a seasonal trend has been highly reliable for many years that it will always repeat. See additional precautionary statements on side 2.

Key to Notations

In order to simplify and condense the seasonals I have used the following notations: - moderate seasonal down tendency; - - strong seasonal down tendency; - - - very high probability seasonal down tendency; + moderate seasonal up tendency; ++ strong seasonal up tendency; +++ very high probability seasonal up tendency; ! larger than average size of move; !! very large size of move; !!! extremely large size average move. A notation of +++!!!, according to this notation, therefore, would indicate a very high probability of large up move in price. Markets are shown by contract symbol and month symbol followed by + or - reading, magnitude reading (!) if any, and dates of moves for given month of the year and indicated contract month. For example, PBK ++! 01-04, means a moderate probability of larger than average up move between the 1st and 4th of the month inclusive. These notations are based on my evaluations which were initially selected by computer but which I then subjectively filtered and evaluated. I have not included S&P Index futures since data history is limited, rather I have included DJIA.

Symbol Listing

LC=Live Cattle FC=Feeder Cattle LH=Live Hogs PB=Pk Bellies C=Corn O=Oats S=Soybeans BO=Soybean Oil SM=Soybean Meal W=Wheat CO=Cocoa
CF=Coffee SU=Sugar OJ=Orange Juice CT=Cotton LB=Lumber GC=Gold PL=Copper Sl=Silver CP=Copper HO=Heating Oil CL=Crude Oil SF=Swiss
Franc BP=Br Pound JY=Japanese Yen CA=Canada $ BD=TBonds TB=TBills DJIA=Dow Industrial Average. Contract Months: Jan=F Feb=G March=H
Apr=J May=K Jun=M Jly=N Aug=Q Sep=U Oct=V Nov=X Dec=Z

JANUARY

LCG -! 24-29; ++ !20-28; LHG ++!04-06; PBG++!02-06; - !28-31; CH - 19-22; OH -16-19; WH -:02-04; -:16-21; SMH -:02-08; BOH ++:!07-07; CFH -:-13-16;
- 28-31; SUK - -:02-05; ++!20-26; OJH -:07-09; ++!!:12-17; GCG +!!! 16-19; PLJ -:27-31; CTH - -03-05; - -14-16; HOH -:!!12-23; CLH - - !!! 19-24; SFH - -!
14-22; - -!!! 26-31; BPH -:- 21-23; CAH ++ 05-07;JYH -!!24-31 BDH -!! 02-06;-29-31; TBH - - !!! 03-06

FEBRUARY

LCM ++!01-09; - -!23-27; FCK ++ !01-08; - -:10-13; -:22-26; LHM -09-11; - :24-27; PBH - -:05-09; CH - -:03-16; - -!!!22-28; OH - -:!!! 18-28; WH - -12-14; -
!! 23-28; SMH - -:01-13; - -:!!19-28; BOH - -:24-26; CCH - -!!16-19; CFH ++!!! 19-24; - -25-27; OJH - -:!! 22-27; SUH - -:!!! 22-28; GCM - -10-15; - !!
22-26; SIH +++!:05-07; -:24-26; CPH +!:12-16; LBH - 16-19; - - !!! 22-28; CTH + 23-28; HOH - -:!06-09; SFH - 01-08; +++!13-17; CAH - !!! 08-
27; JYH - -10-12;+++!13-17; BDH - -:!!! 01-15; TBH - - !!! 01-15; DJIA ++ 91-04; ++ 15-18

MARCH

LCM ++ 23-24; - !!27-30; FCK -:!11-20; PBK +!!! 19-22; ON -:-05-11; - :-20-31; WN -:-08-13; SN ++!17-18; SMN - -25-31; CCH ++!06-08; SUN + 28-
31; OJN - -!! 09-14; GCM - -01-08; ++!17-21; - -:!27-30; SIN - - -:!!24-31; PLN - - !!06-12; - - :18-25; LBN - - - !!! 22-28; CTN - - 03-07; ++!! 19-21; - - 25-27;
HON ++!21-30; SFM - - !!!06-09; - - - !21-26; BPM - - -13-17; CAM ++!!! 11-17; ++ 29-31; BDM - !19-24; TBM - 07-09; - - -12-18; - ! 22-24; DJIA ++ 01-04;
++! 10-18

APRIL

LCM +++!!! 05-08; ++ 21-24; FCK - !! 01-04; ++:!! 05-11; - -!14-18; - - !! 22-28; LHM ++!! 05-09; PBK - -!01-04; CN ++! 06-09; - -10-16; ON - -:24-29; WN - -
09-13; SK ++!!! 04-11; SMN +++!04-09; CPN +!!! 16-22; GCM - -15-16; - -:24-28; PLN +! 10-13; +! 22-24; LBN - 03-06; +! 07-09; - -! 18-27; CTN - 11-15; HON
+!! 01-08; ++!21-23; - -:!27-29; CLN - -:24-30; SFM -!02-06; - -12-14; BPM - - -:21-24; CAM - -03-06; ++!! 07-20;- - !! 21-24; JYM - - - 01-03; - - 15-17; BDM
- 01-04; - 10-13; - - - !! 18-24; TBM - -:19-29; DJIA ++!!! 05-17

MBH PO Box 353 Winnetka, IL 60093 USA 708-291-1870

Figure 12.10   The *Seasonal Cheat Sheet* (Continued)

Jake Bernstein's Seasonal "Cheat Sheet"

MAY

LCM ++ 05-08; LHM -- 24-29; PBQ - - 01-04; - -! 08-14; - - - 24-25; CN ++! 06-08; - ! 09-12; - - 22-28; ON - -16-18; - -! 22-30; WN - -!! 25-31; SN - 01-03; ++!
08-10; - - 26-30; CFN ++! 18-21; - -! 20-29; SUN - - 28-30; SIN + 07-10; - -! 17-21; - - 28-30; PLN + +!! 02-18; LBN ++ 14-16; HON - -02-05; +++ 06-07; - - - !!
27-30; CLIN +++!! 06-11; - -! 26-30; - -! 09-17; - - - ! 27-29; BPM - - 03-06; - -! 16-20; CAM - - !! 01-03; - -! 27-29; - - !!! 11-18; - - - !! 25-31; BDM - - !!
07-12; - - 25-30; DJIA - 18-27

JUNE

LCV - -! 12-14; FCQ - -! 19-22; LHQ ++!! 23-27; - -! 28-30; CN - - - !!! 23-28; ON ++ 04-09; - - - !! 25-29; WN - - 06-08; - - - !!! 22-30; SN ++! 18-21; - - !! 23-29;
SMN - -! 22-29; BON - - 08-12; - - !! 26-29; CCN - -! 10-13; CFN - -! 16-24; SUV - -! 03-16; GCV - - !!! 01-12; CPN - - 02-05; - - !! 24-27; PLN - - 07-10; - - 14-
16; LBN - - 19-27; HON - - - !!! 02-18; +++! 19-25; CLN - - - !!! 03-09; BPU - - 03-04; ++! 06-09; CAU - - - !01-04; +++10-14; JYU - - 07-10; + 12-14; - -! 24-28;
BDU ++! 01-06; - -! 17-26; TBU ++ 12-14; - - - !! 15-24

JULY

FCQ - 13-19; LHQ - ! 08-11; PBQ - - 08-13; - - 17-19; CU - - - !!! 17-30; OU - - - ! 07-12; - - - ! 15-18; SX ++ 12-14; SMU - - !! 22-30; BOU +++!01-03; ++!! 12-17; -
- 23-30; CCU ++! 10-23; - - 25-31; CFU - 24-30; SUV - -! 05-11; OJU + 06-08; GCV - - 11-19; SIU + 15-18; - -!! 26-30; PLV - 09-12; HOU - 05-11; +++ 15-17;
+28-31; CLU ++ 05-10; +++!! 15-17; - - 22-27; SFU - - 11-15; - ! 25-29; BPU + 06-09; ++!! 20-24; CAU - -! 28-31; CAU - - ! 21-24; JYU - - 13-17; - - 27-29; BDU - - 07-13; -
- 21-24; TBU - 07-10; - - 26-28; DJIA +++ 01-05; - - -!! 12-13

AUGUST

FCX ++! 02-07; ++ 23-26; CU - - !! 16-29; WU - -! 26-28; SMU ++! 09-12; BOU - - !! 27-31; CCU - 01-05; ++ 26-30; SUV - - !!! 07-17 SIU - - 07-
09; - 28-31; CPU + 01-04; - - - !! 15-18; PLV +!!! 10-21; - - 29-31; CTZ - 03-09; ++!!! 24-30; HOZ ++ 01-05; + 20-22; CLV + 13-15; - - 22-27; SFU - - - ! 25-31; BPU - -
- !!! 03-07; +++!!! 09-19; CAU - - -! 04-14; +++!!! 19-22; - -! 25-27; JYU - - - !! 02-09; - - - !!! 21-31; BDU ++ 16-20; - -! 22-28; TBU - - 26-28

SEPTEMBER

LCZ ++ 11-15; FCF ++! 03-07; - ! 20-22; PBG - ! 18-24; CZ - -11-22; OZ ++! !! 01-05; - - 20-26; WZ ++ !! 01-06; SX ++! 02-05; - - !! 22-29; SMZ +++!! 01-06; - - !! 19-26;
BOZ ++ 01-06; - - 22-28; BOZ ++ 19-21; - - 26-28; SUV - - - 02-08; OJX - - - !12-15; ++! 21-23; GCV ++!! 01-07; - - 23-26; SIZ - -!! 24-30; PLV ++!! 01-05; - - - !!!
07-12; - - - !!! 24-30; LBF - - - !!! 08-22; - - 24-30; CTV - - ! 06-09; - - !! 13-17; - - ! 20-23; HOZ +++!! 18-21; +++!!! 23-29; CLZ ++ + !!! 23-28;

OCTOBER

LCZ - - !!! 25-30; FCX ++! 08-10; - - !!! 20-29; LHZ - - 19-20; - - ! 24-26; WZ + 03-06; - - 18-20; - - 25-28; BOZ - - 02-12; CFZ - 03-05; OJX - - 06-08; GCG ++!
05-10; - - !! 12-19; CPZ ++! 05-07; PLF - 04-09; ++ 16-18; LBF ++! 06-08; - - 20-26; CTZ - - 20-24; HOZ ++ 07-17; SFZ ++!!! 07-18; CAZ - - !!! 07-20; JYZ - - ! 15-26;
BDZ - - ! 10-16; - - 24-28; TBZ - - 08-10; DJIA ++! 02-06

NOVEMBER

LCZ ++!!! 03-11; ++!!! 19-23; - - ! 25-30; FCF ++!!! 03-12; ++!! 20-24; - - !!! 17-21; PBG ++ 04-05; - - 24-25; CH - - 10-12; OH - - 08-10; WZ ++ 02-07; SH + 25-27;
SMZ + 02-05; BOZ - - !! 07-11; CCZ - - 14-19; CFZ ++ 07-12; - - 22-24; GCG ++11-13; - - 14-16; + 19-25; CPH ++ 21-30; PLF - - 10-15; ++!! 19-29; LBF ++ 24-27;
- - 28-30; SFZ - - 03-08; - - !! 13-17; CAH + 16-19; +++!!! 21-25; JYH ++ 21-24; BDM + 18-21; TBM ++ 18-19; - - 25-30; DJIA ++ 01-05; +++! 22-26

DECEMBER

LCZ ++ 23-24; FCF - ! 03-06; ++ 12-14; ++! 23-24; - -! 27-29; LHG ++ 19-20; - -!! 26-31; CH - - !!! 02-18; OH -21-23; SH - 26-29; BOH - - !!! 26-31; CFH ++!!! 15-
23; SUH - - !!! 01-08; OJH - - 09-15; GCG ++ 09-15; - - 26-31; PLF ++ 19-22; - - 28-31; LBF + 16-18; - - 28-30; CTH -! 08-14; ++! 21-24; HOH - ! 03-09; - 14-16; SFH ++!! 14-21;
BPH +++!!! 26-31; CAH - - !!! 07-15; ++! 20-22; - - 23-26; JYH ++ 02-04; ++! 26-31; BDM - - - !!! 03-11; - 26-30; TBM - - !!! 05-10

Chapter
13

Conclusion

In the preceding chapters I've explained in detail a number of timing indicators that have good profit potential in today's markets. Naturally, only time will tell whether they will continue to work in the future as they have in the past. Here is a review of the indicators discussed, along with a brief synopsis of each indicator, its assets, liabilities and suggested applications.

Moving Averages

The problem with moving averages is their time lag. Traders continue to struggle with moving averages, falling victim to the many whipsaws so common with this approach. This is also true for other lagging indicators, yet the ability of moving averages to ride major trends is their one redeeming quality. Time-lagged indicators sacrifice accuracy for stability. The use of weighted moving averages can overcome some of the delayed response of moving averages by weighting current price activity more heavily than past price activity. Hence, an important turn in the trend that lasts for more than a few time periods will be weighted more heavily, thereby forcing a turn in the MA indicators.

I suggested several specific moving average combinations in a few of the more active markets. The test results were not heavily optimized and the deduction for slippage and commission in each case represented a very reasonable reflection of market reality. In addition to the use of weighted moving averages, I suggest studying and testing triangular moving averages.

Consecutive Closes

This timing method is clearly a trend-following system; however, it tends to enter much sooner than moving-average-based trend-following systems. Since this method is based on intraday data, a trader can quickly jump on board once a move begins, and quickly exit and/or reverse its position once the trend has changed. This approach has great potential in active markets such as S&P and Crude Oil futures, but should not be used on daily data since the results do not appear promising using the current rules.

Since there is still a time delay built into this indicator by virtue of the fact that it must wait for X number of consecutive higher or lower closes, you may use a more responsive market exit procedure. In other words, once a position has moved in your favor by a predetermined amount or once you have been in a profitable position for more than a certain amount of time, you may follow up the position with a stop loss determined by market behavior—a trailing stop loss that is determined by a very short-term moving average. The use of a stop loss based on parabolic timing may prove useful. In so doing you will not be allowing too much of the open profit to dissipate before you exit. While the CC timing indicators I tested have built-in money management stop losses and trailing stop losses as noted in the explanations, these stop losses are rather wide and may not serve the purpose as well as some other alternatives. I'll leave the development of a hybrid approach to you.

You may also consider using the CC timing indicator in conjunction with the seasonal clusters and indicators I've discussed. By closing successively higher or lower during the time frame of a seasonal market turn, the market is giving indications that it is likely to follow its historically valid seasonal pattern.

The theory underlying the use of consecutive closes as a timing indicator is quite valid since it provides a sensitive way of knowing when a trend had changed. Another idea that deserves testing is to use consecutive closes in the upper portion of the trading range for the given time frame you are using. In other words, test X number of consecutive closes in the upper 25 percent of the hourly trading range as a buy signal or vice versa as a sell signal. This may prove to be a more accurate as well as a more sensitive indicator. An hourly higher close in and of itself is not the only way of knowing that a market is becoming strong. Buying pressure may not be sufficient to result in a higher hourly or half-hourly close, but it may be sufficient to result in consecutive higher closes near the upper portion of the trading range. The reverse would likely hold true for sell signals. This will be my next area of research.

Seasonal Clusters and Timing

This is one of my favorite methods because it is based on an underlying truism of market behavior. No matter which market we study and no matter how many days or years of data we study, the results always indicate the presence of seasonal tendencies. Clearly, these tendencies are a function of many variables above and beyond weather. Seasonality and weather are not synonymous terms in the futures and stock markets. While seasonals alone are not as accurate as we might like, when combined with timing they offer great potential of profits in the futures and stock markets. The statistical validity of seasonals has been amply demonstrated both by Art Merrill and by my extensive studies. No matter how statistically valid they may be, the fact remains that timing is an important adjunct other than perhaps in the case of the most reliable seasonals.

I consider seasonal analysis to be a leading indicator of market activity which, when combined with timing, can result not only in a high degree of accuracy but in consistently profitable trading. While we cannot state categorically that this is the best way or the most profitable way to trade, I do feel that this is one of the better ways to enter positions. But be aware that once a seasonal timing entry has been triggered, the market could easily continue its move above and beyond the ideal time frame for the end of the indicated seasonal move. For example, wheat market seasonals turn higher in early September. The ideal time frame for bullish seasonals in wheat based on the September tendency is for an up move through approximately 24 September. Figure

13.1 shows this tendency in December wheat futures from 1967 through 1990. The indicated seasonal has been accurate over 75 percent of the time with considerably larger profits than losses. Just because the ideal exit date is 24 September, do not assume that the move will end on this date. It could end earlier or much later. For example, in 1991 the market continued to rise until mid-October, well beyond the ideal exit. To have exited the trade exactly on 24 September would have been premature. Naturally, I am using 20/20 hindsight. However, one could adjust to such a possibility by using a timing method to exit the trade rather than to exit blindly at the close of trading on 24 September. A trailing stop loss based on some of the other timing indicators I've discussed could be used. And you could easily exit only part of your position according to the rules (i.e., on the 24th) and ride the balance of your position based on other exit timing.

In closing my comments about seasonality I repeat that this area has not received nearly as much attention as it deserves. This is primarily because most traders do not understand seasonality, nor do most traders know how valid seasonals have been. Perhaps seasonality lacks the sex appeal of highly technical methods, or perhaps seasonality is just one of those areas that has hurt traders who have not used it properly. Regardless of the underlying reason(s) I feel that seasonality has been grossly underrated as a basis of systematic stock and futures trading. Those interested in additional information regarding seasonals are advised to read my book *Seasonal Concepts in Futures Trading* or to write me for information about my Daily, Weekly and Monthly seasonal charts or my Seasonal Trading Software.

On-Balance Volume, Quantum Theory

These are trading techniques rather than trading systems or concise timing indicators. They can be converted into relatively mechanical trading systems, or they can be used as an adjunct to timing. Both have good potential as strategic market tools.

Using Multiple Positions

As you know, the most important aspect of any trading system or method is risk management. The old trader at the Alabama Farm Bureau helped me understand this fact better than any actual market experience previous to this encounter, al-/ though I'm certain that it would have meant nothing without my previous experience. There has always been a tendency for traders to exit winning positions quickly and to exit losing positions slowly. The result is costly; profits are small and losses are large. It's idealistic and academic to say that a trader following a system with discipline and consistency will not ride losses and close out profits. That's fine if you also believe in the tooth fairy. I believe, but I know where the tooth fairy's money comes from. You must manage risk effectively if you are to succeed.

To maximize the results of virtually any approach I've discussed or perhaps any method you may be using (unless it is a reversing or always in the market system), I suggest using the Triple Position Method (TPM) that I've developed through my own market experiences. The TPM allows you to *have your market cake and eat it too.* Here's how it works: You enter the market using a minimum of three units. Any quantity above three is acceptable, although, for ease of use a multiple of three is recommended. Market exit will be as follows:

- If you are using a seasonal method, exit one-third of your position on the ideal seasonal exit date.
- Exit one-third of your position using a specific price target determined by using support and resistance methods.
- Exit one-third of your position using a trailing stop loss procedure.
- If you use this approach with other systems or timing indicators, you will need to exit all positions if the indicators themselves turn bearish before you have had an opportunity to exit positions based on the TPM described above.

This technique may be adapted to other timing signals and systems. The idea is to hold positions as long as possible to take full advantage of a strong trend, but at the same time it allows you to exit positions as profits accrue.

Finally, I urge you to use my methods as a starting point for your own work. Remember that dynamic markets require dynamic methods. However, dynamism does not imply complexity. Keep your methods logical, simple, concise and avoid heavy optimization. Simplicity and effective risk management are the two primary rules for consistent success.

Figure 13.1   Seasonal Tendency in Wheat Futures

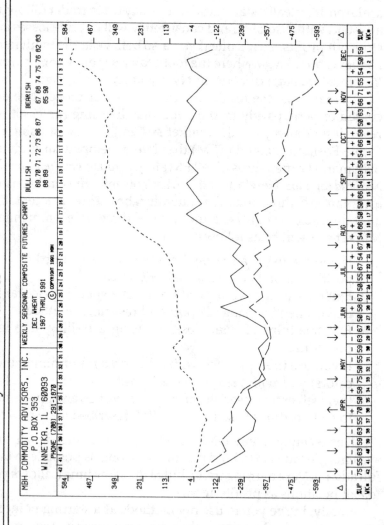

©1991 MBH

Part
4

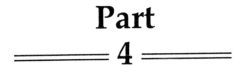

Appendices

Appendix

=== A ===

Signal Computation and Formulae

Stochastic Indicator

1. Assume you want to compute a ten-time-unit SI. Take the highest high and the lowest low of the ten-unit period. Subtract the two.
2. Take the low of the ten units and subtract it from the current close. Divide the difference by the figure arrived at in the first step.
3. The next increment plot is calculated by dropping the oldest data point and recalculating (according to the above steps) using the most recent data as you would do for a moving average. You have now calculated %K.
4. The second line (called %D) is a three-period smoothed moving average of the first figure (%K). This completes the calculation for *fast* stochastic.
5. Slow %K is the Fast %D, and Slow %D is a three-period smoothed moving average of Slow %K.

Simple Moving Average

A simple moving average is calculated as follows:

Simple Moving Average (SMA) = A + B + C ... +N/N

Where A, B, C ... N are the raw data points (i.e., prices), and N = number of data points

To get the next SMA subtract point A and add the next data point. Divide again by N.

Weighted Moving Average

A weighted moving average weights the data points differentially. A WMA may be computed as follows:

WMA = A + B + C(2) + D(3) + E(4) ... / N

Where A-E = data points and N = Total number of data points. Where C-E are weighted by repetition, they are counted as often as used in order to determine N. In other words, since C is used twice, it is counted twice in determining N, D is counted three times and E four times in determining the value for N.

Exponential Moving Average

The formula for computing an exponential moving average is:

EMA= K price(M) + k (1-K) Price(M-1)+

K(1-K) Price(M-2)+ ...

Where K = 2/ (N+1), the smoothing constant
M = today's data
N = Number of days

Consecutive Closes

There is no computation involved in determining the consecutive closes indicator. Simply count the number of consecutive up or down closes for the given time frame and buy or sell according to the rules.

On-Balance Volume

Where Up-close tick or trading volume is assigned a positive value and Down-close tick or trading volume is assigned a negative value

OBV= cumulative total of up and down volumes

Appendix

B

Daily Market Probability Statistics

```
                DAILY MARKET PROBABILITY STATISTICS
                ===================================

File used:      03SF - SWISS FRANC

        Month/    --- % ---   -- Average --   ---------- Years ----------
        Day       Up   Down    Up     Down     Up    Down    Unch    Total
        ======   ==== ====    ====== ======   ====== ====== ====== ======

        DEC 22    45   45     .005  -.004      5     5      1      11
        DEC 23    45   54     .004  -.004      5     6      0      11
        DEC 24    42   57     .005  -.004      3     4      0       7
 +++    DEC 26    80   20     .005  -.003      4     1      0       5
        DEC 27    55   44     .008  -.004      5     4      0       9
        DEC 28    40   50     .009  -.006      4     5      1      10
 ++     DEC 29    72   27     .005  -.001      8     3      0      11
        DEC 30    45   45     .004  -.002      5     5      1      11
 ++     DEC 31    77   22     .008  -.007      7     2      0       9
        JAN  3    50   50     .002  -.015      2     2      0       4
 ---    JAN  4    12   87     .006  -.006      1     7      0       8
 --     JAN  5    27   72     .012  -.011      3     8      0      11
 -      JAN  6    36   63     .004  -.004      4     7      0      11
        JAN  7    50   50     .006  -.006      5     5      0      10
 --     JAN  8    22   77     .007  -.007      2     7      0       9
 -      JAN  9    40   60     .005  -.007      4     6      0      10
        JAN 10    44   55     .004  -.007      4     5      0       9
        JAN 11    50   50     .006  -.010      5     5      0      10
        JAN 12    45   54     .006  -.002      5     6      0      11
 +      JAN 13    63   27     .005  -.006      7     3      1      11
 --     JAN 14    30   70     .011  -.004      3     7      0      10
 ---    JAN 15    11   88     .008  -.010      1     8      0       9
 ++     JAN 16    70   20     .005  -.005      7     2      1      10
 -      JAN 17    33   66     .005  -.005      3     6      0       9
 -      JAN 18    40   60     .006  -.008      4     6      0      10
        JAN 19    45   54     .008  -.005      5     6      0      11
        JAN 20    54   36     .007  -.007      6     4      1      11
 ---    JAN 21    10   80     .003  -.004      1     8      1      10
        JAN 22    33   55     .007  -.003      3     5      1       9
 -      JAN 23    40   60     .006  -.004      4     6      0      10
        JAN 24    55   44     .007  -.008      5     4      0       9
        JAN 25    40   50     .006  -.006      4     5      1      10
 --     JAN 26    27   72     .005  -.005      3     8      0      11
 -      JAN 27    36   63     .005  -.004      4     7      0      11
 +++    JAN 28    80   20     .003  -.005      8     2      0      10
        JAN 29    33   55     .004  -.007      3     5      1       9
 --     JAN 30    30   70     .003  -.008      3     7      0      10
 --     JAN 31    22   77     .008  -.008      2     7      0       9
 -      FEB  1    30   60     .004  -.010      3     6      1      10
 +      FEB  2    63   27     .008  -.004      7     3      1      11
 -      FEB  3    36   63     .003  -.003      4     7      0      11
 --     FEB  4    30   70     .005  -.003      3     7      0      10
        FEB  5    55   44     .006  -.010      5     4      0       9
        FEB  6    50   50     .005  -.007      5     5      0      10
        FEB  7    44   55     .008  -.005      4     5      0       9
```

DAILY MARKET PROBABILITY STATISTICS
==

File used: 06SF - SWISS FRANC

Month/ Day	--- % --- Up	Down	-- Average -- Up	Down	---------- Years ---------- Up	Down	Unch	Total
- MAR 25	33	66	.006	-.005	4	8	0	12
MAR 26	41	58	.006	-.006	5	7	0	12
MAR 27	50	41	.010	-.011	6	5	1	12
++ MAR 28	72	27	.006	-.003	8	3	0	11
MAR 29	41	58	.005	-.003	5	7	0	12
MAR 30	50	50	.007	-.002	6	6	0	12
MAR 31	41	58	.004	-.006	5	7	0	12
- APR 1	40	60	.006	-.009	4	6	0	10
- APR 2	33	66	.004	-.007	4	8	0	12
APR 3	33	58	.004	-.008	4	7	1	12
APR 4	58	41	.004	-.006	7	5	0	12
APR 5	50	40	.006	-.009	5	4	1	10
- APR 6	36	63	.002	-.005	4	7	0	11
APR 7	50	50	.005	-.006	6	6	0	12
APR 8	54	45	.012	-.007	6	5	0	11
APR 9	54	45	.008	-.008	6	5	0	11
++ APR 10	75	25	.009	-.007	9	3	0	12
APR 11	46	46	.007	-.004	6	6	1	13
APR 12	36	54	.004	-.004	4	6	1	11
APR 13	45	54	.005	-.004	5	6	0	11
- APR 14	33	66	.012	-.003	4	8	0	12
APR 15	50	50	.005	-.007	6	6	0	12
+ APR 16	63	36	.009	-.002	7	4	0	11
+ APR 17	60	40	.005	-.006	6	4	0	10
APR 18	53	46	.009	-.006	7	6	0	13
-- APR 19	25	75	.003	-.005	3	9	0	12
+ APR 20	60	40	.004	-.005	6	4	0	10
- APR 21	33	66	.004	-.003	4	8	0	12
APR 22	50	50	.004	-.006	6	6	0	12
APR 23	58	41	.008	-.007	7	5	0	12
- APR 24	33	66	.004	-.005	4	8	0	12
- APR 25	30	69	.007	-.005	4	9	0	13
APR 26	50	41	.004	-.005	6	5	1	12
APR 27	50	41	.004	-.004	6	5	1	12
APR 28	50	50	.004	-.005	6	6	0	12
APR 29	58	41	.007	-.007	7	5	0	12
--- APR 30	16	83	.003	-.004	2	10	0	12
MAY 1	41	50	.003	-.006	5	6	1	12
- MAY 2	23	69	.004	-.007	3	9	1	13
MAY 3	50	50	.004	-.005	6	6	0	12
MAY 4	58	41	.004	-.006	7	5	0	12
MAY 5	50	50	.008	-.005	6	6	0	12
++ MAY 6	75	25	.007	-.003	9	3	0	12
MAY 7	50	50	.011	-.006	6	6	0	12
MAY 8	41	58	.006	-.006	5	7	0	12

DAILY MARKET PROBABILITY STATISTICS
======================================

File used: 09SF - SWISS FRANC

	Month/ Day	% Up	% Down	Average Up	Average Down	Years Up	Years Down	Years Unch	Years Total
	JUN 22	50	50	.004	-.007	5	5	0	10
	JUN 23	54	45	.007	-.002	6	5	0	11
++	JUN 24	72	27	.004	-.012	8	3	0	11
--	JUN 25	30	70	.003	-.005	3	7	0	10
	JUN 26	55	44	.008	-.006	5	4	0	9
	JUN 27	40	50	.007	-.005	4	5	1	10
++	JUN 28	77	22	.003	-.004	7	2	0	9
-	JUN 29	40	60	.007	-.003	4	6	0	10
	JUN 30	54	45	.004	-.004	6	5	0	11
	JUL 1	36	45	.004	-.006	4	5	2	11
+	JUL 2	60	40	.001	-.008	6	4	0	10
+++	JUL 3	85	14	.006	-.011	6	1	0	7
	JUL 5	42	57	.010	-.006	3	4	0	7
---	JUL 6	20	80	.002	-.007	2	8	0	10
-	JUL 7	36	63	.006	-.005	4	7	0	11
	JUL 8	54	45	.004	-.006	6	5	0	11
+	JUL 9	60	30	.007	-.003	6	3	1	10
-	JUL 10	33	66	.009	-.003	3	6	0	9
-	JUL 11	40	60	.004	-.005	4	6	0	10
	JUL 12	55	44	.006	-.004	5	4	0	9
-	JUL 13	40	60	.004	-.003	4	6	0	10
--	JUL 14	30	70	.005	-.003	3	7	0	10
-	JUL 15	27	63	.012	-.005	3	7	1	11
+++	JUL 16	80	20	.008	-.006	8	2	0	10
---	JUL 17	11	88	.021	-.007	1	8	0	9
+	JUL 18	60	40	.006	-.009	6	4	0	10
	JUL 19	44	55	.007	-.004	4	5	0	9
+	JUL 20	60	30	.005	-.006	6	3	1	10
+	JUL 21	63	27	.005	-.004	7	3	1	11
	JUL 22	54	45	.004	-.005	6	5	0	11
	JUL 23	50	50	.005	-.004	5	5	0	10
	JUL 24	55	44	.003	-.003	5	4	0	9
-	JUL 25	30	60	.007	-.005	3	6	1	10
-	JUL 26	33	66	.007	-.005	3	6	0	9
-	JUL 27	40	60	.003	-.004	4	6	0	10
	JUL 28	45	54	.008	-.012	5	6	0	11
-	JUL 29	18	63	.003	-.006	2	7	2	11
+	JUL 30	60	40	.002	-.010	6	4	0	10
	JUL 31	55	44	.009	-.006	5	4	0	9
	AUG 1	50	50	.004	-.005	5	5	0	10
+	AUG 2	66	33	.009	-.003	6	3	0	9
---	AUG 3	20	80	.008	-.006	2	8	0	10
	AUG 4	45	54	.007	-.006	5	6	0	11
	AUG 5	45	54	.006	-.006	5	6	0	11
---	AUG 6	20	80	.006	-.008	2	8	0	10

DAILY MARKET PROBABILITY STATISTICS
===================================

File used: 03TB - TREASURY BILLS

Month/ Day	--- % --- Up	Down	-- Average -- Up	Down	---------- Years ---------- Up	Down	Unch	Total
DEC 22	40	40	.002	-.001	4	4	2	10
+ DEC 23	60	20	.002	-.003	6	2	2	10
+++ DEC 24	83	16	.002	.000	5	1	0	6
DEC 26	20	40	.001	-.002	1	2	2	5
DEC 27	55	33	.001	-.001	5	3	1	9
--- DEC 28	0	90	.000	-.001	0	9	1	10
DEC 29	50	50	.000	-.001	5	5	0	10
+ DEC 30	60	30	.001	-.001	6	3	1	10
+ DEC 31	62	37	.002	-.002	5	3	0	8
++ JAN 3	75	25	.001	.000	3	1	0	4
JAN 4	37	50	.001	-.001	3	4	1	8
JAN 5	50	50	.002	-.001	5	5	0	10
JAN 6	30	40	.000	-.001	3	4	3	10
+++ JAN 7	80	20	.001	-.005	8	2	0	10
JAN 8	44	44	.002	-.002	4	4	1	9
JAN 9	30	50	.001	-.002	3	5	2	10
JAN 10	44	44	.001	-.001	4	4	1	9
- JAN 11	20	60	.001	-.002	2	6	2	10
JAN 12	45	54	.001	.000	5	6	0	11
++ JAN 13	72	27	.001	-.001	8	3	0	11
JAN 14	50	40	.001	-.001	5	4	1	10
JAN 15	55	33	.001	-.002	5	3	1	9
+ JAN 16	60	30	.001	.000	6	3	1	10
JAN 17	44	44	.000	-.001	4	4	1	9
JAN 18	50	50	.001	-.001	5	5	0	10
JAN 19	54	45	.001	-.002	6	5	0	11
--- JAN 20	18	81	.003	-.001	2	9	0	11
- JAN 21	30	60	.001	-.002	3	6	1	10
JAN 22	55	44	.001	-.002	5	4	0	9
++ JAN 23	70	20	.001	-.001	7	2	1	10
JAN 24	33	44	.000	-.002	3	4	2	9
JAN 25	40	50	.001	-.001	4	5	1	10
JAN 26	45	54	.002	-.001	5	6	0	11
JAN 27	54	27	.001	-.001	6	3	2	11
++ JAN 28	70	30	.002	-.001	7	3	0	10
JAN 29	33	55	.001	-.001	3	5	1	9
JAN 30	40	40	.003	-.001	4	4	2	10
JAN 31	33	33	.001	-.001	3	3	3	9
-- FEB 1	20	70	.001	-.002	2	7	1	10
FEB 2	27	54	.001	-.001	3	6	2	11
-- FEB 3	18	72	.000	-.001	2	8	1	11
++ FEB 4	70	30	.002	-.001	7	3	0	10
FEB 5	44	44	.001	-.001	4	4	1	9
--- FEB 6	10	90	.003	-.001	1	9	0	10
FEB 7	55	33	.000	-.001	5	3	1	9

```
              DAILY MARKET PROBABILITY STATISTICS
              =====================================

File used:    09TB - TREASURY BILLS

      Month/   --- % ---   -- Average --   ---------- Years ----------
      Day      Up   Down    Up     Down      Up     Down    Unch    Total
      ======   ==== ====   ====== ======   ====== ====== ====== ======

      JUN 22   50   30     .001   -.001      5      3      2      10
      JUN 23   40   50     .001   -.002      4      5      1      10
  -   JUN 24   40   60     .001   -.002      4      6      0      10
      JUN 25   55   44     .002   -.001      5      4      0       9
      JUN 26   50   37     .001   -.001      4      3      1       8
      JUN 27   44   33     .001   -.001      4      3      2       9
  +   JUN 28   66   33     .001   -.001      6      3      0       9
      JUN 29   50   40     .001   -.001      5      4      1      10
  +   JUN 30   60   30     .001   -.002      6      3      1      10
      JUL  1   50   50     .001   -.002      5      5      0      10
  +   JUL  2   66   33     .001   -.001      6      3      0       9
+++   JUL  3   83   16     .001   -.001      5      1      0       6
 --   JUL  5   14   71     .004   -.001      1      5      1       7
+++   JUL  6   80   10     .001    .000      8      1      1      10
---   JUL  7   10   80     .003   -.002      1      8      1      10
  -   JUL  8   30   60     .004   -.001      3      6      1      10
      JUL  9   44   55     .002   -.001      4      5      0       9
      JUL 10   37   50     .002   -.001      3      4      1       8
      JUL 11   55   44     .001   -.002      5      4      0       9
      JUL 12   55   22     .001   -.001      5      2      2       9
  -   JUL 13   30   60     .001   -.001      3      6      1      10
      JUL 14   55   44     .000   -.001      5      4      0       9
 ++   JUL 15   70   30     .002   -.001      7      3      0      10
      JUL 16   44   55     .003   -.002      4      5      0       9
 ++   JUL 17   75   25     .001   -.001      6      2      0       8
      JUL 18   33   55     .001   -.001      3      5      1       9
 ++   JUL 19   77   22     .000    .000      7      2      0       9
  -   JUL 20   40   60     .001   -.002      4      6      0      10
      JUL 21   50   50     .000   -.002      5      5      0      10
 --   JUL 22   30   70     .002   -.001      3      7      0      10
      JUL 23   55   33     .001   -.001      5      3      1       9
  -   JUL 24   25   62     .002   -.001      2      5      1       8
 ++   JUL 25   77   11     .001    .000      7      1      1       9
      JUL 26   33   44     .000   -.001      3      4      2       9
  -   JUL 27   30   60     .001   -.001      3      6      1      10
---   JUL 28   20   80     .001   -.001      2      8      0      10
      JUL 29   50   30     .001   -.001      5      3      2      10
      JUL 30   55   44     .001   -.001      5      4      0       9
      JUL 31   50   50     .001   -.001      4      4      0       8
      AUG  1   44   55     .000   -.001      4      5      0       9
  +   AUG  2   66   33     .002   -.001      6      3      0       9
  -   AUG  3   40   60     .001   -.002      4      6      0      10
+++   AUG  4   80   20     .001   -.001      8      2      0      10
  -   AUG  5   30   60     .001   -.001      3      6      1      10
      AUG  6   44   44     .001   -.001      4      4      1       9
```

DAILY MARKET PROBABILITY STATISTICS
=====================================

File used: 12TB - TREASURY BILLS

Month/ Day	--- % --- Up	Down	-- Average -- Up	Down	---------- Years ---------- Up	Down	Unch	Total
- SEP 22	30	60	.001	-.003	3	6	1	10
- SEP 23	40	60	.001	.000	4	6	0	10
SEP 24	44	55	.001	-.001	4	5	0	9
SEP 25	50	50	.001	-.003	4	4	0	8
- SEP 26	33	66	.001	-.002	3	6	0	9
SEP 27	55	44	.001	-.001	5	4	0	9
SEP 28	50	50	.002	-.001	5	5	0	10
- SEP 29	30	60	.001	-.002	3	6	1	10
++ SEP 30	70	30	.001	-.002	7	3	0	10
OCT 1	44	44	.001	-.001	4	4	1	9
OCT 2	50	50	.002	-.001	4	4	0	8
+ OCT 3	66	33	.002	-.001	6	3	0	9
OCT 4	44	55	.000	-.002	4	5	0	9
-- OCT 5	30	70	.002	-.001	3	7	0	10
OCT 6	40	40	.003	.000	4	4	2	10
OCT 7	50	50	.002	-.001	5	5	0	10
OCT 8	33	55	.001	-.002	3	5	1	9
OCT 9	37	50	.003	-.002	3	4	1	8
- OCT 10	22	66	.001	-.001	2	6	1	9
+ OCT 11	66	33	.002	-.001	6	3	0	9
+ OCT 12	60	30	.001	-.001	6	3	1	10
- OCT 13	40	60	.001	-.001	4	6	0	10
OCT 14	50	30	.001	-.002	5	3	2	10
OCT 15	44	55	.001	-.002	4	5	0	9
OCT 16	37	50	.001	-.002	3	4	1	8
OCT 17	44	55	.001	-.001	4	5	0	9
OCT 18	55	33	.001	-.002	5	3	1	9
OCT 19	50	50	.002	-.002	5	5	0	10
- OCT 20	30	60	.005	-.001	3	6	1	10
OCT 21	40	50	.001	-.001	4	5	1	10
OCT 22	55	44	.001	-.003	5	4	0	9
OCT 23	50	50	.002	-.001	4	4	0	8
OCT 24	55	44	.002	-.001	5	4	0	9
OCT 25	44	55	.001	-.001	4	5	0	9
++ OCT 26	70	30	.002	-.002	7	3	0	10
OCT 27	50	40	.000	-.003	5	4	1	10
OCT 28	50	50	.001	-.001	5	5	0	10
++ OCT 29	77	22	.001	-.001	7	2	0	9
+ OCT 30	62	37	.002	-.002	5	3	0	8
OCT 31	33	55	.000	-.002	3	5	1	9
+ NOV 1	66	11	.002	-.003	6	1	2	9
- NOV 2	33	66	.001	-.001	3	6	0	9
NOV 3	30	40	.002	-.001	3	4	3	10
NOV 4	44	44	.001	-.001	4	4	1	9
- NOV 5	33	66	.002	-.001	3	6	0	9

```
              DAILY MARKET PROBABILITY STATISTICS
              ========================================

File used:    050J - ORANGE JUICE

    Month/   --- % ---   -- Average --   ---------- Years ----------
    Day      Up   Down    Up     Down      Up     Down    Uncn    Total
    ======   ==== ====   ====== ======   ====== ====== ====== ======

    FEB 24   52   47    .008   -.012      9       8      0      17
--  FEB 25   25   75    .016   -.008      4      12      0      16
 -  FEB 26   31   62    .009   -.015      5      10      1      16
    FEB 27   52   41    .006   -.014      9       7      1      17
    FEB 28   43   50    .012   -.010      7       8      1      16
 -  FEB 29   40   60    .024   -.008      2       3      0       5
    MAR  1   50   50    .009   -.004      8       8      0      16
 +  MAR  2   62   37    .014   -.016     10       6      0      16
    MAR  3   58   41    .013   -.011     10       7      0      17
    MAR  4   50   50    .013   -.013      8       8      0      16
 -  MAR  5   31   68    .017   -.010      5      11      0      16
    MAR  6   58   41    .010   -.022     10       7      0      17
    MAR  7   41   47    .018   -.009      7       8      2      17
    MAR  8   56   43    .008   -.009      9       7      0      16
    MAR  9   43   56    .014   -.013      7       9      0      16
    MAR 10   47   52    .016   -.014      8       9      0      17
    MAR 11   50   50    .013   -.019      8       8      0      16
    MAR 12   56   43    .010   -.016      9       7      0      16
--  MAR 13   23   76    .008   -.010      4      13      0      17
--  MAR 14   17   76    .002   -.006      3      13      1      17
    MAR 15   56   37    .008   -.014      9       6      1      16
 +  MAR 16   68   31    .010   -.016     11       5      0      16
    MAR 17   52   47    .008   -.016      9       8      0      17
    MAR 18   50   50    .014   -.012      8       8      0      16
 -  MAR 19   31   62    .009   -.013      5      10      1      16
    MAR 20   47   47    .010   -.011      8       8      1      17
    MAR 21   52   47    .020   -.011      9       8      0      17
 -  MAR 22   37   62    .009   -.014      6      10      0      16
    MAR 23   50   43    .013   -.007      8       7      1      16
    MAR 24   57   42    .012   -.015      8       6      0      14
    MAR 25   56   43    .015   -.006      9       7      0      16
 -  MAR 26   37   62    .022   -.010      6      10      0      16
    MAR 27   37   56    .010   -.012      6       9      1      16
    MAR 28   53   40    .013   -.011      8       6      1      15
++  MAR 29   75   25    .008   -.007     12       4      0      16
 +  MAR 30   62   31    .021   -.010     10       5      1      16
 +  MAR 31   60   40    .013   -.015      9       6      0      15
--  APR  1   28   71    .010   -.012      4      10      0      14
++  APR  2   75   25    .012   -.010     12       4      0      16
    APR  3   58   41    .018   -.011     10       7      0      17
    APR  4   53   46    .008   -.012      8       7      0      15
    APR  5   46   53    .009   -.004      7       8      0      15
    APR  6   43   56    .014   -.010      7       9      0      16
    APR  7   35   58    .005   -.012      6      10      1      17
 +  APR  8   66   33    .005   -.010     10       5      0      15
```

DAILY MARKET PROBABILITY STATISTICS
=======================================

File used: 07OJ - ORANGE JUICE

Month/	--- % ---		-- Average --		---------- Years ----------			
Day	Up	Down	Up	Down	Up	Down	Unch	Total
APR 23	50	50	.010	-.011	8	8	0	16
APR 24	52	47	.009	-.008	9	8	0	17
+ APR 25	64	23	.007	-.005	11	4	2	17
APR 26	56	43	.011	-.009	9	7	0	16
APR 27	43	50	.011	-.007	7	8	1	16
APR 28	41	52	.012	-.007	7	9	1	17
APR 29	43	56	.006	-.013	7	9	0	16
APR 30	50	43	.012	-.010	8	7	1	16
MAY 1	47	52	.012	-.008	8	9	0	17
MAY 2	52	41	.008	-.007	9	7	1	17
+ MAY 3	68	31	.010	-.007	11	5	0	16
MAY 4	43	43	.016	-.008	7	7	2	16
MAY 5	47	47	.006	-.009	8	8	1	17
MAY 6	43	56	.008	-.007	7	9	0	16
+ MAY 7	62	37	.010	-.003	10	6	0	16
MAY 8	52	41	.011	-.008	9	7	1	17
- MAY 9	35	64	.005	-.008	6	11	0	17
- MAY 10	37	62	.013	-.006	6	10	0	16
+ MAY 11	68	31	.015	-.016	11	5	0	16
- MAY 12	29	64	.013	-.016	5	11	1	17
MAY 13	56	43	.013	-.013	9	7	0	16
++ MAY 14	75	25	.009	-.010	12	4	0	16
MAY 15	41	58	.008	-.015	7	10	0	17
- MAY 16	35	64	.008	-.010	6	11	0	17
MAY 17	43	56	.016	-.017	7	9	0	16
MAY 18	50	43	.010	-.007	8	7	1	16
+ MAY 19	64	35	.009	-.012	11	6	0	17
MAY 20	50	43	.016	-.015	8	7	1	16
MAY 21	56	37	.006	-.008	9	6	1	16
+ MAY 22	64	35	.012	-.019	11	6	0	17
MAY 23	58	41	.005	-.011	10	7	0	17
MAY 24	43	56	.008	-.009	7	9	0	16
MAY 25	57	42	.010	-.014	8	6	0	14
++ MAY 26	71	28	.006	-.017	10	4	0	14
MAY 27	50	35	.016	-.002	7	5	2	14
MAY 28	53	46	.009	-.008	7	6	0	13
MAY 29	53	38	.009	-.004	7	5	1	13
MAY 30	45	36	.004	-.007	5	4	2	11
MAY 31	50	50	.017	-.013	6	6	0	12
JUN 1	43	56	.010	-.021	7	9	0	16
+ JUN 2	64	23	.013	-.012	11	4	2	17
+ JUN 3	68	31	.010	-.009	11	5	0	16
JUN 4	56	37	.006	-.015	9	6	1	16
- JUN 5	23	64	.011	-.010	4	11	2	17
JUN 6	47	52	.013	-.016	8	9	0	17

DAILY MARKET PROBABILITY STATISTICS
=====================================

File used: 110J - ORANGE JUICE

	Month/ Day	--- % --- Up	 Down	-- Average -- Up	 Down	---------- Years ---------- Up	 Down	 Unch	 Total
	AUG 23	46	53	.009	-.009	7	8	0	15
	AUG 24	50	50	.006	-.011	7	7	0	14
++	AUG 25	75	25	.009	-.006	12	4	0	16
-	AUG 26	37	62	.006	-.008	6	10	0	16
	AUG 27	43	56	.007	-.009	7	9	0	16
+	AUG 28	68	25	.010	-.009	11	4	1	16
	AUG 29	43	43	.012	-.008	7	7	2	16
	AUG 30	46	53	.012	-.005	7	8	0	15
+	AUG 31	60	33	.007	-.010	9	5	1	15
	SEP 1	58	41	.012	-.009	7	5	0	12
	SEP 2	38	53	.014	-.009	5	7	1	13
+	SEP 3	61	30	.010	-.013	8	4	1	13
	SEP 4	46	46	.008	-.014	6	6	1	13
+++	SEP 5	84	7	.009	-.004	11	1	1	13
	SEP 6	58	41	.010	-.005	7	5	0	12
	SEP 7	50	50	.004	-.013	6	6	0	12
+++	SEP 8	81	12	.004	-.011	13	2	1	16
+	SEP 9	62	25	.011	-.012	10	4	2	16
	SEP 10	50	37	.014	-.007	8	6	2	16
	SEP 11	56	43	.010	-.014	9	7	0	16
	SEP 12	37	56	.013	-.009	6	9	1	16
	SEP 13	40	53	.012	-.011	6	8	1	15
---	SEP 14	20	80	.004	-.008	3	12	0	15
-	SEP 15	31	68	.008	-.005	5	11	0	16
	SEP 16	50	50	.007	-.007	8	8	0	16
+	SEP 17	62	37	.009	-.009	10	6	0	16
+	SEP 18	68	31	.009	-.009	11	5	0	16
	SEP 19	56	37	.009	-.013	9	6	1	16
	SEP 20	40	53	.012	-.014	6	8	1	15
++	SEP 21	73	20	.014	-.010	11	3	1	15
+	SEP 22	68	18	.012	-.017	11	3	2	16
+	SEP 23	62	37	.008	-.013	10	6	0	16
	SEP 24	50	50	.008	-.008	8	8	0	16
	SEP 25	43	56	.012	-.010	7	9	0	16
+	SEP 26	68	25	.010	-.006	11	4	1	16
	SEP 27	42	42	.013	-.017	6	6	2	14
+	SEP 28	60	40	.008	-.008	9	6	0	15
	SEP 29	56	43	.005	-.005	9	7	0	16
+	SEP 30	62	31	.018	-.009	10	5	1	16
	OCT 1	50	50	.010	-.010	8	8	0	16
+	OCT 2	68	31	.010	-.013	11	5	0	16
	OCT 3	37	56	.011	-.006	6	9	1	16
	OCT 4	53	26	.004	-.009	8	4	3	15
+	OCT 5	60	40	.012	-.006	9	6	0	15
	OCT 6	50	37	.011	-.012	8	6	2	16

DAILY MARKET PROBABILITY STATISTICS

File used: 02PB - PORK BELLIES

Month/ Day	--- % --- Up	Down	-- Average -- Up	Down	---------- Years ---------- Up	Down	Unch	Total
+ NOV 22	61	38	.019	-.012	8	5	0	13
- NOV 23	38	61	.010	-.015	5	8	0	13
NOV 24	45	54	.008	-.012	5	6	0	11
--- NOV 25	15	84	.012	-.016	2	11	0	13
- NOV 26	30	69	.022	-.020	4	9	0	13
NOV 27	58	41	.015	-.011	7	5	0	12
NOV 28	42	57	.018	-.016	6	8	0	14
NOV 29	56	43	.011	-.013	9	7	0	16
- NOV 30	37	62	.022	-.014	6	10	0	16
+ DEC 1	64	35	.010	-.008	11	6	0	17
DEC 2	41	58	.020	-.017	7	10	0	17
- DEC 3	31	68	.015	-.021	5	11	0	16
DEC 4	50	50	.016	-.015	8	8	0	16
DEC 5	47	52	.016	-.012	8	9	0	17
DEC 6	56	43	.013	-.022	9	7	0	16
- DEC 7	37	62	.011	-.018	6	10	0	16
-- DEC 8	29	70	.012	-.017	5	12	0	17
DEC 9	58	41	.017	-.019	10	7	0	17
+ DEC 10	62	37	.011	-.023	10	6	0	16
DEC 11	56	43	.012	-.015	9	7	0	16
DEC 12	47	52	.018	-.017	8	9	0	17
- DEC 13	31	68	.012	-.008	5	11	0	16
++ DEC 14	75	25	.013	-.012	12	4	0	16
DEC 15	47	52	.015	-.019	8	9	0	17
DEC 16	52	47	.017	-.017	9	8	0	17
DEC 17	56	37	.020	-.014	9	6	1	16
- DEC 18	31	68	.010	-.019	5	11	0	16
DEC 19	47	52	.015	-.017	8	9	0	17
- DEC 20	31	68	.008	-.009	5	11	0	16
DEC 21	50	50	.012	-.009	8	8	0	16
+ DEC 22	64	35	.014	-.020	11	6	0	17
DEC 23	47	52	.020	-.014	8	9	0	17
+ DEC 24	63	36	.023	-.027	7	4	0	11
-- DEC 26	30	70	.017	-.017	3	7	0	10
DEC 27	43	56	.022	-.013	7	9	0	16
DEC 28	46	53	.017	-.016	7	8	0	15
DEC 29	41	58	.008	-.014	7	10	0	17
DEC 30	52	47	.018	-.016	9	8	0	17
DEC 31	42	57	.014	-.008	6	8	0	14
JAN 3	55	44	.014	-.023	5	4	0	9
+++ JAN 4	84	15	.014	-.010	11	2	0	13
++ JAN 5	75	12	.015	-.016	12	2	2	16
++ JAN 6	70	29	.019	-.012	12	5	0	17

DAILY MARKET PROBABILITY STATISTICS
==================================

File used: 05PB - PORK BELLIES

Month/	--- % ---		-- Average --		---------- Years ----------			
Day	Up	Down	Up	Down	Up	Down	Uncn	Total
======	====	====	======	======	======	======	======	======
-- FEB 24	29	70	.012	-.019	5	12	0	17
FEB 25	50	50	.014	-.020	8	8	0	16
FEB 26	43	56	.012	-.018	7	9	0	16
FEB 27	41	52	.018	-.019	7	9	1	17
FEB 28	50	50	.007	-.020	8	8	0	16
+ FEB 29	60	40	.012	-.011	3	2	0	5
+ MAR 1	62	37	.018	-.012	10	6	0	16
MAR 2	50	50	.020	-.012	8	8	0	16
MAR 3	52	35	.019	-.024	9	6	2	17
MAR 4	56	43	.011	-.016	9	7	0	16
MAR 5	56	43	.009	-.010	9	7	0	16
+ MAR 6	64	29	.018	-.018	11	5	1	17
MAR 7	58	41	.016	-.011	10	7	0	17
MAR 8	56	43	.016	-.014	9	7	0	16
MAR 9	43	56	.014	-.015	7	9	0	16
+ MAR 10	64	35	.015	-.022	11	6	0	17
MAR 11	56	43	.012	-.017	9	7	0	16
- MAR 12	37	62	.018	-.013	6	10	0	16
MAR 13	41	58	.017	-.014	7	10	0	17
MAR 14	52	47	.011	-.012	9	8	0	17
+ MAR 15	62	31	.021	-.021	10	5	1	16
- MAR 16	37	62	.016	-.014	6	10	0	16
MAR 17	58	41	.018	-.010	10	7	0	17
MAR 18	56	37	.022	-.017	9	6	1	16
+ MAR 19	62	31	.015	-.013	10	5	1	16
MAR 20	52	47	.015	-.016	9	8	0	17
+ MAR 21	64	29	.014	-.018	11	5	1	17
+ MAR 22	68	31	.018	-.022	11	5	0	16
- MAR 23	37	62	.019	-.022	6	10	0	16
- MAR 24	35	64	.022	-.021	5	9	0	14
MAR 25	43	56	.014	-.019	7	9	0	16
- MAR 26	37	62	.026	-.014	6	10	0	16
MAR 27	56	43	.021	-.020	9	7	0	16
- MAR 28	33	66	.015	-.016	5	10	0	15
MAR 29	43	56	.012	-.015	7	9	0	16
- MAR 30	31	62	.019	-.015	5	10	1	16
MAR 31	53	46	.019	-.012	8	7	0	15
-- APR 1	28	71	.012	-.021	4	10	0	14
+ APR 2	62	37	.012	-.018	10	6	0	16
-- APR 3	29	70	.023	-.022	5	12	0	17
APR 4	53	46	.010	-.021	8	7	0	15
APR 5	53	46	.019	-.009	8	7	0	15
APR 6	56	43	.013	-.013	9	7	0	16
APR 7	47	52	.019	-.013	8	9	0	17
++ APR 8	73	26	.016	-.022	11	4	0	15

```
            DAILY MARKET PROBABILITY STATISTICS
            ===================================

File used:  07PB - PORK BELLIES

  Month/    --- % ---    -- Average --    ---------- Years ----------
   Day      Up  Down     Up     Down      Up     Down    Unch    Total
  ======    ==== ====   ====== ======    ====== ====== ====== ======

   APR 23    50   50     .018  -.017      8      8       0      16
   APR 24    58   41     .017  -.016     10      7       0      17
   APR 25    52   47     .016  -.014      9      8       0      17
   APR 26    50   50     .014  -.012      8      8       0      16
   APR 27    50   50     .018  -.012      8      8       0      16
   APR 28    47   52     .013  -.023      8      9       0      17
   APR 29    50   50     .016  -.020      8      8       0      16
   APR 30    50   50     .016  -.015      8      8       0      16
   MAY  1    41   58     .009  -.012      7     10       0      17
   MAY  2    58   41     .016  -.014     10      7       0      17
 - MAY  3    37   62     .008  -.020      6     10       0      16
   MAY  4    56   43     .008  -.013      9      7       0      16
   MAY  5    47   47     .024  -.012      8      8       1      17
   MAY  6    43   56     .012  -.017      7      9       0      16
   MAY  7    43   50     .019  -.019      7      8       1      16
   MAY  8    47   52     .019  -.016      8      9       0      17
   MAY  9    58   41     .019  -.013     10      7       0      17
   MAY 10    50   50     .018  -.011      8      8       0      16
   MAY 11    37   56     .023  -.020      6      9       1      16
   MAY 12    52   47     .020  -.016      9      8       0      17
 - MAY 13    37   62     .015  -.020      6     10       0      16
   MAY 14    43   50     .010  -.025      7      8       1      16
   MAY 15    58   41     .015  -.028     10      7       0      17
   MAY 16    41   58     .021  -.022      7     10       0      17
-- MAY 17    29   70     .030  -.021      5     12       0      17
   MAY 18    52   47     .017  -.021      9      8       0      17
   MAY 19    50   50     .020  -.012      9      9       0      18
   MAY 20    41   58     .013  -.024      7     10       0      17
 + MAY 21    62   37     .014  -.015     10      6       0      16
   MAY 22    58   41     .014  -.017     10      7       0      17
   MAY 23    50   50     .019  -.012      9      9       0      18
---MAY 24    17   82     .013  -.017      3     14       0      17
-- MAY 25    26   73     .013  -.016      4     11       0      15
 + MAY 26    66   33     .021  -.023     10      5       0      15
 + MAY 27    66   33     .018  -.010     10      5       0      15
 - MAY 28    30   69     .021  -.018      4      9       0      13
 - MAY 29    38   61     .014  -.015      5      8       0      13
   MAY 30    54   45     .016  -.020      6      5       0      11
   MAY 31    57   42     .019  -.027      8      6       0      14
   JUN  1    52   47     .020  -.023      9      8       0      17
 - JUN  2    33   66     .015  -.020      6     12       0      18
   JUN  3    58   41     .014  -.022     10      7       0      17
   JUN  4    50   43     .015  -.018      8      7       1      16
   JUN  5    47   52     .025  -.019      8      9       0      17
 - JUN  6    38   61     .012  -.027      7     11       0      18
```

DAILY MARKET PROBABILITY STATISTICS
================================

File used: 06LH - LIVE HOGS

| Month/ | --- % --- | | -- Average -- | | ---------- Years ---------- | | | |
Day	Up	Down	Up	Down	Up	Down	Unch	Total
MAR 25	50	43	.010	-.014	8	7	1	16
MAR 26	50	50	.020	-.016	8	8	0	16
MAR 27	56	43	.009	-.019	9	7	0	16
MAR 28	53	46	.007	-.016	8	7	0	15
MAR 29	50	43	.009	-.011	8	7	1	16
MAR 30	43	56	.010	-.010	7	9	0	16
+ MAR 31	60	33	.010	-.016	9	5	1	15
APR 1	50	50	.010	-.014	7	7	0	14
APR 2	37	50	.014	-.011	6	8	2	16
APR 3	41	52	.015	-.017	7	9	1	17
+ APR 4	60	40	.011	-.013	9	6	0	15
+++ APR 5	80	13	.014	-.008	12	2	1	15
APR 6	56	37	.011	-.007	9	6	1	16
APR 7	52	47	.018	-.006	9	8	0	17
+ APR 8	60	33	.015	-.013	9	5	1	15
+++ APR 9	84	15	.017	-.014	11	2	0	13
APR 10	52	47	.009	-.017	9	8	0	17
APR 11	41	52	.014	-.008	7	9	1	17
APR 12	50	50	.009	-.010	7	7	0	14
- APR 13	40	60	.011	-.008	6	9	0	15
-- APR 14	23	70	.006	-.010	4	12	1	17
APR 15	50	50	.008	-.009	8	8	0	16
+ APR 16	66	33	.011	-.010	10	5	0	15
+ APR 17	60	40	.012	-.015	9	6	0	15
APR 18	41	58	.010	-.006	7	10	0	17
APR 19	50	43	.007	-.009	8	7	1	16
APR 20	50	50	.008	-.009	7	7	0	14
APR 21	41	58	.017	-.007	7	10	0	17
- APR 22	37	62	.010	-.012	6	10	0	16
APR 23	43	50	.009	-.012	7	8	1	16
++ APR 24	70	29	.008	-.013	12	5	0	17
APR 25	52	47	.014	-.008	9	8	0	17
APR 26	37	50	.007	-.007	6	8	2	16
APR 27	50	43	.010	-.012	8	7	1	16
APR 28	35	58	.013	-.009	6	10	1	17
APR 29	56	43	.011	-.014	9	7	0	16
APR 30	50	50	.015	-.013	8	8	0	16
MAY 1	47	41	.008	-.009	8	7	2	17
MAY 2	58	29	.013	-.010	10	5	2	17
MAY 3	50	43	.010	-.015	8	7	1	16
MAY 4	37	50	.013	-.009	6	8	2	16
MAY 5	58	41	.009	-.008	10	7	0	17
MAY 6	56	37	.009	-.009	9	6	1	16
MAY 7	43	50	.010	-.008	7	8	1	16
++ MAY 8	70	29	.013	-.015	12	5	0	17

DAILY MARKET PROBABILITY STATISTICS
■■■■■■■■■■■■■■■■■■■■■■■■■■■■■■■■■■■■■■

File used: 10LH - LIVE HOGS

Month/ Day	--- % ---		-- Average --		---------- Years ----------			
	Up	Down	Up	Down	Up	Down	Unch	Total
JUL 23	56	43	.015	-.007	9	7	0	16
+ JUL 24	68	18	.007	-.018	11	3	2	16
JUL 25	52	35	.012	-.016	9	6	2	17
JUL 26	50	37	.014	-.031	8	6	2	16
- JUL 27	25	62	.016	-.013	4	10	2	16
JUL 28	41	41	.013	-.011	7	7	3	17
JUL 29	41	41	.020	-.015	7	7	3	17
JUL 30	43	50	.013	-.012	7	8	1	16
+ JUL 31	68	25	.017	-.010	11	4	1	16
AUG 1	35	58	.015	-.016	6	10	1	17
AUG 2	37	56	.010	-.011	6	9	1	16
AUG 3	43	43	.012	-.011	7	7	2	16
AUG 4	35	58	.014	-.006	6	10	1	17
+ AUG 5	64	29	.016	-.022	11	5	1	17
AUG 6	50	43	.011	-.009	8	7	1	16
AUG 7	56	37	.016	-.015	9	6	1	16
- AUG 8	35	64	.017	-.011	6	11	0	17
AUG 9	31	56	.019	-.013	5	9	2	16
AUG 10	56	43	.024	-.015	9	7	0	16
AUG 11	58	41	.012	-.012	10	7	0	17
AUG 12	47	41	.019	-.010	8	7	2	17
AUG 13	50	43	.015	-.014	8	7	1	16
AUG 14	56	25	.013	-.012	9	4	3	16
AUG 15	47	47	.014	-.018	8	8	1	17
AUG 16	43	50	.012	-.017	7	8	1	16
AUG 17	56	43	.009	-.008	9	7	0	16
++ AUG 18	76	23	.015	-.016	13	4	0	17
++ AUG 19	70	29	.013	-.013	12	5	0	17
AUG 20	50	43	.012	-.011	8	7	1	16
AUG 21	50	43	.012	-.016	8	7	1	16
AUG 22	35	52	.011	-.016	6	9	2	17
AUG 23	43	50	.007	-.013	7	8	1	16
+ AUG 24	62	37	.013	-.014	10	6	0	16
AUG 25	41	52	.012	-.012	7	9	1	17
+ AUG 26	64	29	.012	-.017	11	5	1	17
AUG 27	50	50	.017	-.020	8	8	0	16
--- AUG 28	12	87	.013	-.015	2	14	0	16
AUG 29	47	47	.011	-.018	8	8	1	17
AUG 30	37	56	.012	-.013	6	9	1	16
AUG 31	50	43	.007	-.012	8	7	1	16
+ SEP 1	69	30	.012	-.005	9	4	0	13
SEP 2	57	35	.009	-.013	8	5	1	14
SEP 3	38	53	.019	-.016	5	7	1	13
SEP 4	38	46	.013	-.014	5	6	2	13
+ SEP 5	61	30	.018	-.014	8	4	1	13

DAILY MARKET PROBABILITY STATISTICS
■■■■■■■■■■■■■■■■■■■■■■■■■■■■■■■■■■■■■■■

File used: 02LH - LIVE HOGS

Month/	--- % ---		-- Average --		---------- Years ----------			
Day	Up	Down	Up	Down	Up	Down	Unch	Total
■■■■■■	■■■■	■■■■	■■■■■■	■■■■■■	■■■■■■	■■■■■■	■■■■■■	■■■■■■
+ NOV 22	66	33	.011	-.004	8	4	0	12
NOV 23	41	58	.010	-.013	5	7	0	12
NOV 24	50	50	.009	-.006	5	5	0	10
NOV 25	38	53	.008	-.009	5	7	1	13
- NOV 26	16	66	.013	-.012	2	8	2	12
NOV 27	58	25	.009	-.012	7	3	2	12
+ NOV 28	64	35	.010	-.019	9	5	0	14
NOV 29	40	53	.006	-.010	6	8	1	15
NOV 30	46	40	.013	-.016	7	6	2	15
+ DEC 1	68	25	.010	-.007	11	4	1	16
DEC 2	43	56	.012	-.008	7	9	0	16
DEC 3	53	46	.015	-.022	8	7	0	15
DEC 4	43	50	.011	-.010	7	8	1	16
DEC 5	47	41	.012	-.012	8	7	2	17
DEC 6	53	46	.011	-.010	8	7	0	15
DEC 7	53	40	.008	-.015	8	6	1	15
- DEC 8	31	62	.012	-.012	5	10	1	16
DEC 9	43	50	.012	-.009	7	8	1	16
DEC 10	46	53	.012	-.017	7	8	0	15
- DEC 11	31	62	.013	-.011	5	10	1	16
DEC 12	41	35	.014	-.012	7	6	4	17
DEC 13	46	46	.012	-.011	7	7	1	15
+ DEC 14	60	40	.010	-.011	9	6	0	15
DEC 15	50	50	.013	-.016	8	8	0	16
+ DEC 16	62	37	.010	-.014	10	6	0	16
DEC 17	53	46	.013	-.010	8	7	0	15
DEC 18	50	50	.008	-.019	8	8	0	16
DEC 19	29	52	.014	-.008	5	9	3	17
DEC 20	40	53	.012	-.007	6	8	1	15
+ DEC 21	60	33	.012	-.004	9	5	1	15
DEC 22	56	37	.010	-.019	9	6	1	16
++ DEC 23	75	25	.016	-.009	12	4	0	16
DEC 24	54	45	.025	-.021	6	5	0	11
-- DEC 26	30	70	.004	-.016	3	7	0	10
+ DEC 27	60	33	.011	-.011	9	5	1	15
DEC 28	35	57	.008	-.005	5	8	1	14
--- DEC 29	0	87	.000	-.012	0	14	2	16
DEC 30	37	43	.009	-.019	6	7	3	16
- DEC 31	38	61	.017	-.006	5	8	0	13
JAN 3	44	55	.012	-.009	4	5	0	9
+++ JAN 4	83	16	.010	-.003	10	2	0	12
++ JAN 5	73	26	.012	-.013	11	4	0	15
++ JAN 6	75	25	.016	-.004	12	4	0	16
- JAN 7	33	60	.011	-.010	5	9	1	15
- JAN 8	31	68	.014	-.015	5	11	0	16

```
DAILY MARKET PROBABILITY STATISTICS
===================================
```

File used: 01SM - SOYBEAN MEAL

Month/ Day	Up	Down	Up	Down	Up	Down	Unch	Total
	--- % ---		-- Average --		---------- years ----------			
OCT 22	37	43	.153	-.083	6	7	3	16
+ OCT 23	62	31	.082	-.134	10	5	1	16
OCT 24	52	41	.141	-.158	9	7	1	17
OCT 25	50	37	.101	-.106	8	6	2	16
OCT 26	50	50	.104	-.149	8	8	0	16
OCT 27	41	58	.153	-.129	7	10	0	17
OCT 28	52	47	.106	-.067	9	8	0	17
- OCT 29	37	62	.148	-.121	6	10	0	16
++ OCT 30	75	25	.078	-.086	12	4	0	16
++ OCT 31	70	29	.145	-.146	12	5	0	17
NOV 1	43	56	.129	-.113	7	9	0	16
+ NOV 2	64	28	.178	-.092	9	4	1	14
NOV 3	43	56	.125	-.118	7	9	0	16
+ NOV 4	62	37	.083	-.041	10	6	0	16
+ NOV 5	64	28	.131	-.050	9	4	1	14
- NOV 6	25	68	.047	-.087	4	11	1	16
NOV 7	46	53	.143	-.089	7	8	0	15
- NOV 8	33	60	.203	-.101	5	9	1	15
NOV 9	56	43	.091	-.164	9	7	0	16
NOV 10	47	52	.073	-.087	8	9	0	17
NOV 11	41	58	.070	-.176	7	10	0	17
NOV 12	56	37	.131	-.146	9	6	1	16
NOV 13	43	56	.153	-.075	7	9	0	16
NOV 14	52	47	.136	-.058	9	8	0	17
- NOV 15	37	62	.092	-.147	6	10	0	16
NOV 16	56	43	.137	-.159	9	7	0	16
NOV 17	52	47	.077	-.093	9	8	0	17
- NOV 18	35	64	.091	-.155	6	11	0	17
NOV 19	50	43	.207	-.048	8	7	1	16
+ NOV 20	68	18	.155	-.053	11	3	2	16
NOV 21	52	47	.153	-.165	9	8	0	17
NOV 22	53	46	.142	-.096	7	6	0	13
- NOV 23	30	69	.162	-.058	4	9	0	13
NOV 24	53	46	.227	-.135	7	6	0	13
NOV 25	57	35	.090	-.101	8	5	1	14
+ NOV 26	69	30	.121	-.234	9	4	0	13
NOV 27	58	41	.119	-.168	7	5	0	12
NOV 28	42	50	.143	-.165	6	7	1	14
- NOV 29	37	62	.162	-.110	6	10	0	16
+ NOV 30	68	31	.094	-.078	11	5	0	16
DEC 1	47	47	.125	-.105	8	8	1	17
DEC 2	41	58	.068	-.143	7	10	0	17
DEC 3	56	43	.137	-.102	9	7	0	16
DEC 4	56	37	.154	-.137	9	6	1	16
-- DEC 5	29	70	.132	-.149	5	12	0	17

DAILY MARKET PROBABILITY STATISTICS
=====================================

File used: 07SM - SOYBEAN MEAL

| Month/ | --- % --- | | -- Average -- | | ---------- Years ---------- | | | |
Day	Up	Down	Up	Down	Up	Down	Unch	Total
APR 23	50	37	.072	- .143	8	6	2	16
APR 24	52	47	.075	- .120	9	8	0	17
APR 25	47	47	.188	- .107	8	8	1	17
APR 26	43	56	.072	- .192	7	9	0	16
- APR 27	31	68	.100	- .112	5	11	0	16
APR 28	52	47	.064	- .118	9	8	0	17
APR 29	43	56	.169	- .145	7	9	0	16
APR 30	56	43	.175	- .076	9	7	0	16
MAY 1	52	47	.119	- .094	9	8	0	17
MAY 2	43	56	.107	- .073	7	9	0	16
MAY 3	50	37	.118	- .056	8	6	2	16
+ MAY 4	68	31	.072	- .137	11	5	0	16
MAY 5	47	52	.104	- .108	8	9	0	17
- MAY 6	31	68	.067	- .107	5	11	0	16
+ MAY 7	62	37	.160	- .092	10	6	0	16
MAY 8	58	35	.115	- .078	10	6	1	17
MAY 9	47	47	.127	- .060	8	8	1	17
++ MAY 10	75	18	.100	- .159	12	3	1	16
MAY 11	56	43	.131	- .192	9	7	0	16
MAY 12	47	52	.106	- .107	8	9	0	17
MAY 13	56	43	.136	- .099	9	7	0	16
+ MAY 14	68	31	.100	- .051	11	5	0	16
MAY 15	35	58	.109	- .087	6	10	1	17
MAY 16	35	58	.228	- .094	6	10	1	17
MAY 17	37	56	.091	- .149	6	9	1	16
MAY 18	50	50	.132	- .110	8	8	0	16
+ MAY 19	64	35	.093	- .078	11	6	0	17
MAY 20	43	56	.156	- .126	7	9	0	16
MAY 21	56	37	.146	- .081	9	6	1	16
MAY 22	47	52	.101	- .105	8	9	0	17
MAY 23	58	41	.124	- .121	10	7	0	17
MAY 24	47	41	.226	- .076	8	7	2	17
+ MAY 25	60	40	.130	- .210	9	6	0	15
-- MAY 26	26	73	.087	- .071	4	11	0	15
MAY 27	46	46	.102	- .128	7	7	1	15
MAY 28	53	46	.087	- .080	7	6	0	13
MAY 29	53	30	.110	- .073	7	4	2	13
MAY 30	45	54	.110	- .079	5	6	0	11
+ MAY 31	64	35	.176	- .126	9	5	0	14
JUN 1	47	52	.168	- .078	8	9	0	17
JUN 2	44	55	.107	- .129	8	10	0	18
JUN 3	41	58	.145	- .124	7	10	0	17
JUN 4	56	31	.159	- .043	9	5	2	16
JUN 5	58	41	.106	- .039	10	7	0	17
JUN 6	44	55	.110	- .222	8	10	0	18

```
          DAILY MARKET PROBABILITY STATISTICS
          ===================================

File used:    07BO - SOYBEAN OIL

   Month/    --- % ---    -- Average --    ---------- Years ----------
   Day       Up  Down     Up    Down       Up    Down    Unch    Total
   ======    ==== ====    ====== ======    ====== ====== ====== ======

      APR 23  50   50     .010  -.019       8      8      0      16
      APR 24  35   58     .022  -.011       6     10      1      17
      APR 25  58   35     .022  -.010      10      6      1      17
   -  APR 26  37   62     .015  -.012       6     10      0      16
   -  APR 27  31   68     .010  -.017       5     11      0      16
      APR 28  52   35     .007  -.017       9      6      2      17
      APR.29  56   43     .013  -.013       9      7      0      16
   +  APR 30  62   37     .018  -.006      10      6      0      16
      MAY  1  41   58     .012  -.015       7     10      0      17
   +  MAY  2  68   31     .009  -.013      11      5      0      16
      MAY  3  43   56     .012  -.006       7      9      0      16
      MAY  4  56   37     .007  -.011       9      6      1      16
      MAY  5  47   52     .011  -.011       8      9      0      17
      MAY  6  50   43     .010  -.019       8      7      1      16
      MAY  7  56   43     .011  -.011       9      7      0      16
      MAY  8  41   58     .017  -.008       7     10      0      17
  ++  MAY  9  70   29     .012  -.007      12      5      0      17
      MAY 10  56   43     .012  -.013       9      7      0      16
      MAY 11  50   50     .012  -.010       8      8      0      16
  --  MAY 12  29   70     .012  -.012       5     12      0      17
   +  MAY 13  62   37     .013  -.013      10      6      0      16
   +  MAY 14  62   31     .011  -.009      10      5      1      16
      MAY 15  35   58     .011  -.013       6     10      1      17
      MAY 16  41   52     .016  -.009       7      9      1      17
      MAY 17  43   43     .007  -.007       7      7      2      16
   +  MAY 18  68   31     .014  -.023      11      5      0      16
      MAY 19  47   47     .009  -.005       8      8      1      17
   +  MAY 20  68   25     .011  -.016      11      4      1      16
      MAY 21  56   37     .022  -.016       9      6      1      16
      MAY 22  41   58     .010  -.013       7     10      0      17
      MAY 23  41   58     .011  -.013       7     10      0      17
      MAY 24  52   47     .021  -.008       9      8      0      17
      MAY 25  46   53     .022  -.011       7      8      0      15
   -  MAY 26  40   60     .015  -.010       6      9      0      15
      MAY 27  53   46     .008  -.018       8      7      0      15
 ---  MAY 28  15   84     .007  -.009       2     11      0      13
   +  MAY 29  61   38     .010  -.015       8      5      0      13
 ---  MAY 30  18   81     .023  -.015       2      9      0      11
      MAY 31  42   57     .023  -.010       6      8      0      14
      JUN  1  35   58     .004  -.017       6     10      1      17
   -  JUN  2  27   66     .011  -.018       5     12      1      18
      JUN  3  52   41     .013  -.015       9      7      1      17
   +  JUN  4  62   37     .013  -.010      10      6      0      16
      JUN  5  41   58     .007  -.015       7     10      0      17
      JUN  6  50   50     .017  -.015       9      9      0      18
```

DAILY MARKET PROBABILITY STATISTICS
==

File used: 12BO - SOYBEAN OIL

| Month/ | --- % --- | | -- Average -- | | ---------- Years ---------- | | | |
Day	Up	Down	Up	Down	Up	Down	Unch	Total
SEP 22	41	58	.012	-.013	7	10	0	17
SEP 23	41	58	.019	-.013	7	10	0	17
SEP 24	56	37	.016	-.014	9	6	1	16
SEP 25	50	50	.023	-.014	8	8	0	16
--- SEP 26	11	82	.028	-.015	2	14	1	17
SEP 27	50	50	.017	-.010	8	8	0	16
- SEP 28	37	62	.015	-.013	6	10	0	16
SEP 29	41	58	.011	-.015	7	10	0	17
+ SEP 30	64	35	.012	-.014	11	6	0	17
OCT 1	50	43	.010	-.013	8	7	1	16
- OCT 2	31	62	.012	-.020	5	10	1	16
OCT 3	58	41	.018	-.008	10	7	0	17
OCT 4	31	56	.015	-.013	5	9	2	16
- OCT 5	31	62	.026	-.008	5	10	1	16
OCT 6	58	41	.015	-.015	10	7	0	17
OCT 7	52	41	.012	-.016	9	7	1	17
- OCT 8	33	66	.012	-.008	5	10	0	15
OCT 9	43	50	.015	-.007	7	8	1	16
- OCT 10	29	64	.013	-.008	5	11	1	17
+ OCT 11	62	37	.011	-.011	10	6	0	16
OCT 12	31	56	.024	-.016	5	9	2	16
++ OCT 13	70	29	.020	-.020	12	5	0	17
OCT 14	47	52	.013	-.018	8	9	0	17
-- OCT 15	25	75	.010	-.017	4	12	0	16
+ OCT 16	62	37	.014	-.021	10	6	0	16
- OCT 17	35	64	.007	-.010	6	11	0	17
-- OCT 18	25	75	.006	-.013	4	12	0	16
OCT 19	43	50	.012	-.010	7	8	1	16
OCT 20	47	52	.018	-.018	8	9	0	17
OCT 21	58	41	.012	-.016	10	7	0	17
OCT 22	43	56	.025	-.012	7	9	0	16
OCT 23	43	50	.007	-.010	7	8	1	16
OCT 24	52	47	.020	-.013	9	8	0	17
OCT 25	56	43	.010	-.013	9	7	0	16
OCT 26	43	56	.014	-.017	7	9	0	16
OCT 27	41	58	.022	-.012	7	10	0	17
OCT 28	58	41	.009	-.013	10	7	0	17
OCT 29	43	56	.022	-.016	7	9	0	16
OCT 30	56	37	.015	-.008	9	6	1	16
OCT 31	52	41	.013	-.015	9	7	1	17
NOV 1	50	50	.015	-.011	8	8	0	16
NOV 2	57	35	.009	-.010	8	5	1	14
NOV 3	50	43	.010	-.019	8	7	1	16
NOV 4	50	50	.020	-.010	8	8	0	16
++ NOV 5	78	7	.015	-.003	11	1	2	14

```
          DAILY MARKET PROBABILITY STATISTICS
          ===================================

File used:    013  - SOYBEANS

     Month/   --- % ---   -- Average --   ---------- Years ----------
      Day     Up  Down     Up    Down      Up    Down   Uncn    Total
     ======   ==== ====   ====== ======   ====== ====== ====== ======

       DEC  6   55   40    .099  -.086      15    11      1      27
    ++ DEC  7   70   29    .065  -.103      19     8      0      27
       DEC  8   50   50    .089  -.120      14    14      0      28
    -  DEC  9   35   60    .084  -.072      10    17      1      28
       DEC 10   48   51    .046  -.110      13    14      0      27
       DEC 11   48   51    .088  -.096      13    14      0      27
       DEC 12   57   42    .075  -.106      16    12      0      28
  _ -  DEC 13   33   66    .056  -.075       9    18      0      27
       DEC 14   51   40    .075  -.075      14    11      2      27
    +  DEC 15   64   35    .086  -.102      18    10      0      28
    +  DEC 16   64   28    .072  -.078      18     8      2      28
       DEC 17   44   51    .060  -.083      12    14      1      27
       DEC 18   33   59    .084  -.060       9    16      2      27
    ++ DEC 19   75   14    .084  -.098      21     4      3      28
       DEC 20   51   48    .038  -.045      14    13      0      27
       DEC 21   59   40    .078  -.053      16    11      0      27
       DEC 22   46   46    .069  -.062      13    13      2      28
       DEC 23   44   55    .064  -.051      12    15      0      27
       DEC 24   52   47    .050  -.064      10     9      0      19
    -  DEC 26   38   61    .032  -.104       7    11      0      18
       DEC 27   55   37    .056  -.089      15    10      2      27
    -  DEC 28   38   61    .060  -.082      10    16      0      26
    -  DEC 29   32   67    .076  -.099       9    19      0      28
       DEC 30   55   40    .063  -.069      15    11      1      27
       DEC 31   52   47    .080  -.046      12    11      0      23
       JAN  3   50   43    .084  -.059       8     7      1      16
       JAN  4   54   45    .067  -.088      12    10      0      22
       JAN  5   55   44    .090  -.050      15    12      0      27
    +  JAN  6   64   35    .081  -.099      18    10      0      28
       JAN  7   53   46    .103  -.077      14    12      0      26
       JAN  8   50   50    .061  -.075      13    13      0      26
       JAN  9   46   53    .056  -.093      13    15      0      28
       JAN 10   48   48    .131  -.058      13    13      1      27
       JAN 11   55   40    .052  -.056      15    11      1      27
   +++ JAN 12   82   14    .086  -.099      23     4      1      28
       JAN 13   39   57    .073  -.065      11    16      1      28
    +  JAN 14   62   33    .053  -.055      17     9      1      27
       JAN 15   51   48    .098  -.079      14    13      0      27
       JAN 16   35   57    .103  -.123      10    16      2      28
       JAN 17   48   48    .108  -.129      13    13      1      27
       JAN 18   55   40    .088  -.069      15    11      1      27
    +  JAN 19   67   28    .083  -.097      19     8      1      28
```

DAILY MARKET PROBABILITY STATISTICS
==

File used: 05S   - SOYBEANS

Month/ Day	--- % --- Up	Down	-- Average -- Up	Down	---------- Years ---------- Up	Down	Unch	Total
FEB 24	52	47	.034	-.061	9	8	0	17
- FEB 25	37	62	.084	-.091	6	10	0	16
- FEB 26	25	68	.113	-.089	4	11	1	16
- FEB 27	35	64	.069	-.088	6	11	0	17
- FEB 28	37	62	.073	-.125	6	10	0	16
FEB 29	40	40	.213	-.030	2	2	1	5
++ MAR 1	75	25	.120	-.067	12	4	0	16
MAR 2	56	43	.110	-.119	9	7	0	16
+ MAR 3	64	35	.088	-.074	11	6	0	17
MAR 4	50	50	.053	-.085	8	8	0	16
MAR 5	43	43	.107	-.067	7	7	2	16
++ MAR 6	76	23	.105	-.061	13	4	0	17
MAR 7	41	47	.111	-.067	7	8	2	17
MAR 8	43	56	.113	-.117	7	9	0	16
+ MAR 9	64	29	.094	-.071	11	5	1	17
-- MAR 10	27	72	.046	-.101	5	13	0	18
MAR 11	41	52	.102	-.041	7	9	1	17
MAR 12	56	37	.103	-.116	9	6	1	16
MAR 13	47	52	.110	-.096	8	9	0	17
MAR 14	50	50	.071	-.090	9	9	0	18
MAR 15	47	47	.103	-.057	8	8	1	17
MAR 16	41	52	.086	-.086	7	9	1	17
++ MAR 17	72	27	.133	-.078	13	5	0	18
++ MAR 18	70	29	.071	-.103	12	5	0	17
+ MAR 19	62	31	.066	-.082	10	5	1	16
-- MAR 20	29	70	.096	-.086	5	12	0	17
MAR 21	50	44	.115	-.077	9	8	1	18
MAR 22	41	52	.087	-.039	7	9	1	17
MAR 23	41	47	.150	-.061	7	8	2	17
MAR 24	53	46	.080	-.034	8	7	0	15
MAR 25	41	58	.072	-.078	7	10	0	17
MAR 26	43	56	.077	-.078	7	9	0	16
- MAR 27	31	62	.103	-.119	5	10	1	16
MAR 28	43	50	.074	-.071	7	8	1	16
-- MAR 29	29	70	.081	-.105	5	12	0	17
- MAR 30	35	64	.060	-.098	6	11	0	17
+ MAR 31	68	25	.107	-.092	11	4	1	16
APR 1	46	53	.096	-.100	7	8	0	15
APR 2	43	56	.111	-.101	7	9	0	16
APR 3	41	58	.094	-.180	7	10	0	17
+ APR 4	68	25	.133	-.118	11	4	1	16
+ APR 5	68	31	.094	-.144	11	5	0	16

DAILY MARKET PROBABILITY STATISTICS
==

File used: 03C   - CORN

Month/ Day	--- % --- Up	--- % --- Down	-- Average -- Up	-- Average -- Down	---------- Years Up	---------- Years Down	---------- Years Unch	---------- Years Total
FEB 8	42	57	.099	-.061	8	11	0	19
FEB 9	57	42	.084	-.097	12	9	0	21
FEB 10	55	35	.068	-.071	11	7	2	20
FEB 11	45	45	.063	-.086	9	9	2	20
-- FEB 12	21	71	.151	-.078	3	10	1	14
- FEB 13	40	60	.068	-.081	8	12	0	20
FEB 14	35	50	.113	-.076	7	10	3	20
FEB 15	43	43	.074	-.029	7	7	2	16
FEB 16	41	52	.092	-.086	7	9	1	17
+ FEB 17	66	33	.055	-.066	12	6	0	18
- FEB 18	35	64	.050	-.075	6	11	0	17
- FEB 19	35	64	.084	-.072	6	11	0	17
+ FEB 20	61	27	.086	-.081	11	5	2	18
FEB 21	43	43	.102	-.098	7	7	2	16
FEB 22	42	50	.120	-.056	6	7	1	14
-- FEB 23	22	72	.039	-.071	4	13	1	18
FEB 24	40	55	.041	-.071	8	11	1	20
-- FEB 25	30	70	.078	-.085	6	14	0	20
FEB 26	42	52	.065	-.053	8	10	1	19
FEB 27	38	57	.064	-.104	8	12	1	21
-- FEB 28	23	76	.066	-.123	5	16	0	21
FEB 29	50	50	.130	-.052	3	3	0	6
MAR 1	52	31	.102	-.021	10	6	3	19
MAR 2	47	42	.105	-.103	9	8	2	19
+ MAR 3	60	40	.059	-.049	12	8	0	20
MAR 4	52	36	.083	-.113	10	7	2	19
MAR 5	55	35	.087	-.073	11	7	2	20
+ MAR 6	66	33	.100	-.039	14	7	0	21
MAR 7	47	42	.073	-.069	10	9	2	21
- MAR 8	36	63	.052	-.115	7	12	0	19
++ MAR 9	70	30	.073	-.055	14	6	0	20
- MAR 10	28	66	.065	-.086	6	14	1	21
- MAR 11	40	60	.082	-.059	8	12	0	20
MAR 12	45	50	.082	-.111	9	10	1	20
+ MAR 13	61	33	.076	-.122	13	7	1	21
MAR 14	54	40	.069	-.070	12	9	1	22
MAR 15	55	40	.100	-.078	11	8	1	20
+ MAR 16	60	35	.081	-.040	12	7	1	20
+ MAR 17	66	28	.124	-.059	14	6	1	21
MAR 18	36	52	.097	-.059	7	10	2	19
+ MAR 19	65	35	.103	-.081	13	7	0	20
MAR 20	33	55	.080	-.112	6	10	2	18
MAR 21	57	35	.107	-.059	8	5	1	14

DAILY MARKET PROBABILITY STATISTICS
====================================

File used: 12C   - CORN

Month/ Day	--- % --- Up	Down	-- Average -- Up	Down	---------- Years ---------- Up	Down	Unch	Total
- SEP 22	32	68	.106	-.117	8	17	0	25
SEP 23	37	58	.129	-.103	9	14	1	24
SEP 24	58	37	.132	-.074	14	9	1	24
- SEP 25	39	60	.070	-.096	9	14	0	23
SEP 26	46	50	.152	-.123	12	13	1	26
SEP 27	50	50	.142	-.125	12	12	0	24
SEP 28	37	54	.082	-.099	9	13	2	24
SEP 29	40	52	.131	-.839	10	13	2	25
SEP 30	45	50	******	-.054	11	12	1	24
OCT 1	45	50	.108	-.090	11	12	1	24
+ OCT 2	60	39	.110	-.148	14	9	0	23
+ OCT 3	69	30	.128	-.107	18	8	0	26
OCT 4	50	45	.092	-.108	12	11	1	24
+ OCT 5	60	30	.073	-.085	14	7	2	23
+ OCT 6	64	28	.091	-.112	16	7	2	25
OCT 7	54	41	.059	-.104	13	10	1	24
OCT 8	43	56	.049	-.138	10	13	0	23
OCT 9	52	43	.123	-.074	12	10	1	23
- OCT 10	38	61	.086	-.065	10	16	0	26
OCT 11	45	50	.085	-.119	11	12	1	24
OCT 12	56	43	.074	-.118	9	7	0	16
OCT 13	52	47	.157	-.140	12	11	0	23
- OCT 14	37	62	.147	-.100	9	15	0	24
- OCT 15	37	62	.071	-.147	9	15	0	24
OCT 16	52	43	.086	-.118	12	10	1	23
OCT 17	42	53	.088	-.114	11	14	1	26
- OCT 18	33	62	.066	-.056	8	15	1	24
OCT 19	34	52	.062	-.143	8	12	3	23
OCT 20	40	52	.144	-.096	10	13	2	25
OCT 21	45	45	.076	-.088	11	11	2	24
OCT 22	45	54	.082	-.068	11	13	0	24
- OCT 23	34	60	.101	-.082	8	14	1	23
OCT 24	53	42	.122	-.123	14	11	1	26
OCT 25	41	58	.092	-.105	10	14	0	24
OCT 26	47	52	.110	-.112	11	12	0	23
OCT 27	44	56	.072	-.108	11	14	0	25
++ OCT 28	70	20	.072	-.109	17	5	2	24
OCT 29	58	41	.115	-.137	14	10	0	24
- OCT 30	34	65	.090	-.065	8	15	0	23
OCT 31	50	46	.109	-.104	13	12	1	26
NOV 1	54	41	.095	-.093	13	10	1	24
NOV 2	54	45	.090	-.118	12	10	0	22
NOV 3	37	45	.093	-.095	9	11	4	24
NOV 4	52	42	.084	-.083	11	9	1	21
NOV 5	54	36	.133	-.072	12	8	2	22

DAILY MARKET PROBABILITY STATISTICS
=======================================

File used: 03NY - COTTON

Month/ Day	--- % --- Up	Down	-- Average -- Up	Down	---------- Years ---------- Up	Down	Unch	Total
+ DEC 22	66	33	.007	-.008	8	4	0	12
+ DEC 23	69	30	.008	-.007	9	4	0	13
+ DEC 24	62	37	.007	-.001	5	3	0	8
DEC 26	50	50	.012	-.010	4	4	0	8
DEC 27	58	33	.012	-.005	7	4	1	12
DEC 28	45	54	.009	-.007	5	6	0	11
DEC 29	50	41	.014	-.007	6	5	1	12
-- DEC 30	23	76	.005	-.010	3	10	0	13
DEC 31	50	50	.005	-.007	5	5	0	10
- JAN 3	37	62	.009	-.015	3	5	0	8
- JAN 4	22	66	.012	-.005	2	6	1	9
JAN 5	50	50	.014	-.010	5	5	0	10
+ JAN 6	61	38	.009	-.011	8	5	0	13
JAN 7	50	42	.007	-.012	7	6	1	14
+ JAN 8	64	35	.007	-.007	9	5	0	14
JAN 9	53	38	.007	-.010	7	5	1	13
+ JAN 10	66	25	.007	-.014	8	3	1	12
JAN 11	41	58	.013	-.010	5	7	0	12
JAN 12	41	50	.008	-.010	5	6	1	12
+ JAN 13	69	30	.006	-.010	9	4	0	13
JAN 14	42	50	.013	-.004	6	7	1	14
-- JAN 15	21	78	.003	-.011	3	11	0	14
JAN 16	38	53	.005	-.005	5	7	1	13
JAN 17	41	58	.013	-.011	5	7	0	12
JAN 18	50	50	.008	-.013	6	6	0	12
JAN 19	41	58	.015	-.007	5	7	0	12
+ JAN 20	69	30	.008	-.008	9	4	0	13
JAN 21	57	42	.006	-.011	8	6	0	14
JAN 22	57	42	.010	-.006	8	6	0	14
- JAN 23	30	69	.008	-.012	4	9	0	13
- JAN 24	33	66	.011	-.008	4	8	0	12
--- JAN 25	9	81	.000	-.010	1	9	1	11
JAN 26	50	41	.012	-.015	6	5	1	12
+ JAN 27	61	38	.009	-.014	8	5	0	13
-- JAN 28	28	71	.012	-.013	4	10	0	14
+ JAN 29	64	35	.007	-.013	9	5	0	14
JAN 30	46	53	.008	-.010	6	7	0	13
+ JAN 31	66	33	.007	-.007	8	4	0	12
FEB 1	50	50	.011	-.005	6	6	0	12
FEB 2	58	41	.006	-.012	7	5	0	12
FEB 3	46	53	.009	-.007	6	7	0	13
FEB 4	57	42	.011	-.005	8	6	0	14
FEB 5	42	57	.007	-.012	6	8	0	14
- FEB 6	30	69	.005	-.017	4	9	0	13
FEB 7	58	41	.009	-.008	7	5	0	12

DAILY MARKET PROBABILITY STATISTICS
==================================

File used: 07NY - COTTON

	Month/ Day	--- % --- Up	Down	-- Average -- Up	Down	--------- Years --------- Up	Down	Unch	Total
+	APR 23	66	33	.012	-.008	10	5	0	15
+	APR 24	68	31	.011	-.008	11	5	0	16
-	APR 25	25	68	.010	-.010	4	11	1	16
+	APR 26	64	28	.010	-.015	9	4	1	14
	APR 27	42	42	.004	-.007	6	6	2	14
	APR 28	53	33	.006	-.007	8	5	2	15
++	APR 29	73	26	.007	-.004	11	4	0	15
	APR 30	53	40	.014	-.006	8	6	1	15
	MAY 1	50	43	.011	-.013	8	7	1	16
	MAY 2	43	50	.010	-.014	7	8	1	16
-	MAY 3	28	64	.011	-.005	4	9	1	14
	MAY 4	42	50	.008	-.008	6	7	1	14
	MAY 5	40	53	.009	-.003	6	8	1	15
	MAY 6	53	46	.008	-.010	8	7	0	15
+	MAY 7	66	26	.014	-.015	10	4	1	15
	MAY 8	43	50	.013	-.005	7	8	1	16
+	MAY 9	68	25	.013	-.013	11	4	1	16
	MAY 10	42	50	.007	-.007	6	7	1	14
	MAY 11	42	50	.007	-.011	6	7	1	14
	MAY 12	53	40	.006	-.006	8	6	1	15
+	MAY 13	60	40	.008	-.013	9	6	0	15
--	MAY 14	26	73	.013	-.015	4	11	0	15
-	MAY 15	31	68	.008	-.010	5	11	0	16
+	MAY 16	68	25	.011	-.017	11	4	1	16
	MAY 17	42	50	.008	-.010	6	7	1	14
	MAY 18	57	35	.011	-.014	8	5	1	14
	MAY 19	40	53	.008	-.007	6	8	1	15
+	MAY 20	60	40	.008	-.015	9	6	0	15
	MAY 21	53	40	.013	-.004	8	6	1	15
--	MAY 22	25	75	.016	-.011	4	12	0	16
-	MAY 23	25	68	.005	-.011	4	11	1	16
	MAY 24	42	50	.012	-.008	6	7	1	14
-	MAY 25	25	66	.012	-.006	3	8	1	12
	MAY 26	58	33	.010	-.010	7	4	1	12
-	MAY 27	38	61	.010	-.013	5	8	0	13
	MAY 28	58	41	.006	-.014	7	5	0	12
+	MAY 29	61	30	.012	-.009	8	4	1	13
--	MAY 30	30	70	.011	-.010	3	7	0	10
	MAY 31	45	45	.018	-.008	5	5	1	11
-	JUN 1	28	64	.010	-.011	4	9	1	14
	JUN 2	33	53	.008	-.009	5	8	2	15
++	JUN 3	73	26	.008	-.005	11	4	0	15
+	JUN 4	60	40	.020	-.009	9	6	0	15
	JUN 5	37	56	.010	-.009	6	9	1	16
	JUN 6	50	43	.009	-.013	8	7	1	16

DAILY MARKET PROBABILITY STATISTICS
■■■■■■■■■■■■■■■■■■■■■■■■■■■■■■■■■■■■■■

File used: 1ONY - COTTON

	Month/	--- % ---		-- Average --		---------- Years ----------			
	Day	Up	Down	Up	Down	Up	Down	Unch	Total
	JUL 23	50	50	.020	-.010	7	7	0	14
	JUL 24	53	46	.011	-.011	7	6	0	13
+	JUL 25	69	30	.010	-.017	9	4	0	13
-	JUL 26	30	69	.007	-.015	4	9	0	13
--	JUL 27	21	78	.007	-.009	3	11	0	14
	JUL 28	57	42	.012	-.016	8	6	0	14
	JUL 29	50	50	.016	-.007	7	7	0	14
--	JUL 30	28	71	.025	-.010	4	10	0	14
	JUL 31	46	53	.005	-.008	6	7	0	13
-	AUG 1	38	61	.010	-.013	5	8	0	13
-	AUG 2	38	61	.006	-.013	5	8	0	13
	AUG 3	42	57	.018	-.011	6	8	0	14
	AUG 4	50	50	.007	-.014	7	7	0	14
+	AUG 5	64	35	.008	-.012	9	5	0	14
	AUG 6	50	50	.012	-.004	7	7	0	14
-	AUG 7	38	61	.012	-.011	5	8	0	13
	AUG 8	46	46	.010	-.011	6	6	1	13
	AUG 9	46	53	.013	-.011	6	7	0	13
	AUG 10	57	42	.011	-.008	8	6	0	14
	AUG 11	57	42	.014	-.011	8	6	0	14
--	AUG 12	28	71	.020	-.013	4	10	0	14
+	AUG 13	64	35	.022	-..009	9	5	0	14
	AUG 14	46	53	.007	-.010	6	7	0	13
-	AUG 15	38	61	.010	-.009	5	8	0	13
	AUG 16	53	46	.006	-.010	7	6	0	13
	AUG 17	50	50	.010	-.012	7	7	0	14
--	AUG 18	28	71	.008	-.010	4	10	0	14
	AUG 19	57	42	.009	-.009	8	6	0	14
	AUG 20	57	42	.010	-.009	8	6	0	14
-	AUG 21	38	61	.011	-.011	5	8	0	13
	AUG 22	53	38	.016	-.008	7	5	1	13
+	AUG 23	61	38	.010	-.013	8	5	0	13
	AUG 24	42	57	.011	-.009	6	8	0	14
	AUG 25	42	50	.015	-.005	6	7	1	14
	AUG 26	57	35	.013	-.011	8	5	1	14
	AUG 27	57	35	.012	-.012	8	5	1	14
	AUG 28	46	46	.011	-.010	6	6	1	13
++	AUG 29	76	23	.009	-.004	10	3	0	13
-	AUG 30	38	61	.012	-.008	5	8	0	13
--	AUG 31	28	71	.009	-.009	4	10	0	14
++	SEP. 1	72	27	.007	-.013	8	3	0	11
	SEP 2	50	41	.018	-.013	6	5	1	12
	SEP 3	54	45	.006	-.011	6	5	0	11
--	SEP 4	27	72	.012	-.011	3	8	0	11
+++	SEP 5	80	20	.011	-.006	8	2	0	10

DAILY MARKET PROBABILITY STATISTICS

File used: 07LB - LUMBER

Month/ Day	--- % --- Up	Down	-- Average -- Up	Down	---------- Years ---------- Up	Down	Unch	Total
APR 23	35	57	.017	-.012	5	8	1	14
APR 24	42	50	.019	-.007	6	7	1	14
APR 25	57	42	.015	-.013	8	6	0	14
- APR 26	35	64	.009	-.012	5	9	0	14
- APR 27	33	66	.006	-.011	5	10	0	15
+ APR 28	60	40	.014	-.010	9	6	0	15
APR 29	57	35	.011	-.021	8	5	1	14
-- APR 30	21	71	.010	-.016	3	10	1	14
MAY 1	35	57	.008	-.014	5	8	1	14
MAY 2	35	57	.014	-.012	5	8	1	14
MAY 3	42	57	.009	-.012	6	8	0	14
- MAY 4	40	60	.010	-.016	6	9	0	15
-- MAY 5	26	73	.011	-.010	4	11	0	15
-- MAY 6	28	71	.014	-.009	4	10	0	14
MAY 7	42	50	.018	-.013	6	7	1	14
MAY 8	50	50	.016	-.011	7	7	0	14
++ MAY 9	71	28	.015	-.012	10	4	0	14
MAY 10	50	50	.015	-.012	7	7	0	14
- MAY 11	26	66	.007	-.010	4	10	1	15
MAY 12	53	46	.009	-.013	8	7	0	15
MAY 13	42	50	.013	-.014	6	7	1	14
+ MAY 14	64	35	.012	-.010	9	5	0	14
+ MAY 15	64	35	.009	-.015	9	5	0	14
+ MAY 16	64	35	.011	-.016	9	5	0	14
-- MAY 17	21	78	.005	-.015	3	11	0	14
MAY 18	46	46	.012	-.012	7	7	1	15
MAY 19	46	46	.011	-.020	7	7	1	15
MAY 20	35	57	.022	-.010	5	8	1	14
MAY 21	57	35	.013	-.020	8	5	1	14
MAY 22	50	42	.017	-.016	7	6	1	14
- MAY 23	35	64	.016	-.013	5	9	0	14
MAY 24	57	35	.015	-.016	8	5	1	14
+ MAY 25	69	23	.013	-.002	9	3	1	13
+++ MAY 26	91	8	.016	-.001	11	1	0	12
MAY 27	50	33	.018	-.011	6	4	2	12
MAY 28	45	45	.010	-.023	5	5	1	11
-- MAY 29	30	70	.007	-.012	3	7	0	10
MAY 30	54	45	.015	-.010	6	5	0	11
MAY 31	45	54	.017	-.013	5	6	0	11
- JUN 1	33	66	.009	-.012	5	10	0	15
JUN 2	53	46	.008	-.019	8	7	0	15
JUN 3	42	50	.011	-.012	6	7	1	14
JUN 4	57	42	.012	-.019	8	6	0	14
JUN 5	50	50	.014	-.016	7	7	0	14
JUN 6	57	42	.013	-.012	8	6	0	14

```
            DAILY MARKET PROBABILITY STATISTICS
            =====================================

File used:      11LB - LUMBER

    Month/    --- % ---    -- Average --    ---------- Years ----------
     Day      Up   Down     Up     Down      Up    Down   Unch    Total
    ======    ==== ====    ====== ======    ====== ====== ======  ======

 +  AUG 23    61    38     .013   -.013      8      5      0      13
    AUG 24    50    35     .016   -.019      7      5      2      14
    AUG 25    35    57     .015   -.016      5      8      1      14
 +  AUG 26    64    35     .009   -.012      9      5      0      14
    AUG 27    57    42     .015   -.020      8      6      0      14
    AUG 28    46    53     .010   -.009      6      7      0      13
 +  AUG 29    61    38     .016   -.014      8      5      0      13
 -  AUG 30    38    61     .013   -.008      5      8      0      13
    AUG 31    57    42     .014   -.015      8      6      0      14
    SEP  1    36    54     .009   -.012      4      6      1      11
    SEP  2    41    58     .012   -.012      5      7      0      12
++  SEP  3    72    27     .012   -.014      8      3      0      11
++  SEP  4    72    27     .012   -.024      8      3      0      11
+++ SEP  5    80    20     .012   -.017      8      2      0      10
 +  SEP  6    60    40     .015   -.009      6      4      0      10
    SEP  7    54    45     .018   -.021      6      5      0      11
--  SEP  8    21    78     .006   -.014      3     11      0      14
    SEP  9    50    50     .009   -.011      7      7      0      14
 -  SEP 10    35    64     .019   -.015      5      9      0      14
 +  SEP 11    61    38     .015   -.019      8      5      0      13
 -  SEP 12    38    61     .008   -.014      5      8      0      13
 -  SEP 13    30    69     .020   -.012      4      9      0      13
 -  SEP 14    28    64     .017   -.011      4      9      1      14
    SEP 15    42    50     .010   -.008      6      7      1      14
    SEP 16    50    50     .013   -.014      7      7      0      14
--  SEP 17    28    71     .011   -.017      4     10      0      14
--  SEP 18    15    76     .011   -.017      2     10      1      13
    SEP 19    38    53     .016   -.016      5      7      1      13
    SEP 20    46    53     .017   -.021      6      7      0      13
    SEP 21    57    42     .021   -.018      8      6      0      14
--  SEP 22    21    71     .020   -.014      3     10      1      14
    SEP 23    57    35     .009   -.016      8      5      1      14
--  SEP 24    28    71     .008   -.012      4     10      0      14
 +  SEP 25    61    38     .009   -.012      8      5      0      13
    SEP 26    46    46     .011   -.025      6      6      1      13
    SEP 27    53    46     .011   -.014      7      6      0      13
 -  SEP 28    28    64     .018   -.012      4      9      1      14
    SEP 29    42    57     .009   -.009      6      8      0      14
    SEP 30    57    35     .013   -.011      8      5      1      14
++  OCT  1    78    21     .010   -.015     11      3      0      14
 -  OCT  2    30    69     .012   -.012      4      9      0      13
 +  OCT  3    69    30     .019   -.017      9      4      0      13
    OCT  4    38    53     .007   -.013      5      7      1      13
    OCT  5    57    28     .012   -.016      8      4      2      14
++  OCT  6    78    21     .011   -.014     11      3      0      14
```

DAILY MARKET PROBABILITY STATISTICS
■■■■■■■■■■■■■■■■■■■■■■■■■■■■■■■■■■■■■

File used: 01LB - LUMBER

	Month/ Day	--- % --- Up	Down	-- Average -- Up	Down	--------- Years --------- Up	Down	Unch	Total
	OCT 22	50	42	.019	-.007	7	6	1	14
+	OCT 23	61	38	.015	-.015	8	5	0	13
	OCT 24	53	46	.010	-.012	7	6	0	13
-	OCT 25	30	69	.014	-.014	4	9	0	13
--	OCT 26	28	71	.008	-.014	4	10	0	14
	OCT 27	50	50	.015	-.014	7	7	0	14
	OCT 28	50	42	.012	-.014	7	6	1	14
+	OCT 29	64	35	.019	-.006	9	5	0	14
	OCT 30	53	46	.012	-.012	7	6	0	13
	OCT 31	46	53	.015	-.008	6	7	0	13
+	NOV 1	61	38	.010	-.011	8	5	0	13
	NOV 2	46	53	.013	-.010	6	7	0	13
	NOV 3	53	46	.015	-.014	7	6	0	13
-	NOV 4	30	61	.012	-.011	4	8	1	13
+	NOV 5	69	15	.014	-.005	9	2	2	13
	NOV 6	46	53	.011	-.016	6	7	0	13
	NOV 7	45	54	.011	-.010	5	6	0	11
+	NOV 8	61	38	.008	-.011	8	5	0	13
	NOV 9	50	50	.009	-.008	7	7	0	14
	NOV 10	50	50	.010	-.015	7	7	0	14
	NOV 11	50	42	.008	-.007	7	6	1	14
	NOV 12	50	28	.023	-.010	7	4	3	14
--	NOV 13	23	76	.024	-.014	3	10	0	13
+	NOV 14	61	30	.010	-.023	8	4	1	13
-	NOV 15	30	69	.013	-.020	4	9	0	13
+++	NOV 16	92	7	.012	-.034	13	1	0	14
++	NOV 17	71	28	.016	-.017	10	4	0	14
	NOV 18	50	42	.016	-.012	7	6	1	14
	NOV 19	42	57	.013	-.014	6	8	0	14
	NOV 20	46	53	.017	-.015	6	7	0	13
+	NOV 21	61	38	.014	-.014	8	5	0	13
--	NOV 22	30	70	.025	-.007	3	7	0	10
+	NOV 23	66	25	.013	-.006	8	3	1	12
	NOV 24	55	33	.015	-.015	5	3	1	9
+++	NOV 25	80	20	.010	-.030	8	2	0	10
++	NOV 26	72	27	.016	-.030	8	3	0	11
+++	NOV 27	80	20	.013	-.023	8	2	0	10
	NOV 28	45	54	.021	-.011	5	6	0	11
-	NOV 29	30	69	.012	-.009	4	9	0	13
	NOV 30	35	50	.012	-.014	5	7	2	14
+	DEC 1	64	35	.008	-.013	9	5	0	14
	DEC 2	42	50	.009	-.009	6	7	1	14
++	DEC 3	78	21	.008	-.018	11	3	0	14
	DEC 4	53	46	.016	-.014	7	6	0	13
-	DEC 5	38	61	.015	-.013	5	8	0	13

```
       DAILY MARKET PROBABILITY STATISTICS
       ===================================

File used:    03CC - COFFEE

   Month/    --- % ---    -- Average --    ---------- Years ----------
    Day      Up   Down     Up     Down      Up    Down    Unch    Total
   ======    ==== ====    ====== ======    ====== ====== ====== ======

 +  DEC 22   63    36     .016   -.013      7      4       0      11
    DEC 23   50    50     .015   -.003      6      6       0      12
 -- DEC 24   25    75     .016   -.002      1      3       0       4
    DEC 26   50    50     .009   -.016      3      3       0       6
    DEC 27   50    50     .006   -.024      6      6       0      12
 -  DEC 28   36    63     .017   -.010      4      7       0      11
    DEC 29   58    41     .014   -.010      7      5       0      12
    DEC 30   41    58     .015   -.012      5      7       0      12
 ++ DEC 31   70    30     .012   -.004      7      3       0      10
    JAN  3   42    57     .005   -.012      3      4       0       7
 +  JAN  4   60    40     .011   -.013      6      4       0      10
 +  JAN  5   66    33     .014   -.016      6      3       0       9
 -  JAN  6   33    66     .010   -.012      4      8       0      12
 -  JAN  7   33    66     .025   -.011      4      8       0      12
    JAN  8   41    50     .010   -.013      5      6       1      12
    JAN  9   46    53     .012   -.017      6      7       0      13
    JAN 10   58    41     .017   -.021      7      5       0      12
 -  JAN 11   33    66     .034   -.021      4      8       0      12
 +  JAN 12   66    33     .017   -.021      8      4       0      12
 -  JAN 13   33    66     .007   -.021      4      8       0      12
 +  JAN 14   66    33     .016   -.010      8      4       0      12
--- JAN 15   16    83     .008   -.020      2     10       0      12
    JAN 16   46    46     .010   -.008      6      6       1      13
    JAN 17   50    41     .012   -.011      6      5       1      12
    JAN 18   41    58     .016   -.010      5      7       0      12
    JAN 19   50    50     .010   -.010      6      6       0      12
+++ JAN 20   81    18     .013   -.006      9      2       0      11
 -  JAN 21   33    66     .010   -.013      4      8       0      12
    JAN 22   41    58     .008   -.010      5      7       0      12
 -  JAN 23   38    61     .004   -.016      5      8       0      13
    JAN 24   41    58     .018   -.018      5      7       0      12
 +  JAN 25   63    36     .009   -.005      7      4       0      11
    JAN 26   41    58     .014   -.016      5      7       0      12
 ++ JAN 27   75    25     .009   -.017      9      3       0      12
 -  JAN 28   33    66     .014   -.015      4      8       0      12
    JAN 29   41    58     .016   -.017      5      7       0      12
    JAN 30   38    53     .011   -.005      5      7       1      13
    JAN 31   41    58     .019   -.011      5      7       0      12
    FEB  1   50    41     .011   -.004      6      5       1      12
 ++ FEB  2   75    25     .011   -.003      9      3       0      12
    FEB  3   50    50     .006   -.011      6      6       0      12
 ++ FEB  4   75    25     .014   -.017      9      3       0      12
    FEB  5   58    41     .025   -.014      7      5       0      12
 +  FEB  6   61    38     .013   -.015      8      5       0      13
    FEB  7   54    45     .024   -.010      6      5       0      11
```

DAILY MARKET PROBABILITY STATISTICS
===================================

File used: 07CC - COFFEE

Month/ Day	--- % --- Up	Down	-- Average -- Up	Down	---------- Years ---------- Up	Down	Unch	Total
APR 23	50	50	.012	-.007	6	6	0	12
APR 24	58	41	.009	-.009	7	5	0	12
- APR 25	30	69	.005	-.009	4	9	0	13
APR 26	50	50	.015	-.010	6	6	0	12
APR 27	58	41	.010	-.013	7	5	0	12
- APR 28	33	66	.007	-.013	4	8	0	12
APR 29	50	50	.015	-.008	6	6	0	12
APR 30	50	50	.004	-.013	6	6	0	12
+ MAY 1	66	33	.014	-.005	8	4	0	12
MAY 2	53	46	.010	-.007	7	6	0	13
MAY 3	50	50	.009	-.012	6	6	0	12
+ MAY 4	66	33	.009	-.008	8	4	0	12
MAY 5	33	58	.013	-.008	4	7	1	12
- MAY 6	33	66	.019	-.019	4	8	0	12
MAY 7	58	41	.007	-.013	7	5	0	12
MAY 8	50	50	.010	-.007	6	6	0	12
MAY 9	53	46	.008	-.013	7	6	0	13
++ MAY 10	75	25	.010	-.014	9	3	0	12
MAY 11	50	41	.018	-.006	6	5	1	12
MAY 12	41	58	.016	-.009	5	7	0	12
- MAY 13	33	66	.007	-.011	4	8	0	12
- MAY 14	33	66	.014	-.007	4	8	0	12
MAY 15	50	50	.008	-.015	6	6	0	12
MAY 16	46	53	.023	-.006	6	7	0	13
MAY 17	50	50	.009	-.012	6	6	0	12
+ MAY 18	66	33	.015	-.015	8	4	0	12
MAY 19	50	41	.011	-.024	6	5	1	12
MAY 20	58	41	.012	-.009	7	5	0	12
++ MAY 21	75	25	.024	-.006	9	3	0	12
MAY 22	41	58	.010	-.009	5	7	0	12
- MAY 23	38	61	.008	-.011	5	8	0	13
-- MAY 24	25	75	.018	-.008	3	9	0	12
++ MAY 25	70	30	.013	-.031	7	3	0	10
MAY 26	44	55	.016	-.010	4	5	0	9
MAY 27	50	40	.021	-.020	5	4	1	10
MAY 28	55	44	.007	-.016	5	4	0	9
-- MAY 29	30	70	.014	-.020	3	7	0	10
++ MAY 30	70	30	.005	-.013	7	3	0	10
MAY 31	50	50	.013	-.021	5	5	0	10
-- JUN 1	25	75	.052	-.021	3	9	0	12
JUN 2	58	41	.016	-.009	7	5	0	12
JUN 3	58	33	.008	-.009	7	4	1	12
- JUN 4	33	66	.025	-.017	4	8	0	12
+ JUN 5	66	33	.014	-.011	8	4	0	12
+ JUN 6	61	38	.016	-.027	8	5	0	13

```
DAILY MARKET PROBABILITY STATISTICS
===================================

File used:     12CC - COFFEE
```

Month/	--- % ---		-- Average --		---------- Years ----------			
Day	Up	Down	Up	Down	Up	Down	Unch	Total

		Up	Down	Up	Down	Up	Down	Unch	Total
	SEP 22	54	45	.016	-.020	6	5	0	11
	SEP 23	58	41	.014	-.016	7	5	0	12
	SEP 24	58	41	.016	-.012	7	5	0	12
	SEP 25	54	45	.029	-.009	6	5	0	11
---	SEP 26	16	83	.010	-.015	2	10	0	12
+++	SEP 27	80	20	.015	-.007	8	2	0	10
-	SEP 28	36	63	.011	-.011	4	7	0	11
	SEP 29	54	45	.015	-.012	6	5	0	11
	SEP 30	41	58	.009	-.016	5	7	0	12
	OCT 1	58	41	.012	-.017	7	5	0	12
+++	OCT 2	100	0	.011	.000	11	0	0	11
	OCT 3	58	41	.011	-.012	7	5	0	12
	OCT 4	45	54	.009	-.014	5	6	0	11
-	OCT 5	36	63	.016	-.007	4	7	0	11
++	OCT 6	72	27	.015	-.017	8	3	0	11
+	OCT 7	66	33	.016	-.013	8	4	0	12
+	OCT 8	63	36	.010	-.016	7	4	0	11
	OCT 9	50	50	.007	-.015	5	5	0	10
++	OCT 10	72	27	.010	-.032	8	3	0	11
--	OCT 11	20	70	.016	-.008	2	7	1	10
	OCT 12	45	54	.016	-.016	5	6	0	11
-	OCT 13	40	60	.019	-.006	4	6	0	10
---	OCT 14	20	80	.002	-.016	2	8	0	10
++	OCT 15	75	25	.016	-.011	9	3	0	12
	OCT 16	45	54	.007	-.011	5	6	0	11
	OCT 17	50	50	.010	-.015	6	6	0	12
	OCT 18	45	54	.010	-.009	5	6	0	11
-	OCT 19	40	60	.019	-.015	4	6	0	10
-	OCT 20	36	63	.004	-.027	4	7	0	11
	OCT 21	50	50	.014	-.010	6	6	0	12
	OCT 22	50	50	.008	-.006	6	6	0	12
	OCT 23	45	36	.016	-.004	5	4	2	11
+	OCT 24	66	33	.017	-.010	8	4	0	12
	OCT 25	45	54	.017	-.009	5	6	0	11
--	OCT 26	27	72	.004	-.006	3	8	0	11
	OCT 27	54	45	.022	-.009	6	5	0	11
	OCT 28	58	41	.026	-.013	7	5	0	12
-	OCT 29	33	66	.003	-.015	4	8	0	12
+	OCT 30	63	36	.010	-.010	7	4	0	11
+	OCT 31	66	33	.017	-.005	8	4	0	12
	NOV 1	45	54	.011	-.012	5	6	0	11
	NOV 2	44	55	.017	-.012	4	5	0	9
-	NOV 3	36	63	.025	-.010	4	7	0	11
	NOV 4	50	40	.024	-.019	5	4	1	10
	NOV 5	45	54	.009	-.010	5	6	0	11

DAILY MARKET PROBABILITY STATISTICS
=====================================

File used: 03SU - SUGAR

	Month/ Day	--- % --- Up	Down	-- Average -- Up	Down	---------- Years ---------- Up	Down	Unch	Total
	DEC 22	50	37	.020	-.013	8	6	2	16
	DEC 23	41	52	.029	-.018	7	9	1	17
	DEC 24	42	57	.014	-.009	3	4	0	7
	DEC 26	42	42	.030	-.019	3	3	1	7
	DEC 27	46	53	.015	-.022	7	8	0	15
	DEC 28	50	42	.012	-.016	7	6	1	14
	DEC 29	41	58	.021	-.018	7	10	0	17
	DEC 30	47	52	.019	-.014	8	9	0	17
+	DEC 31	66	16	.019	-.034	8	2	2	12
-	JAN 3	37	62	.008	-.023	3	5	0	8
	JAN 4	46	38	.019	-.033	6	5	2	13
	JAN 5	42	57	.025	-.016	6	8	0	14
	JAN 6	55	44	.018	-.029	10	8	0	18
	JAN 7	37	56	.019	-.020	6	9	1	16
	JAN 8	46	46	.028	-.029	7	7	1	15
	JAN 9	43	56	.028	-.019	7	9	0	16
+	JAN 10	62	37	.024	-.016	10	6	0	16
	JAN 11	50	43	.027	-.025	8	7	1	16
	JAN 12	55	44	.020	-.027	10	8	0	18
+	JAN 13	61	38	.026	-.026	11	7	0	18
+++	JAN 14	81	18	.025	-.027	13	3	0	16
	JAN 15	46	53	.024	-.020	7	8	0	15
	JAN 16	31	50	.020	-.023	5	8	3	16
+	JAN 17	62	31	.025	-.015	10	5	1	16
	JAN 18	53	46	.014	-.018	8	7	0	15
	JAN 19	55	44	.020	-.018	10	8	0	18
+	JAN 20	64	35	.013	-.019	11	6	0	17
+	JAN 21	68	31	.024	-.022	11	5	0	16
-	JAN 22	40	60	.037	-.017	6	9	0	15
++	JAN 23	75	25	.042	-.028	12	4	0	16
	JAN 24	50	50	.019	-.032	8	8	0	16
+	JAN 25	66	33	.024	-.020	10	5	0	15
+	JAN 26	66	33	.018	-.018	12	6	0	18
	JAN 27	55	44	.022	-.021	10	8	0	18
-	JAN 28	31	68	.025	-.028	5	11	0	16
-	JAN 29	26	60	.047	-.021	4	9	2	15
+	JAN 30	62	37	.013	-.015	10	6	0	16
	JAN 31	50	43	.032	-.015	8	7	1	16
	FEB 1	50	50	.020	-.027	8	8	0	16
	FEB 2	44	44	.022	-.017	8	8	2	18
-	FEB 3	27	66	.020	-.021	5	12	1	18
	FEB 4	50	50	.016	-.023	8	8	0	16
-	FEB 5	33	60	.025	-.023	5	9	1	15
	FEB 6	37	56	.039	-.026	6	9	1	16
	FEB 7	40	53	.022	-.021	6	8	1	15

```
DAILY MARKET PROBABILITY STATISTICS
===================================

File used:    07SU - SUGAR

   Month/   --- % ---   -- Average --   ---------- Years ----------
   Day      Up  Down     Up     Down      Up    Down   Unch   Total
   ======   ==== ====   ====== ======   ====== ====== ====== ======

   APR 23    43   56    .015   -.020      7      9      0      16
   APR 24    47   52    .026   -.025      8      9      0      17
   APR 25    55   44    .022   -.020     10      8      0      18
   APR 26    52   47    .019   -.026      9      8      0      17
-- APR 27    17   76    .013   -.018      3     13      1      17
   APR 28    50   50    .017   -.029      9      9      0      18
   APR 29    58   35    .023   -.020     10      6      1      17
   APR 30    50   31    .020   -.023      8      5      3      16
   MAY  1    41   52    .027   -.029      7      9      1      17
   MAY  2    44   44    .026   -.027      8      8      2      18
   MAY  3    58   41    .020   -.024     10      7      0      17
--- MAY  4    17   82    .019   -.017      3     14      0      17
   MAY  5    33   55    .014   -.018      6     10      2      18
   MAY  6    41   52    .025   -.018      7      9      1      17
   MAY  7    31   56    .049   -.029      5      9      2      16
++ MAY  8    70   29    .026   -.010     12      5      0      17
 + MAY  9    61   38    .025   -.018     11      7      0      18
-- MAY 10    29   70    .010   -.018      5     12      0      17
 - MAY 11    35   64    .026   -.025      6     11      0      17
 - MAY 12    38   61    .023   -.023      7     11      0      18
   MAY 13    52   41    .020   -.029      9      7      1      17
   MAY 14    50   50    .021   -.024      8      8      0      16
   MAY 15    52   41    .022   -.016      9      7      1      17
   MAY 16    50   44    .019   -.014      9      8      1      18
   MAY 17    41   52    .019   -.012      7      9      1      17
   MAY 18    47   41    .018   -.019      8      7      2      17
 + MAY 19    61   38    .017   -.025     11      7      0      18
   MAY 20    41   52    .033   -.028      7      9      1      17
   MAY 21    50   50    .030   -.021      8      8      0      16
   MAY 22    47   41    .027   -.025      8      7      2      17
   MAY 23    55   38    .024   -.013     10      7      1      18
   MAY 24    41   58    .013   -.016      7     10      0      17
 - MAY 25    33   66    .022   -.014      5     10      0      15
   MAY 26    53   46    .029   -.015      8      7      0      15
   MAY 27    40   53    .021   -.013      6      8      1      15
 - MAY 28    30   61    .012   -.035      4      8      1      13
   MAY 29    41   50    .037   -.022      5      6      1      12
 - MAY 30    27   63    .013   -.025      3      7      1      11
 + MAY 31    64   35    .035   -.028      9      5      0      14
   JUN  1    35   58    .037   -.033      6     10      1      17
 + JUN  2    61   38    .021   -.025     11      7      0      18
   JUN  3    47   52    .019   -.043      8      9      0      17
 - JUN  4    31   68    .024   -.015      5     11      0      16
   JUN  5    47   52    .029   -.023      8      9      0      17
 - JUN  6    38   61    .032   -.042      7     11      0      18
```

DAILY MARKET PROBABILITY STATISTICS

File used: 10SU - SUGAR

	Month/ Day	--- % --- Up	Down	-- Average -- Up	Down	---------- Years ---------- Up	Down	Unch	Total
-	JUL 23	25	68	.023	-.027	4	11	1	16
	JUL 24	43	50	.026	-.023	7	8	1	16
+	JUL 25	64	29	.039	-.027	11	5	1	17
	JUL 26	56	37	.029	-.045	9	6	1	16
	JUL 27	43	56	.019	-.020	7	9	0	16
	JUL 28	52	47	.024	-.027	9	8	0	17
	JUL 29	47	52	.023	-.026	8	9	0	17
	JUL 30	37	56	.020	-.023	6	9	1	16
	JUL 31	50	37	.018	-.028	8	6	2	16
	AUG 1	58	35	.026	-.011	10	6	1	17
+	AUG 2	68	31	.024	-.029	11	5	0	16
	AUG 3	50	50	.019	-.036	8	8	0	16
+	AUG 4	64	35	.030	-.015	11	6	0	17
	AUG 5	47	47	.019	-.019	8	8	1	17
	AUG 6	56	43	.017	-.015	9	7	0	16
	AUG 7	43	50	.025	-.036	7	8	1	16
	AUG 8	41	58	.030	-.019	7	10	0	17
	AUG 9	31	56	.011	-.025	5	9	2	16
	AUG 10	50	50	.016	-.017	8	8	0	16
--	AUG 11	23	70	.021	-.017	4	12	1	17
	AUG 12	52	41	.022	-.032	9	7	1	17
	AUG 13	43	56	.023	-.029	7	9	0	16
-	AUG 14	31	62	.011	-.024	5	10	1	16
	AUG 15	41	52	.020	-.031	7	9	1	17
	AUG 16	50	50	.034	-.026	8	8	0	16
	AUG 17	31	56	.014	-.018	5	9	2	16
+	AUG 18	64	35	.023	-.027	11	6	0	17
--	AUG 19	29	70	.023	-.032	5	12	0	17
	AUG 20	43	50	.016	-.026	7	8	1	16
+	AUG 21	62	37	.017	-.025	10	6	0	16
	AUG 22	58	41	.027	-.021	10	7	0	17
	AUG 23	43	56	.036	-.030	7	9	0	16
	AUG 24	50	50	.014	-.028	8	8	0	16
	AUG 25	41	52	.011	-.029	7	9	1	17
	AUG 26	41	58	.027	-.024	7	10	0	17
	AUG 27	56	37	.035	-.011	9	6	1	16
+	AUG 28	62	37	.021	-.010	10	6	0	16
	AUG 29	41	52	.022	-.029	7	9	1	17
	AUG 30	43	50	.020	-.020	7	8	1	16
	AUG 31	56	31	.007	-.015	9	5	2	16
+	SEP 1	61	38	.026	-.038	8	5	0	13
--	SEP 2	21	71	.015	-.025	3	10	1	14
	SEP 3	46	46	.041	-.037	6	6	1	13
---	SEP 4	15	84	.021	-.019	2	11	0	13
	SEP 5	38	53	.027	-.031	5	7	1	13

```
DAILY MARKET PROBABILITY STATISTICS
===================================

File used:   03CO - COCOA
```

Month/ Day	% Up	% Down	Average Up	Average Down	Years Up	Years Down	Years Unch	Years Total
- FEB 8	35	64	.019	-.011	6	11	0	17
FEB 9	50	50	.013	-.011	9	9	0	18
FEB 10	58	41	.012	-.013	10	7	0	17
FEB 11	41	58	.018	-.014	7	10	0	17
--- FEB 12	14	85	.011	-.014	1	6	0	7
+ FEB 13	62	31	.015	-.013	10	5	1	16
FEB 14	47	47	.025	-.019	8	8	1	17
FEB 15	57	35	.010	-.015	8	5	1	14
- FEB 16	33	60	.017	-.019	5	9	1	15
FEB 17	31	56	.007	-.019	5	9	2	16
FEB 18	50	50	.013	-.012	7	7	0	14
FEB 19	35	57	.014	-.011	5	8	1	14
FEB 20	50	50	.020	-.018	7	7	0	14
FEB 21	46	46	.019	-.022	6	6	1	13
FEB 22	57	42	.011	-.013	8	6	0	14
FEB 23	58	41	.017	-.014	10	7	0	17
++ FEB 24	72	27	.018	-.014	13	5	0	18
FEB 25	41	52	.016	-.019	7	9	1	17
FEB 26	37	56	.008	-.020	6	9	1	16
++ FEB 27	70	29	.015	-.026	12	5	0	17
-- FEB 28	23	70	.012	-.013	4	12	1	17
--- FEB 29	20	80	.019	-.005	1	4	0	5
MAR 1	58	41	.021	-.010	10	7	0	17
- MAR 2	35	64	.020	-.013	6	11	0	17
+ MAR 3	61	38	.015	-.013	11	7	0	18
MAR 4	52	41	.011	-.014	9	7	1	17
MAR 5	37	56	.014	-.020	6	9	1	16
MAR 6	52	47	.018	-.014	9	8	0	17
+ MAR 7	61	33	.018	-.017	11	6	1	18
++ MAR 8	70	29	.013	-.021	12	5	0	17
MAR 9	47	52	.010	-.017	8	9	0	17
MAR 10	50	50	.012	-.026	9	9	0	18
++ MAR 11	76	23	.018	-.008	13	4	0	17
MAR 12	43	56	.016	-.009	7	9	0	16
MAR 13	58	35	.023	-.016	10	6	1	17
+ MAR 14	61	38	.025	-.025	11	7	0	18
+ MAR 15	64	29	.020	-.013	11	5	1	17
MAR 16	43	56	.012	-.021	7	9	0	16
MAR 17	46	53	.018	-.020	7	8	0	15
MAR 18	41	58	.026	-.012	5	7	0	12
++ MAR 19	75	25	.011	-.013	9	3	0	12
MAR 20	45	54	.010	-.015	5	6	0	11
MAR 21	44	55	.019	-.011	4	5	0	9
MAR 22	42	57	.022	-.008	3	4	0	7
+ MAR 23	66	33	.024	-.023	2	1	0	3

DAILY MARKET PROBABILITY STATISTICS
==================================

File used: 07CO - COCOA

Month/ Day	--- % --- Up	Down	-- Average -- Up	Down	---------- Years ---------- Up	Down	Uncn	Tota
APR 23	43	56	.020	-.009	7	9	0	16
-- APR 24	29	70	.022	-.013	5	12	0	17
APR 25	50	50	.013	-.018	9	9	0	18
+ APR 26	64	35	.014	-.016	11	6	0	17
APR 27	47	52	.010	-.013	8	9	0	17
- APR 28	33	61	.014	-.022	6	11	1	18
APR 29	58	41	.018	-.012	10	7	0	17
APR 30	50	50	.012	-.017	8	8	0	16
++ MAY 1	70	29	.010	-.013	12	5	0	17
MAY 2	55	44	.013	-.009	10	8	0	18
-- MAY 3	29	70	.013	-.011	5	12	0	17
MAY 4	47	52	.016	-.021	8	9	0	17
MAY 5	50	50	.007	-.015	9	9	0	18
MAY 6	41	52	.014	-.018	7	9	1	17
MAY 7	56	43	.016	-.009	9	7	0	16
MAY 8	41	58	.017	-.012	7	10	0	17
MAY 9	44	55	.013	-.017	8	10	0	18
MAY 10	52	47	.009	-.018	9	8	0	17
MAY 11	41	58	.012	-.016	7	10	0	17
MAY 12	44	55	.016	-.014	8	10	0	18
- MAY 13	35	64	.019	-.017	6	11	0	17
- MAY 14	37	62	.009	-.012	6	10	0	16
MAY 15	58	41	.010	-.017	10	7	0	17
MAY 16	50	50	.016	-.016	9	9	0	18
MAY 17	58	41	.012	-.006	10	7	0	17
+ MAY 18	64	29	.018	-.013	11	5	1	17
MAY 19	55	44	.024	-.010	10	8	0	18
MAY 20	47	52	.020	-.013	8	9	0	17
+ MAY 21	62	31	.013	-.015	10	5	1	16
MAY 22	58	35	.014	-.014	10	6	1	17
MAY 23	44	55	.014	-.011	8	10	0	18
MAY 24	41	58	.011	-.015	7	10	0	17
MAY 25	53	46	.020	-.009	8	7	0	15
- MAY 26	40	60	.022	-.023	6	9	0	15
- MAY 27	40	60	.011	-.012	6	9	0	15
MAY 28	53	46	.011	-.012	7	6	0	13
MAY 29	58	41	.016	-.015	7	5	0	12
-- MAY 30	27	72	.010	-.023	3	8	0	11
MAY 31	46	53	.018	-.019	6	7	0	13
JUN 1	41	58	.013	-.020	7	10	0	17
JUN 2	50	50	.013	-.018	9	9	0	18
JUN 3	41	47	.009	-.011	7	8	2	17
JUN 4	56	43	.016	-.018	9	7	0	16
JUN 5	41	58	.018	-.017	7	10	0	17
JUN 6	44	55	.015	-.012	8	10	0	18

```
          DAILY MARKET PROBABILITY STATISTICS
          ====================================

File used:    12CO - COCOA

     Month/   --- % ---   -- Average --   ---------- Years ----------
      Day     Up  Down     Up    Down       Up   Down   Unch   Total
     ======   ==== ====   ====== ======   ====== ====== ====== ======

      SEP 22   52   47    .017  -.020       9     8      0      17
      SEP 23   47   47    .016  -.019       8     8      1      17
      SEP 24   56   43    .019  -.009       9     7      0      16
   +  SEP 25   62   37    .010  -.015      10     6      0      16
  --  SEP 26   29   70    .019  -.015       5    12      0      17
   -  SEP 27   40   60    .021  -.020       6     9      0      15
   -  SEP 28   37   62    .014  -.019       6    10      0      16
      SEP 29   58   41    .015  -.023      10     7      0      17
      SEP 30   52   47    .015  -.012       9     8      0      17
      OCT  1   56   43    .011  -.016       9     7      0      16
      OCT  2   50   50    .014  -.009       8     8      0      16
      OCT  3   52   41    .014  -.014       9     7      1      17
      OCT  4   37   56    .012  -.017       6     9      1      16
      OCT  5   50   43    .022  -.012       8     7      1      16
      OCT  6   41   58    .012  -.015       7    10      0      17
   +  OCT  7   64   35    .017  -.025      11     6      0      17
   -  OCT  8   40   60    .012  -.016       6     9      0      15
      OCT  9   57   42    .022  -.009       8     6      0      14
   +  OCT 10   62   37    .016  -.018      10     6      0      16
  --  OCT 11   28   71    .015  -.017       4    10      0      14
   -  OCT 12   38   61    .012  -.025       5     8      0      13
   +  OCT 13   60   40    .013  -.012       9     6      0      15
      OCT 14   53   46    .014  -.014       8     7      0      15
   -  OCT 15   37   62    .021  -.015       6    10      0      16
   +  OCT 16   62   31    .015  -.016      10     5      1      16
      OCT 17   58   41    .012  -.015      10     7      0      17
   +  OCT 18   62   37    .017  -.012      10     6      0      16
   +  OCT 19   62   37    .007  -.019      10     6      0      16
  ++  OCT 20   70   29    .011  -.023      12     5      0      17
      OCT 21   58   41    .015  -.010      10     7      0      17
   +  OCT 22   66   33    .009  -.009      10     5      0      15
   -  OCT 23   33   60    .012  -.009       5     9      1      15
      OCT 24   35   58    .014  -.013       6    10      1      17
      OCT 25   53   46    .013  -.024       8     7      0      15
      OCT 26   43   56    .010  -.014       7     9      0      16
      OCT 27   41   58    .006  -.013       7    10      0      17
      OCT 28   58   41    .013  -.027      10     7      0      17
   -  OCT 29   31   68    .015  -.012       5    11      0      16
      OCT 30   43   50    .016  -.013       7     8      1      16
  ++  OCT 31   76   23    .016  -.019      13     4      0      17
   +  NOV  1   68   31    .012  -.018      11     5      0      16
  ++  NOV  2   76   23    .014  -.016      10     3      0      13
      NOV  3   43   56    .021  -.016       7     9      0      16
      NOV  4   50   50    .024  -.013       7     7      0      14
      NOV  5   50   50    .011  -.014       7     7      0      14
```

DAILY MARKET PROBABILITY STATISTICS
==

File used: 05CP - COPPER

Month/ Day	--- % --- Up	Down	-- Average -- Up	Down	---------- Years ---------- Up	Down	Unch	Total
FEB 24	38	55	.014	-.008	7	10	1	18
FEB 25	35	58	.011	-.014	6	10	1	17
+ FEB 26	62	37	.015	-.021	10	6	0	16
++ FEB 27	70	23	.014	-.010	12	4	1	17
FEB 28	41	47	.014	-.019	7	8	2	17
- FEB 29	40	60	.017	-.015	2	3	0	5
+ MAR 1	64	35	.017	-.012	11	6	0	17
MAR 2	41	58	.015	-.014	7	10	0	17
MAR 3	44	50	.012	-.011	8	9	1	18
++ MAR 4	70	29	.014	-.018	12	5	0	17
+ MAR 5	62	37	.011	-.019	10	6	0	16
MAR 6	52	41	.017	-.013	9	7	1	17
MAR 7	50	50	.016	-.011	9	9	0	18
MAR 8	52	47	.009	-.017	9	8	0	17
MAR 9	47	52	.014	-.011	8	9	0	17
+ MAR 10	61	27	.012	-.021	11	5	2	18
MAR 11	41	58	.016	-.007	7	10	0	17
- MAR 12	31	62	.016	-.010	5	10	1	16
+ MAR 13	64	29	.008	-.027	11	5	1	17
+ MAR 14	61	38	.015	-.005	11	7	0	18
+ MAR 15	62	37	.008	-.016	10	6	0	16
MAR 16	41	58	.021	-.007	7	10	0	17
+ MAR 17	66	33	.011	-.017	12	6	0	18
MAR 18	52	47	.018	-.009	9	8	0	17
++ MAR 19	75	25	.016	-.007	12	4	0	16
MAR 20	41	52	.013	-.015	7	9	1	17
MAR 21	44	50	.012	-.015	8	9	1	18
MAR 22	41	58	.014	-.010	7	10	0	17
MAR 23	52	41	.012	-.008	9	7	1	17
MAR 24	46	53	.017	-.010	7	8	0	15
--- MAR 25	17	82	.023	-.010	3	14	0	17
MAR 26	50	50	.013	-.016	8	8	0	16
+ MAR 27	68	31	.013	-.021	11	5	0	16
+ MAR 28	62	37	.022	-.012	10	6	0	16
MAR 29	47	47	.016	-.010	8	8	1	17
MAR 30	47	52	.016	-.008	8	9	0	17
MAR 31	50	50	.007	-.012	8	8	0	16
- APR 1	40	60	.015	-.013	6	9	0	15
APR 2	56	43	.018	-.014	9	7	0	16
-- APR 3	29	70	.007	-.016	5	12	0	17
APR 4	56	37	.018	-.009	9	6	1	16
APR 5	43	56	.014	-.016	7	9	0	16
APR 6	58	41	.010	-.014	10	7	0	17
APR 7	55	38	.013	-.008	10	7	1	18
- APR 8	40	60	.013	-.012	6	9	0	15

DAILY MARKET PROBABILITY STATISTICS
==

File used: 07CP - COPPER

Month/ Day	--- % --- Up	Down	-- Average -- Up	Down	---------- Years ---------- Up	Down	Unch	Total
APR 23	56	43	.009	-.011	9	7	0	16
APR 24	35	58	.019	-.015	6	10	1	17
- APR 25	38	61	.015	-.015	7	11	0	18
APR 26	41	52	.013	-.014	7	9	1	17
- APR 27	35	64	.013	-.017	6	11	0	17
- APR 28	33	66	.008	-.015	6	12	0	18
APR 29	47	52	.017	-.011	8	9	0	17
APR 30	56	43	.012	-.015	9	7	0	16
-- MAY 1	23	70	.007	-.011	4	12	1	17
MAY 2	55	44	.012	-.013	10	8	0	18
MAY 3	58	41	.011	-.010	10	7	0	17
MAY 4	35	58	.011	-.013	6	10	1	17
MAY 5	44	50	.008	-.012	8	9	1	18
MAY 6	47	52	.014	-.011	8	9	0	17
MAY 7	56	31	.016	-.017	9	5	2	16
MAY 8	41	58	.009	-.014	7	10	0	17
MAY 9	55	33	.012	-.008	10	6	2	18
MAY 10	47	47	.009	-.014	8	8	1	17
- MAY 11	35	64	.011	-.014	6	11	0	17
MAY 12	44	38	.008	-.009	8	7	3	18
MAY 13	41	58	.013	-.010	7	10	0	17
+ MAY 14	62	31	.006	-.011	10	5	1	16
MAY 15	58	35	.012	-.014	10	6	1	17
MAY 16	44	50	.008	-.016	8	9	1	18
MAY 17	47	52	.015	-.016	8	9	0	17
MAY 18	47	52	.012	-.016	8	9	0	17
MAY 19	50	50	.012	-.011	9	9	0	18
MAY 20	52	41	.011	-.019	9	7	1	17
MAY 21	50	50	.011	-.010	8	8	0	16
+ MAY 22	64	29	.008	-.020	11	5	1	17
MAY 23	44	50	.015	-.011	8	9	1	18
MAY 24	47	52	.009	-.018	8	9	0	17
MAY 25	46	53	.013	-.015	7	8	0	15
+ MAY 26	66	33	.012	-.012	10	5	0	15
MAY 27	53	46	.010	-.012	8	7	0	15
- MAY 28	30	61	.010	-.017	4	8	1	13
- MAY 29	38	61	.009	-.011	5	8	0	13
- MAY 30	27	63	.010	-.010	3	7	1	11
- MAY 31	38	61	.011	-.008	5	8	0	13
JUN 1	47	52	.007	-.016	8	9	0	17
- JUN 2	38	61	.026	-.009	7	11	0	18
-- JUN 3	29	70	.014	-.016	5	12	0	17
+ JUN 4	62	37	.017	-.012	10	6	0	16
-- JUN 5	29	70	.022	-.016	5	12	0	17
JUN 6	55	44	.008	-.017	10	8	0	18

```
                 DAILY MARKET PROBABILITY STATISTICS
                 ===================================

File used:       12CP - COPPER

        Month/   --- % ---   -- Average --   ---------- Years ----------
        Day      Up   Down   Up      Down    Up      Down    Unch    Total
        ======   ==== ====   ======  ======  ======  ======  ======  ======

        SEP 22   47    52    .018   -.013     8       9       0       17
   ++   SEP 23   70    29    .013   -.017    12       5       0       17
    +   SEP 24   62    37    .014   -.017    10       6       0       16
        SEP 25   50    50    .012   -.020     8       8       0       16
        SEP 26   41    58    .021   -.009     7      10       0       17
        SEP 27   37    56    .018   -.012     6       9       1       16
        SEP 28   56    43    .011   -.015     9       7       0       16
    -   SEP 29   35    64    .012   -.011     6      11       0       17
        SEP 30   47    47    .017   -.008     8       8       1       17
    +   OCT  1   62    37    .014   -.016    10       6       0       16
    -   OCT  2   31    62    .018   -.015     5      10       1       16
        OCT  3   41    58    .012   -.014     7      10       0       17
    +   OCT  4   62    37    .008   -.012    10       6       0       16
        OCT  5   56    43    .013   -.011     9       7       0       16
        OCT  6   52    35    .014   -.011     9       6       2       17
    +   OCT  7   64    35    .016   -.009    11       6       0       17
   --   OCT  8   26    73    .009   -.015     4      11       0       15
        OCT  9   46    46    .016   -.012     7       7       1       15
        OCT 10   47    52    .012   -.021     8       9       0       17
        OCT 11   53    46    .011   -.016     8       7       0       15
        OCT 12   46    53    .019   -.009     6       7       0       13
        OCT 13   40    53    .019   -.010     6       8       1       15
        OCT 14   50    50    .019   -.006     8       8       0       16
        OCT 15   43    50    .011   -.017     7       8       1       16
        OCT 16   43    56    .010   -.020     7       9       0       16
        OCT 17   35    52    .012   -.011     6       9       2       17
        OCT 18   56    37    .011   -.011     9       6       1       16
    -   OCT 19   31    68    .020   -.015     5      11       0       16
        OCT 20   58    41    .012   -.026    10       7       0       17
        OCT 21   58    41    .012   -.007    10       7       0       17
    -   OCT 22   40    60    .016   -.009     6       9       0       15
  +++   OCT 23   86    13    .015   -.017    13       2       0       15
    -   OCT 24   35    64    .011   -.010     6      11       0       17
        OCT 25   53    46    .017   -.015     8       7       0       15
        OCT 26   31    56    .012   -.018     5       9       2       16
    +   OCT 27   64    29    .011   -.013    11       5       1       17
        OCT 28   47    35    .015   -.010     8       6       3       17
        OCT 29   50    37    .010   -.013     8       6       2       16
    +   OCT 30   68    31    .014   -.005    11       5       0       16
   ++   OCT 31   70    29    .018   -.012    12       5       0       17
        NOV  1   50    43    .013   -.011     8       7       1       16
    +   NOV  2   61    38    .019   -.006     8       5       0       13
        NOV  3   43    56    .008   -.011     7       9       0       16
        NOV  4   57    42    .013   -.009     8       6       0       14
        NOV  5   57    35    .008   -.010     8       5       1       14
```

DAILY MARKET PROBABILITY STATISTICS
■■■■■■■■■■■■■■■■■■■■■■■■■■■■■■■■■■■■■■

File used: 02GC - GOLD

Month/	--- % ---		-- Average --		---------- Years ----------			
Day	Up	Down	Up	Down	Up	Down	Unch	Total
NOV 22	57	28	.147	-.113	4	2	1	7
NOV 23	44	55	.091	-.084	4	5	0	9
++ NOV 24	75	25	.082	-.170	6	2	0	8
+++ NOV 25	87	12	.119	-.070	7	1	0	8
--- NOV 26	12	87	.395	-.124	1	7	0	8
NOV 27	50	50	.134	-.172	3	3	0	6
++ NOV 28	77	22	.186	-.186	7	2	0	9
- NOV 29	33	66	.084	-.039	3	6	0	9
++ NOV 30	70	30	.128	-.081	7	3	0	10
-- DEC 1	27	72	.099	-.064	3	8	0	11
DEC 2	45	54	.185	-.059	5	6	0	11
++ DEC 3	70	30	.093	-.044	7	3	0	10
-- DEC 4	11	77	.023	-.080	1	7	1	9
+ DEC 5	60	40	.051	-.036	6	4	0	10
DEC 6	55	44	.081	-.056	5	4	0	9
- DEC 7	40	60	.107	-.080	4	6	0	10
- DEC 8	36	63	.144	-.176	4	7	0	11
DEC 9	54	45	.050	-.155	6	5	0	11
+ DEC 10	60	40	.109	-.176	6	4	0	10
DEC 11	44	55	.108	-.112	4	5	0	9
+ DEC 12	60	40	.124	-.085	6	4	0	10
DEC 13	44	55	.165	-.087	4	5	0	9
+ DEC 14	60	40	.092	-.109	6	4	0	10
DEC 15	45	45	.073	-.200	5	5	1	11
++ DEC 16	72	27	.064	-.130	8	3	0	11
-- DEC 17	30	70	.085	-.103	3	7	0	10
DEC 18	44	55	.224	-.095	4	5	0	9
DEC 19	50	50	.244	-.072	5	5	0	10
+ DEC 20	66	33	.060	-.111	6	3	0	9
DEC 21	50	40	.171	-.091	5	4	1	10
DEC 22	54	45	.072	-.097	6	5	0	11
- DEC 23	36	63	.095	-.056	4	7	0	11
DEC 24	50	50	.039	-.020	3	3	0	6
++ DEC 26	75	25	.212	-.015	3	1	0	4
+ DEC 27	66	33	.122	-.065	6	3	0	9
DEC 28	50	40	.024	-.102	5	4	1	10
+ DEC 29	63	36	.084	-.141	7	4	0	11
DEC 30	54	36	.052	-.092	6	4	1	11
+ DEC 31	62	37	.167	-.024	5	3	0	8
- JAN 3	40	60	.238	-.035	2	3	0	5
JAN 4	50	50	.154	-.129	4	4	0	8
JAN 5	45	54	.092	-.093	5	6	0	11
JAN 6	50	50	.036	-.083	6	6	0	12
JAN 7	45	54	.182	-.105	5	6	0	11
- JAN 8	40	60	.116	-.164	4	6	0	10

```
              DAILY MARKET PROBABILITY STATISTICS
              ===================================

File used:    06GC - GOLD

        Month/   --- % ---   -- Average --   ---------- Years ----------
        Day      Up  Down     Up     Down     Up    Down    Unch    Total
        ======   ==== ====   ====== ======   ====== ====== ======  ======

   --  MAR 25    27   72     .044  -.120       3      8      0       11
   +   MAR 26    60   40     .147  -.225       6      4      0       10
   --  MAR 27    30   70     .168  -.163       3      7      0       10
   -   MAR 28    33   66     .241  -.095       3      6      0        9
   --  MAR 29    30   70     .072  -.071       3      7      0       10
   -   MAR 30    36   63     .073  -.094       4      7      0       11
       MAR 31    50   50     .109  -.114       6      6      0       12
       APR  1    33   55     .064  -.097       3      5      1        9
       APR  2    40   50     .078  -.093       4      5      1       10
   -   APR  3    40   60     .048  -.122       4      6      0       10
       APR  4    50   40     .106  -.075       5      4      1       10
   -   APR  5    33   66     .196  -.102       3      6      0        9
   ++  APR  6    72   18     .102  -.069       8      2      1       11
       APR  7    50   50     .131  -.147       6      6      0       12
  +++  APR  8    80   20     .136  -.069       8      2      0       10
   -   APR  9    22   66     .158  -.119       2      6      1        9
   -   APR 10    40   60     .046  -.057       4      6      0       10
   +   APR 11    63   36     .113  -.085       7      4      0       11
       APR 12    50   50     .039  -.109       5      5      0       10
   +   APR 13    60   30     .087  -.120       6      3      1       10
       APR 14    41   58     .213  -.167       5      7      0       12
   -   APR 15    27   63     .098  -.095       3      7      1       11
   -   APR 16    33   66     .136  -.118       3      6      0        9
   +   APR 17    62   37     .088  -.132       5      3      0        8
   +   APR 18    63   36     .148  -.041       7      4      0       11
  ---  APR 19    20   80     .035  -.137       2      8      0       10
   +   APR 20    60   40     .087  -.096       6      4      0       10
   --  APR 21    25   75     .032  -.118       3      9      0       12
   ++  APR 22    72   27     .070  -.057       8      3      0       11
   ++  APR 23    70   20     .136  -.081       7      2      1       10
   -   APR 24    40   60     .146  -.096       4      6      0       10
   -   APR 25    27   63     .081  -.047       3      7      1       11
   -   APR 26    40   60     .044  -.049       4      6      0       10
   +   APR 27    63   36     .072  -.160       7      4      0       11
  ---  APR 28     8   91     .195  -.083       1     11      0       12
       APR 29    54   27     .080  -.050       6      3      2       11
       APR 30    50   50     .051  -.248       5      5      0       10
       MAY  1    50   50     .097  -.074       5      5      0       10
       MAY  2    54   45     .050  -.053       6      5      0       11
       MAY  3    50   30     .060  -.085       5      3      2       10
       MAY  4    54   45     .056  -.082       6      5      0       11
   -   MAY  5    25   66     .051  -.063       3      8      1       12
       MAY  6    36   54     .085  -.094       4      6      1       11
   ++  MAY  7    70   30     .087  -.054       7      3      0       10
   --  MAY  8    30   70     .102  -.071       3      7      0       10
```

```
DAILY MARKET PROBABILITY STATISTICS
===================================

File used:    10GC - GOLD
```

Month/ Day	--- % --- Up	Down	-- Average -- Up	Down	---------- Years ---------- Up	Down	Unch	Total
JUL 23	50	50	.041	-.090	5	5	0	10
JUL 24	55	44	.046	-.043	5	4	0	9
++ JUL 25	70	30	.115	-.158	7	3	0	10
JUL 26	44	55	.076	-.110	4	5	0	9
JUL 27	50	50	.109	-.078	5	5	0	10
JUL 28	54	45	.102	-.115	6	5	0	11
- JUL 29	36	63	.052	-.133	4	7	0	11
JUL 30	50	40	.055	-.179	5	4	1	10
JUL 31	55	44	.137	-.128	5	4	0	9
- AUG 1	30	60	.143	-.079	3	6	1	10
AUG 2	55	44	.089	-.085	5	4	0	9
++ AUG 3	70	30	.090	-.248	7	3	0	10
AUG 4	54	45	.099	-.036	6	5	0	11
- AUG 5	36	63	.036	-.088	4	7	0	11
AUG 6	50	50	.080	-.074	5	5	0	10
+ AUG 7	66	33	.075	-.172	6	3	0	9
AUG 8	50	50	.144	-.100	5	5	0	10
- AUG 9	33	66	.180	-.101	3	6	0	9
+++ AUG 10	80	20	.084	-.136	8	2	0	10
AUG 11	54	36	.148	-.106	6	4	1	11
AUG 12	45	54	.099	-.098	5	6	0	11
- AUG 13	40	60	.114	-.112	4	6	0	10
+ AUG 14	66	33	.114	-.070	6	3	0	9
AUG 15	50	50	.117	-.100	5	5	0	10
AUG 16	44	55	.091	-.055	4	5	0	9
++ AUG 17	70	30	.058	-.168	7	3	0	10
+ AUG 18	63	36	.177	-.143	7	4	0	11
AUG 19	36	54	.116	-.023	4	6	1	11
- AUG 20	40	60	.215	-.100	4	6	0	10
+ AUG 21	66	22	.128	-.088	6	2	1	9
- AUG 22	40	60	.142	-.115	4	6	0	10
AUG 23	44	55	.132	-.133	4	5	0	9
AUG 24	50	50	.067	-.171	5	5	0	10
- AUG 25	36	63	.134	-.106	4	7	0	11
AUG 26	54	36	.145	-.045	6	4	1	11
+ AUG 27	60	40	.055	-.219	6	4	0	10
+ AUG 28	66	33	.092	-.030.	6	3	0	9
- AUG 29	40	60	.133	-.083	4	6	0	10
AUG 30	44	44	.072	-.039	4	4	1	9
--- AUG 31	20	80	.045	-.045	2	8	0	10
++ SEP 1	75	25	.100	-.049	6	2	0	8
++ SEP 2	70	20	.246	-.325	7	2	1	10
SEP 3	50	50	.279	-.090	4	4	0	8
+ SEP 4	62	37	.115	-.158	5	3	0	8
++ SEP 5	71	28	.163	-.096	5	2	0	7

Bibliography

Allen, R.C. *How To Use the 4-Day, 9-Day and 19-Day Moving Average To Earn Larger Profits from Commodities*. Chicago: Best Books, 1974.

Angell, George. *Winning in the Commodities Market*. New York: Doubleday, 1979.

Angrist, Stanley W. *Sensible Speculating in Commodities*. New York: Simon & Schuster, 1972.

Babcock, Bruce, Jr. *The Dow Jones-Irwin Guide to Trading Systems*. Homewood, Ill.: Richard D. Irwin Inc., 1989.

Barnes, Robert M. *Taming the Pits: A Technical Approach to Commodity Trading*. New York: Wiley, 1979.

Bernstein, Jacob. *The Investor's Quotient*. New York: Wiley, 1980.

———. *The Handbook of Commodity Cycles: A Window on Time*. New York: Wiley, 1982.

———. *Facts on Futures*. Chicago: Probus Publishing, 1987.

———. *Short-Term Trading in Futures*. Chicago: Probus Publishing, 1987.

———. *Beyond the Investor's Quotient*. New York: Wiley, 1988.

———. *Seasonal Concepts in Futures Trading*. New York: Wiley, 1988.

———. *Short-Term Trader's Manual*. Chicago: Probus Publishing, 1989.

———. *Handbook of Economics Cycles*. Homewood, Ill.: Business One Irwin, 1991.

———. *MBH Seasonal Futures Charts: A Study of Weekly Seasonal Tendencies in the Commodity Futures Markets*. Winnetka, Ill.: MBH Commodity Advisors Inc., 1992.

———. *Timing Signals*. Chicago: Probus Publishing, 1992.

———. *Why Traders Lose and How Traders Win*. Forthcoming.

Darvas, Nicholas. *How I Made $2,000,000 in the Stock Market.* Larchmont, N.Y.: American Research Council, 1960.

Gold, Gerald. *Modern Commodity Futures Trading.* 7th ed. New York: Commodity Research Bureau, 1975.

Granville, Joseph. *Granville's New Strategy of Daily Stock Market Timing for Maximum Profit.* Englewood Cliffs, N.J.: Prentice Hall, 1976.

Hill, John R. *Stock and Commodity Market Trend Trading by Advanced Technical Analysis.* Hendersonville, N.C.: Commodity Research Institute, 1977.

——. *Scientific Interpretation of Bar Charts.* Hendersonville, N.C.: Commodity Research Institute, 1979.

Jiler, Harry, ed. *Forecasting Commodity Prices: How the Experts Analyze the Market.* New York: Commodity Research Bureau, 1975.

Kaufman, Perry J. *Commodity Trading Systems and Methods.* New York: Wiley, 1978.

——. *The New Commodity Trading Systems and Methods.* New York: Wiley, 1987.

Merrill, Art. *The Behavior of Prices on Wall Street.* Chappaqua, N.Y.: Analysis Press, 1980.

Pugh, Burton. *The Science and Secrets of Wheat Trading.* Pomeroy, Wash.: Lambert-Gann, 1978.

Robbins, Anthony. *Unlimited Power.* New York: Simon & Schuster, 1986.

Williams, Larry R. *The Definitive Guide to Futures Trading.* Brightwaters, N.Y.: Windsor Books, 1990.

Williams, Larry R. and Michelle Noseworthy. *Sure Thing Commodity Trading, How Seasonal Factors Influence Commodity Prices.* Brightwaters, N.Y.: Windsor, 1977.

Index